To See Ourselves as Others See Us

To See Ourselves as Others See Us

How Publics Abroad View the United States after 9/11

OLE R. HOLSTI

The University of Michigan Press

Ann Arbor

2011   2010   2009   2008   4   3   2   1

A CIP catalog record for this book is available from the British Library.

Library of Congress Cataloging-in-Publication Data

Holsti, Ole R.

To see ourselves as others see us : how publics abroad view the
    United States after 9/11 / Ole R. Holsti.
        p.   cm.
    Includes bibliographical references and index.
    ISBN-13: 978-0-472-07036-7 (cloth : alk. paper)
    ISBN-10: 0-472-07036-3 (cloth : alk. paper)
    ISBN-13: 978-0-472-05036-9 (pbk. : alk. paper)
    ISBN-10: 0-472-05036-2 (pbk. : alk. paper)
    1. United States—Foreign public opinion.   2. United States—
Foreign relations—2001—Public opinion.   3. United States—Social
conditions—21st century—Public opinion.   4. United States—Foreign
public opinion—Case studies.   5. Anti-Americanism.   6. United
States—Relations—Foreign countries. I. Title.

E895.H65   2008
303.48'27300905—dc22   2007046328

For
Maija and Brad, Aksel and Mikko

Contents

Tables

Preface

The ruins of the World Trade Center towers and the Pentagon were still smoldering from the September 11 terrorist attacks when many stunned Americans joined President Bush in wondering, as he did in his speech to Congress nine days later, "Why do they hate us?" What could have caused nineteen mostly well-educated men from longtime ally Saudi Arabia to plan and execute the deadliest attacks on American soil since the Japanese strike against the U.S. Navy at Pearl Harbor almost exactly six decades earlier?

The initial reaction to the 9/11 attacks in much of the world was sympathy and support for America and the more than three thousand victims who died that day. To be sure, a few rejoiced that an arrogant Uncle Sam was finally getting a long overdue comeuppance, and a much smaller number espoused conspiracy theories that the attacks were an "inside job," perpetrated by the Central Intelligence Agency or Israel's Mossad intelligence service—or both. Yet even the leaders of countries with which the United States has had less than cordial relations were quick to express their condolences. The most impressive display of support came from NATO allies that, despite Washington's preference for acting alone in Afghanistan, provided material and other assistance for the invasion, and in most cases they did so with strong support from their publics. Help was not limited to NATO members, as some of the republics of the former Soviet Union also contributed with intelligence, basing rights, and overflight rights.

In many countries, the final quarter of 2001 represented the high-water mark for favorable opinions of America and its policies. A series of important events and actions by the United States highlighted the months and years that followed: President Bush's State of the Union message that identified Iraq, Iran, and North Korea as an "axis of evil"; the 2002 National Security Strategy, predicated on the proposition that deterrence and containment, the foundations of Cold War defense policies, were no longer adequate bases for ensuring the country's safety; the long run-up to and subsequent invasion of Iraq in the face of widespread opposition within NATO and with the support of only a handful of allies in "the coalition of the willing"; undeniable photographic evidence that Iraqi prisoners were mistreated at Abu Ghraib prison, along with less-well-documented charges of similar misconduct at the Guantanamo prison; the reelection of President Bush in 2004; three successful elections that led to a democratic constitution and an elected government in Baghdad; the capture, trial, and execution of Saddam Hussein and two of his colleagues; and an increasingly bloody insurgency that threatens to engulf Iraq in a full-fledged civil war. These and other important events provided the American people as well as publics abroad ample material for judging this country and its policies.

There is a vast literature on how America is viewed abroad, ranging from Alexis de Tocqueville's classic nineteenth-century study *Democracy in America* to recent editorials supporting or criticizing the United States and its policies. This book has a more limited goal, focusing largely on the post-9/11 years and attempting to understand how publics abroad view America; its people, values, and institutions; and Washington's foreign policies. Do they judge this country primarily because of what it *is,* or are their views mostly based on what it *does?* The obvious answer is that both judgments are important, and the chapters that follow present a wealth of international survey data on opinions about both American society and its conduct in world affairs.

If the goal is to understand substantial changes about how America is viewed by publics abroad over such a short period of time as the years since the 9/11 attacks, the underlying hypothesis is that actions are likely to be more significant. The qualities that constitute what America *is*—modern, capitalistic, wealthy, powerful, democratic, nationalistic, religious, materialistic, innovative, optimistic, sports loving, and many others that characterize this country today—were also prominent features of the country during the decade prior to the 9/11 attacks, and thus they probably cannot fully explain significant changes in how others see us. What America *does,* on the other hand, may have a powerful impact, even in the short run.

That thesis, if valid, contains an optimistic message for the future. Without overlooking the existence of deeply committed "America haters" whose views are cast in concrete, it suggests that the United States has within its powers the ability to influence how most others will see us. Foreign policies that are wise, generous, and reflect a thoughtful long-term vision for a more secure world are likely to be judged accordingly—certainly not by all because some will always hate America for whatever it does, or fails to do, but by enough to make a significant difference. Perhaps Winston Churchill was engaging in hyperbole when he described the Marshall Plan as "the most unsordid act in history," but even if he was, it stands as one of the great triumphs of twentieth-century

American foreign policy. It certainly demonstrated that the term "enlightened self-interest" is not an oxymoron.

In undertaking this book, I have been the fortunate beneficiary of the talents, kindness, and insights of many individuals and organizations. The Carnegie Corporation provided Duke University with a grant to study constraints on the uses of force in the twenty-first century. My colleagues Peter Feaver and Bruce Jentleson, principal investigators, urged me to undertake this study, and they provided some useful comments along the way, as did Bob Keohane, now a member of the faculty at Princeton University. Kal Holsti and Bruce Kuniholm provided useful suggestions on the Canada and Turkey mini–care studies. The Duke Arts and Science Research Council provided a small grant in 2006 to fund undergraduate research assistants for the year following the expiration of the Carnegie grant. Natasha Roetter, Elizabeth Kelly, Erika Seeler, Mark Dubois, and Caleb Seeley were model research assistants, especially in finding materials for the mini–case studies in chapter 4.

Papers for two American Political Science Association annual meetings and lectures at Harvard's Kennedy School of Government and the Technologico de Monterrey in Mexico City provided an opportunity to present some preliminary results and to get useful comments and suggestions; those from my longtime friend Richard Sobel of Harvard University were especially helpful.

Even a casual reader of the tables in chapters 2 and 3 will note the importance of data from the Pew Global Attitudes Project and the Program on International Policy Attitudes. The surveys conducted in recent years by Andrew Kohut and Steve Kull, directors of the Pew and PIPA projects, have greatly enriched our understanding of international public opinion.

Since August 2000 I have had the great good fortune to work with Anne Marie Boyd on this and several other projects. Her title, "research secretary," does not begin to do full justice to her many contributions. Whether searching the Internet for obscure sources, formatting tables, identifying poorly worded sentences in draft chapters, or helping to prepare the index, she does it all with skill, dedication, and good humor. She is also an exceptionally pleasant person with whom it has always been a pleasure to work.

This is my second book project with Jim Reische, political science editor at the University of Michigan Press. His unfailing help, support, and patience have been exemplary. Sarah Remington, acquisitions editorial assistant at the Press, and Kevin Rennells were also immensely helpful in the process of transforming a manuscript into a book. Betsy Hovey provided excellent copyediting.

All of the above have my heartfelt thanks, and they are absolved from the remaining weaknesses and errors.

Last but not least, I dedicate this book to my wonderful family—daughter Maija, her husband Brad, and their delightful sons Aksel and Mikko. One of my fondest hopes is they will someday see an America that ranks not only among the wealthiest and most powerful countries but also among the most highly respected among publics abroad.

Ole R. Holsti

CHAPTER 1

Introduction

It was the best of times, it was the worst of times.
—Charles Dickens

A decent respect to the opinions of mankind.
—Declaration of Independence

Oh wad some power the giftie gie us,
  To see oursels as others see us!
It wad frae monie a blunder free us,
  An' foolish notion.
—Robert Burns

The opening sentence of Charles Dickens's classic novel of the French Revolution, *A Tale of Two Cities,* could serve as an apt description of contemporary American foreign policy. In fact, each of these familiar quotations frames some central themes in this book, which studies the ways publics abroad have assessed the United States, its institutions, and its policies in recent years.

By conventional measures of power and status, the United States unquestionably sits at the apex of the international pecking order. Its military capabilities outstrip those of any potential challenger or, indeed, those of any potential coalition of challengers. Because the Pentagon's annual budget is higher than that of the next sixteen countries combined, accounting for 48 percent of global military spending in 2005, the American position at the top of the world's military hierarchy seems certain to persist into the foreseeable future. The next four countries—Great Britain, France, China, and Japan—each contributed 4 to 5 percent of the world total.[1]

---

1. For extensive data on military capabilities and defense spending, see the annual reports of the International Institute of Strategic Studies, *The Military Balance* (London: Routledge); and Stockholm International Peace Research Institute, *Military Expenditure Database,* http://www.sipri.org/GlobalSecurity.org.

When our attention turns to the economic realm, the picture is much the same. In 2000 the United States accounted for 29.3 percent of the world gross domestic product, a figure that is estimated to have risen to 29.5 percent in 2005 and to decline only slightly to 28.8 percent in 2025, while the countries that two decades ago were sometimes identified as challengers to American economic superiority—the Soviet Union, Japan, and Germany—have either disintegrated (the Soviet Union) or have suffered serious economic difficulties (Japan and Germany) that have all but eliminated their chances of approaching, much less surpassing, the United States. To be sure, reckless American tax policies since 2001 have resulted in unprecedented budget and trade deficits that will almost surely have serious consequences at some point in the future. It is also possible, though by no means inevitable, that China's economy will surpass the U.S. economy in several decades, but for the time being the American position as the world's top economy is beyond serious debate.[2] Given the disparity in the present sizes of the American and Chinese economies, even should China maintain its spectacular GDP growth rate of 9.3 percent annually while the United States continues growing at a pedestrian 3.3 percent, the gap between the two countries will grow rather than contract.[3] Analysts have even come to rethink their views of two decades ago that as a result of "imperial overreach" the United States would follow the declining path of previous hegemonic powers—Spain, the Netherlands, France, and Great Britain among them.[4]

These figures clearly point to "the best of times" for the material bases of American foreign policy. How, then, can the phrase "the worst of times" possibly be used in any sentence or paragraph that deals with American foreign policy? By another measure of power—the ability to get others to do one's bidding—the situation is somewhat less clear. Recent years have witnessed an increasing number of episodes in which the United States found itself unable to achieve its foreign policy goals as other countries have balked at following America's lead. That the United States has been unable to gain much cooperation from China on such issues as the future of Taiwan or Iran's nuclear pro-

---

2. According to Department of Energy projections, China's share of the world gross domestic product will rise from 3.5 percent in 2000 to 7.6 percent in 2025. Data on American and Chinese contributions to the world gross domestic product are drawn from Energy Information Administration, *Annual Energy Outlook, 2004* (Washington, DC, 2004), table 4. These figures are based on U.S. dollars and would be somewhat different if based on the Chinese yuan.

3. The economic growth rate data are from the Economist, *Pocket World in Figures* (London: Profile Books, 2007).

4. Paul Kennedy, *The Rise and Fall of the Great Powers: Economic Change and Military Conflict from 1500 to 2000* (New York: Random House, 1987). Kennedy's views were almost immediately challenged, most notably by Joseph Nye, "Understating U.S. Strength," *Foreign Policy* 72 (fall 1988): 105–29; and Nye, *Bound to Lead: The Changing Nature of American Power* (New York: Basic Books, 1991).

gram is not especially surprising, given the history of Sino-American relations and China's own status as a nuclear-armed major power and, perhaps, as an emerging superpower. Moreover, China's leading role in financing America's budget deficit provides Beijing with considerable potential leverage in its relations with Washington. But in many cases the foreign policy setbacks have come at the hands of much less powerful countries, some of which have long been among America's allies in such organizations as the North Atlantic Treaty Organization (NATO) and the Organization of American States (OAS). A few examples illustrate Washington's recent difficulties in translating its exceptional reservoir of "hard power" into effective influence on some important foreign policy issues.

- In the summer of 2002, as the George W. Bush administration was gearing up a full-scale effort to gain congressional and international support for military action to overthrow the Saddam Hussein regime in Iraq, Chancellor Gerhard Schroeder faced a very difficult reelection campaign. Schroeder publicly declared that Germany, which in the wake of the 9/11 terrorist attacks had sent troops to assist in the U.S.-led campaign against the Taliban and al Qaeda in Afghanistan, would not in any circumstances join in military action against Iraq. That promise was probably sufficient to ensure his reelection.
- During the run-up to the Iraq war the United States put intense pressure on the recently elected Turkish government to permit deployment of the U.S. Fourth Infantry Division there to open a northern front against Iraq. Despite American use of both carrots (offers of aid and loans) and sticks (possible withdrawal of support for Turkey's bid for European Union membership), in a close vote the recently elected Turkish Grand National Assembly rejected the U.S. demands, thereby faithfully reflecting overwhelming public opposition to the U.S. plan.
- Apparently at the insistence of Secretary of State Colin Powell and against the advice of other key foreign policy officials, including Vice President Dick Cheney, and Defense Department officials Donald Rumsfeld and Paul Wolfowitz, the Bush administration reluctantly took its case for the use of force against Iraq to the UN Security Council. Washington realized that France or Russia might well veto an American resolution authorizing the invasion of Iraq, and it was all but certain that Germany would not support it, but the United States expected to obtain support from at least nine of the fifteen Security Council members, thereby gaining a measure of legitimacy

for its Iraq policy while simultaneously isolating naysayers in Paris, Moscow, and Berlin. The issue never came to a vote because preliminary canvassing revealed that the resolution would result in an embarrassing American defeat. The three African members of the Security Council—Angola, Cameroon, Guinea—let it be known that they agreed with French opposition to the use of force in Iraq. The United States was unable to gain the support of even Mexico or Chile, hemispheric neighbors with which it has special trade relationships. Only seven of thirty-three Latin American and Caribbean countries supported military action against Iraq.[5]

- After the Iraqi invasion of Kuwait in August 1990, President George H. W. Bush was able to gain Security Council authorization to use force against Iraq should it fail to withdraw from Kuwait, and he put together a coalition of twenty-six countries to contribute to the war effort against Iraq. That coalition notably included two important Islamic regional powers—Egypt and Turkey. In contrast, President George W. Bush not only failed to gain Security Council support for the invasion of Iraq in 2003, but his "coalition of the willing" included significant contributions of armed forces only from Great Britain, with much smaller, mostly symbolic military units from Poland and Australia and, later, from Italy, Spain, and several other countries. Notably missing were any Arab or Muslim countries.
- Even after the war successfully toppled the brutal Saddam Hussein regime that had previously committed aggression against two neighbors—Iran and Kuwait—predictions by administration officials and their cheerleaders that an awesome display of American military power would lead to at least grudging support from Islamic countries and their publics (the so-called Arab street) proved to be wildly off the mark.
- After President Bush announced the end of hostilities in Iraq on May 1, 2003—"Mission Accomplished," as a banner at an aircraft carrier photo opportunity famously proclaimed—many countries, including those that opposed the war, were informed that they were expected to make significant financial contributions, including debt forgiveness, toward rebuilding post-Saddam Iraq and arranging for the transition to a stable democratic government. Such contributions were not forthcoming, perhaps in part because the administration also made it clear that contracts for rebuilding Iraq would be issued only to firms from countries that joined the U.S.-led

5. Christopher Marquis, "Latin American Allies of the U.S.: Docile and Reliable No Longer," *New York Times,* January 9, 2004.

S

invasion of Iraq, thereby excluding France, Germany, Russia, and Canada, among others.[6]

• As the June 30, 2004, deadline for a partial handover of sovereignty to an interim Iraqi government approached, the administration once again demanded that NATO members contribute more troops to help quell an increasingly serious Iraqi insurgency and to maintain security during the transition period leading up to full sovereignty for Iraq. At the June 2004 Group of Eight meeting at Sea Island, Georgia, it became clear that such additional assistance would not be forthcoming; President Bush conceded that it was an "unrealistic expectation" to count on additional NATO troops.[7] France, Germany, and other hesitant NATO members apparently saw no advantage in becoming involved in Iraq, probably in part because of the growing toll inflicted by insurgents. Both Germany and France later offered to help train Iraqi military personnel, but not in Iraq.

• South Korea has been a longtime American ally, and U.S. troops have been stationed there since the July 1953 armistice that brought the Korean War to an end. For various reasons, including misbehavior by U.S. troops stationed in Korea, anti-American sentiments have risen, especially among the younger generation who did not experience the international effort, led by the United States, to repel the North Korean aggression during the bloody 1950–53 war. North Korea has openly boasted of violating agreements to terminate its nuclear weapons program, but how to deal with the issue has divided rather than united Washington and Seoul. In his 2002 State of the Union address, President Bush included North Korea in the "axis of evil," whereas South Korea has generally followed a softer line—the "sunshine" policy—perhaps fearing a flood of refugees across the 38th parallel should the totalitarian North Korean regime collapse.[8] In presidential elections on December 19, 2002, liberal candidate Roh Moo-hyun won by taking a very critical stance toward the United States, even in the face of nuclear threats from North Korea. According to one analyst: "In the past, security threats

6. Erin E. Arvedlund and Clifford Krauss, "A Region Inflamed: Reconstruction; Allies Angered at Exclusion from Bidding," *New York Times,* December 11, 2003.
7. Richard W. Stevenson and David E. Sanger, "Bush Doesn't Expect NATO to Provide Troops for Iraq," *New York Times,* June 11, 2004.
8. For an overview of differences between U.S. and South Korean approaches to North Korea, see James Brooke, "South Korea Sidesteps U.S. to Forge Political and Pragmatic Links," *New York Times,* August 26, 2004, A1. C. Kenneth Quinones, a U.S. expert on Korea, is quoted: "South Koreans have gone the full circle. Ten years ago anyone who went north was painted pink. Today, anyone who does not go north is not a real Korean." See also the case study in chapter 4.

from the North would have made Koreans favor a conservative candidate and seek solidarity with the United States. In 2002, however, a pro-U.S. image was a burden in the election."[9]

- Although Canada has not always followed Washington's lead in foreign affairs—for example, it maintains diplomatic and trade relations with Cuba—it has generally been a faithful ally of the United States and Britain on major international issues. Canada fought alongside the United States and Great Britain as an ally in every war through the end of the twentieth century, but it declined to join them in the "coalition of the willing" for the invasion of Iraq in March 2003.[10] Canada also served as an integral part of NORAD and the DEW Line, the air defense systems erected during the Cold War, but in 2005 the government in Ottawa pulled out of the missile defense system, one of the centerpieces of Bush administration defense planning. Perhaps the long record of test failures of the missile defense system contributed to the withdrawal, but like the decision not to participate in the invasion of Iraq, it may also have been rooted in the opposition of the Canadian public. "Polls have shown the system to be unpopular with the public, particularly in Quebec."[11] However, the 2006 elections brought to power a minority conservative government, headed by Stephen Harper, that appears more willing to participate in the missile defense system as a part of an effort to improve relations with Washington.
- In June 2005 the United States proposed a resolution that would authorize the Organization of American States to appraise the state of democracy among member countries as a way of putting some teeth in the "Democratic Charter" adopted four years earlier. The American effort met strong resistance among other members, in part because they feared that the resolution might be used by the United States against Venezuela, whose populist president, Hugo Chávez, has used vitriolic anti-American rhetoric to bolster his popularity at home. OAS members had earlier broken precedent by declining to support an American-backed candidate for secretary general of the organization, electing José Miguel Insulza instead.[12]

9. Lee Sook-jung, "Anti-Americanism in Korean Society: A Survey Based Analysis," in *The United States and South Korea: Reinvigorating the Partnership*, U.S.-Korea Academic Symposium (2003), proceedings available in *Joint U.S.-Korea Academic Studies* 14 (2004): 184 (available at www.keia.org).
10. Clifford Krauss, "Chrétien Leaves at Ease, Even If Bush Is Displeased," *New York Times*, November 14, 2003.
11. Clifford Krauss, "Canada May Be a Close Neighbor, but It Proudly Keeps Its Distance," *New York Times*, March 23, 2005; and Krauss, "Canada Says It Won't Join Missile Shield with the U.S." *New York Times*, February 24, 2005.
12. Larry Rohter, "O.A.S. to Pick Chile Socialist U.S. Opposed as Its Leader," *New York Times*, April 30, 2005; and Joel Brinkley, "Latin States Shun U.S. Plan to Watch Over Democracy," *New York Times*, June 9, 2005.

• In September 2006, the newly elected leader of Britain's Conservative Party, David Cameron, made his first major foreign policy address. With a view toward possible elections in 2009, and in recognition that Labor prime minister Tony Blair would shortly leave office under a dark cloud owing to his close ties to President Bush on the Iraq war, Cameron took special pains to distinguish his policies from those of Blair. Speaking on the fifth anniversary of the terrorist attacks on New York and Washington, he went on to criticize a core tenet of the Bush administration's post–September 11 policies: "The danger is that by positing a single source of terrorism—a global jihad—and opposing it with a single global response—American-backed force—we will simply fulfill our own prophecy." After assuring his audience, the British American Project, that "I and my party are instinctive friends of America, and passionate supporters of the Atlantic Alliance," Cameron went on to assert, "Britain does not need to establish her identity by recklessly poking the United States in the eye, as some like to do." Although he had earlier acknowledged that since the Churchill-Roosevelt era during World War II, Britain has been America's junior partner, he then issued something of a declaration of quasi-independence. "But we will serve neither our own, nor America's, nor the world's interests if we are seen as America's unconditional associate in every endeavor. Our duty is to our own citizens, and to our own conception of what is right for the world. We should be solid but not slavish in our friendship with America. . . . I fear that if we continue as at present we may combine the maximum of exposure with the minimum of real influence over decisions." He also pointed to the problems with unilateralism in world affairs. "But as we have found out in recent years, a country may act alone—but it cannot always succeed alone. The United States has learnt this lesson painfully." In closing, he quoted a warning from nineteenth-century prime minister William Gladstone against imperial hubris and international arrogance: "even when you do a good thing, you may do it in so bad a way that you entirely spoil the beneficial effect."[13] It is unlikely that anyone in the audience failed to grasp the target of Cameron's polite but devastating critique. Whether or not Cameron's diagnosis of terrorism or the American response is valid, it reflected the belief that his electoral prospects can be improved by avoiding the label—"Bush's poodle"—that was often applied to Tony Blair. An ICM

---

13. "David Cameron's Speech," *Guardian Unlimited,* September 11, 2006, http://politics.guardian.co.uk/speeches /story/0,,1869970,00.html.

poll in 2006 revealed that 63 percent of British voters felt that Britain is "too close to the United States," 30 percent stated that the relationship is "about right," and only 3 percent responded that Britain is "not close enough to the USA."

• Nicholas Sarkozy, the center-right Union pour un Movement Populaire (UMP) party candidate in the 2007 election for the French presidency, has a pro-American image. He was photographed with President Bush in September 2006 and has been branded by his Socialist opponent as an "American neo-conservative with a French passport." Locked in a close race that he ultimately won, Sarkozy gave a 90-minute interview, conducted in French and translated into English, with Charlie Rose on American public television in which he sought to distance himself from American foreign policy. "I want to say this to my American friends. The world does not come to a halt at the borders of your country. . . . Beyond the Pacific and beyond the Atlantic, there are men and women like you. Get interested in the world and the world will learn to love you. . . . The world is not just the American empire. There's more to it than that." Since winning the presidency, Sarkozy has taken several significant steps toward improving relations with the United States, including considering whether France should rejoin NATO as a full-fledged member, but he has shown no inclination to send French forces into Iraq. Although no friend of President Jacques Chirac, Sarkozy paid him homage: "Jacques Chirac's international policy, particularly on Iraq, was the right one. He made the right choice at the right time."[14]

What do these episodes have in common? With only a few exceptions (the "Arab street") they involve actions by allies and countries with which the United States has long had good relations. They are also at least electoral democracies in which leaders must periodically face electorates. Moreover, in each case there was evidence that in defying Washington, the leaders in question were acting in ways that reflected the policy preferences of their publics. It is of course important to point out that there is no direct evidence that they were consciously guided by polls or other expressions of public opinion; evidence on that score would be hard to find as virtually all leaders insist that they are guided by "the national interest" rather than by surveys or focus groups. Nevertheless, the ubiquity of polling in virtually all democratic countries, including surveys that are commissioned by governments, makes it likely that

---

14. Martin Arnold, "Sarkozy Tells Americans to Broaden Horizon," *Financial Times*, February 1, 2007.

there was at least an awareness of the domestic political costs and benefits of refusing to go along with the United States. Is it conceivable, for example, that British Conservative leader David Cameron and his advisers were unaware of the ICM survey that revealed the breadth and depth of British opinions that the Blair government had been "too close to the U.S."?

These and many similar examples suggest that there are limits on the goals that even a hegemonic superpower can achieve with threats and inducements, backed by the kinds of "hard power" that the United States possesses in plentitude. "Soft power" constitutes a less direct means by which a country can achieve its foreign policy goals: "A country may obtain the outcomes it wants in world politics because other countries want to follow it, admiring its values, emulating its examples, aspiring to its level of prosperity and openness."[15]

"A DECENT RESPECT TO THE OPINIONS OF MANKIND"

Although Thomas Jefferson and his colleagues, in writing the Declaration of Independence, were not aware of the concept "soft power," the phrase "a decent respect to the opinions of mankind" in that historic document reflected a belief that the manner in which others viewed the legitimacy of claims to independence by the upstart colonies might in fact influence the prospects for a successful divorce from the mother country. To be sure, much of the subsequent assistance from abroad—for example from the French government of Louis XVI—had more to do with strategic support for a revolution that would weaken archrival Great Britain than any sympathy for such subversive ideas as "all men are created equal." Nevertheless, the document that emerged from the July 1776 meeting of the founding fathers reflected the hope that a compelling statement of the reasons for the assertion of independence would gain support not only at home but also abroad. Because the rebelling colonies hardly enjoyed a surfeit of military and economic resources (hard power), sympathy from abroad (soft power) took on greater significance.

In contrast to hard power, the base of soft power resides in the "hearts and minds" of other countries, especially among the leaders of their political, economic, military, cultural, and other major institutions. There are also reasons to believe that, especially in countries with regular competitive elections, the opinions and preferences of the general public may be of some consequence

---

15. Joseph Nye, *The Paradox of American Power: Why the World's Only Superpower Can't Go It Alone* (New York: Oxford University Press, 2002), 8. A fuller development of the concept appears in Nye, *Soft Power: The Means to Success in World Politics* (New York: Public Affairs, 2005).

because in at least some instances its leaders may harbor concerns that they will be held accountable for their foreign policy decisions. Although it is not always possible to establish a causal link between public opinion and government policy, in the episodes cited earlier in the chapter, leaders in Germany, South Korea, Mexico, Turkey, Canada, France, and elsewhere who chose to defy Washington acted in ways that were consistent with the preferences of their publics. The extent to which publics abroad want to follow the United States, admire its values and institutions, and agree with its foreign policy goals may have an impact on the willingness of their governments to cooperate with the United States. But because governments do not conduct their foreign affairs by plebiscite, the impact of public views of the United States is a question to be explored rather than a relationship to be assumed.

Many of the episodes in which Washington failed to get its way were also linked directly or indirectly to the American-led war in Iraq. The September 11 terrorist attacks on New York and Washington gave rise to an almost unanimous outpouring of sympathy and support from leaders and publics abroad. For the first time in its history, NATO invoked Article 5 of the North Atlantic Treaty: "The parties agree that an armed attack against one or more of them in Europe or North America shall be considered an attack on all of them." The subsequent American invasion of Afghanistan to capture the al Qaeda leaders who openly claimed responsibility for the 9/11 attacks and to oust the Taliban regime that had given sanctuary to al Qaeda received widespread support. Numerous countries, including but not limited to NATO allies, provided troops, equipment, intelligence, basing rights, overflight rights, and the like. The American military action was generally regarded as a legitimate response to a barbaric terrorist attack in which there was no ambiguity about the identity or purposes of the perpetrators.

Shortly after expulsion of the Taliban government in Afghanistan, President Bush identified Iraq, Iran, and North Korea as an "axis of evil" in his 2002 State of the Union address. Later that summer he initiated a campaign to gain congressional and international support for a military campaign to oust Saddam Hussein, alleging that Iraq had accumulated an arsenal of weapons of mass destruction and, moreover, that Iraq was implicated in the 9/11 terrorist attacks by virtue of close links to al Qaeda. The United Nations Security Council unanimously passed Resolution 1441 on November 8, 2002, requiring that Iraq readmit UN inspectors to determine whether it had violated agreements not to acquire WMDs. In the absence of compelling evidence of Iraqi violations or of ties between Baghdad and al Qaeda, Washington's proposal to use force against Iraq generated widespread opposition abroad. The debates on Iraq coincided with an unprecedented amount of international polling that yielded a mountain of evidence during the run-up to and conduct of the Iraq war.

"TO SEE OURSELS AS OTHERS SEE US"

Even before Robert Burns wrote "To a Louse" in 1786, from which this line is drawn, the American experiment had attracted the attention of visitors from abroad—for example, St. Jean de Crevecoeur who had written "What Is an American?" four years earlier. Many other observers of American society followed, including Charles Dickens, Frances Trollope, James Bryce, D. H. Lawrence, and Alexis de Tocqueville. The last wrote the classic study *Democracy in America*, which, more than a century and a half after its initial publication, remains in print and continues to be cited and debated.

In order to gain a sense of how the United States is viewed abroad today, we are no longer dependent solely on the observations of a few travelers and intellectuals. The dramatic events of the past two decades, including disintegration of the Soviet Union, the end of the Cold War, two wars against Iraq, and the terrorist attacks against New York and Washington, have provided both incentives and opportunities for unprecedented efforts to gauge "as others see us" by means of public opinion surveys in scores of countries. The U.S. Information Agency undertook extensive polling throughout much of the Cold War period, and private firms such as Gallup International, the Eurobarometer, and their counterparts in many countries have been involved in similar undertakings for several decades. Nevertheless, the polling efforts of the past few years have dwarfed those of previous periods. Policymakers have long been interested in gauging public sentiments, but efforts to do so, once viewed as somewhat questionable activities that they tried to shield from public view, now constitute a growth industry in many countries. The end of the Cold War and the expansion of democratic governments have opened up areas that were previously inaccessible to pollsters, and new technologies, including computer-assisted telephone surveys, have opened up opportunities for almost instantaneous measures of public sentiments at a lower cost. Global turbulence and often controversial events, combined with the growth in the number of democracies, have enhanced interest in how publics react to these events. For example, John Mueller described the first Persian Gulf War as the "mother of all polling events."[16] The September 11 terrorist attacks and the 2003 war against Iraq have relegated the first war against Iraq to a distant runner-up position as a stimulant to surveys.

The many recent international surveys by Gallup International, the Pew Research Center for the People and the Press, the German Marshall Fund, the Program on International Policy Attitudes (PIPA), and the British Broadcasting Corporation have provided relevant data about how the United States and its policies are viewed from about five dozen countries. Many of the tables in this study focus on twenty-seven countries, including ten NATO allies and seventeen other key countries. Not only do these include many of America's allies but they are also countries for which results of multiple surveys are available. The vast majority of these countries are also at least electoral democracies in which leaders must face electorates periodically and, thus, cannot be wholly indifferent to public sentiments. It is, of course, an open question whether elites in these countries feel as constrained by public views on foreign affairs as they do on domestic issues.

Before turning to data, two caveats are worth mentioning. One of the "iron laws" of public opinion research is that responses are often highly sensitive to wording of the questions. The data presented here are drawn from a broad array of survey organizations, few of which used identical wording even when they sought to measure opinions on the same issue. Because even minor variations in phrasing questions may yield significantly different responses, comparison of responses across surveys should be undertaken with caution. A corollary to this "iron law" is that when differently worded questions on a given issue give rise to essentially similar responses, our confidence in the results is materially enhanced. The plethora of tables in this study arises from a deliberate decision to use multiple surveys, when available, in order to unearth findings that do not rely excessively on responses that might merely be an artifact of any single question format or the sampling designs of a single polling organization.

A more general caveat centers on the entire polling enterprise. Despite immense technical improvements since the disastrous *Literary Digest* presidential poll of 1936 that confidently predicted a landslide victory for Alf Landon over incumbent Franklin D. Roosevelt, there continues to be an active debate about whether surveys tap "real" opinions rather than merely casual answers by largely uninterested and uninformed respondents. That is not the place to re-

---

16. John Mueller, *Policy and Opinion in the Gulf War* (Chicago: University of Chicago Press, 1994), xiv.

view the vast literature on that ongoing debate. For present purposes it is perhaps appropriate to paraphrase Winston Churchill's observation about democracy being the worst form of government—except for all the alternatives. In order to understand the opinions and preferences of general publics, a well-designed survey is the worst research instrument for doing so—except for all the alternatives.

There is little doubt that some respondents in mass surveys not only are poorly informed about world affairs but also may give "off the top of the head" responses rather than appear to be ignorant. There is, nevertheless, striking evidence that, in the aggregate, responses to well-designed surveys reveal considerable stability. Moreover, when aggregate responses on a given issue change significantly, they usually reflect important events.[17] Thus, changes in opinions are not necessarily indications of ignorance and mindless volatility; they are more likely to indicate that respondents are paying at least some attention to new information rather than being permanently wedded to a particular point of view.

There are, of course, other methods that may be used to assess how countries are viewed abroad. Analyses of writings, speeches, novels, movies and other cultural products, and the media have often been used, and indeed, there were few alternatives prior to development of systematic mass surveys in the 1930s. But just as surveys cannot provide bulletproof assurances of validity, even if sophisticated content analyses designs are employed, the volume of materials is such that only samples can be studied. Because not all such studies have grappled with sampling problems, the results are heavily dependent on which materials are selected, and that choice may at least in some cases reflect the investigator's preconceptions. One admittedly extreme hypothetical example illustrates the problem. Suppose that a study designed to assess the nature and impact of religion on American politics focused on the extensive writings, sermons, and political commentaries of James Dobson, Pat Robertson, and Jerry Falwell. To understate the case, the results would be a skewed representation of the rich diversity in American religious thought, and they would suggest

---

17. The extensive literature on this point, to which Bruce Russett, Benjamin Page, Richard Sobel, Eugene Wittkopf, Robert Shapiro, Richard Eichenburg, Laurence Jacobs, Steven Kull, John Zaller, John Mueller, and James Rosenau are among the many contributors, is reviewed in Ole R. Holsti, *Public Opinion and American Foreign Policy,* 2nd edition (Ann Arbor: University of Michigan Press, 2004), chap. 3. While the evidence cited there is largely based on studies of the American public, there is reason to believe that this is equally true of most non-American publics, many of which have been shown to outstrip Americans in their knowledge of world affairs. Michael A. Dimock and Samuel L. Popkin, "Political Knowledge in Comparative Perspective," in *Do the Media Govern?* ed. Shanto Iyengar and Richard Reeves (Thousand Oaks, CA: Sage), 217–24.

that the study was designed to portray an especially somber view of an important aspect of U.S. society, with the goal of constructing a straw man that can easily be knocked down.

There are ways of avoiding such obvious traps, but not all have done so. In an especially impressive effort to gauge public opinion by means other than surveys, Marc Lynch translated and content analyzed 1,350 editorials and op-ed articles in twelve Arab newspapers.[18] In contrast, some depictions of French thinking about the United States have emphasized the views of those on the fringes who have argued, for example, that the September 11 terrorist attacks were a justified response to American sins or, worse yet, were actually orchestrated by elements in Washington. At the same time they have given less attention to those, such as Jean François Revel, who have long been vocal and articulate admirers of the United States.[19]

But even the best polls—many of those cited here represent the "gold standard" in survey research—cannot fully address questions about the sources and consequences of public opinion. The brief country studies in chapter 4 attempt to deal with those limitations by exploring the extent to which, if any, public assessments of the United States may have had an impact on policy.

OVERVIEW

Chapters 2 and 3 present and discuss extensive survey findings about how the United States is viewed by publics abroad. Many of these surveys analyzed included questions assessing levels of approval of President George W. Bush and his conduct of foreign affairs, but they are not considered here because this book focuses on broader questions of how publics abroad view the United States and its policies. Suffice it to say that assessments of the president and his conduct of foreign affairs are almost universally very critical, and they have generally become more so in the light of developments in Iraq, including abuses of prisoners and the insurgency that has put the country on the brink of civil war. In any case, it is not altogether clear whether the responses to questions that mention President Bush are appraisals of the president, his policies, or both. For that reason, such questions are not central to the analyses that follow.

18. Marc Lynch, "Beyond the Arab Street: Iraq and the Arab Public Sphere," *Politics and Society* 31 (March 2003): 55–91.
19. Jean-François Revel, *Anti-Americanism* (San Francisco: Encounter Books, 2003). For an excellent and balanced assessment of French opinions see Sophie Meunier, "The Distinctiveness of French Anti-Americanism," in *Anti-Americanisms in World Politics*, ed. Peter J. Katzenstein and Robert O. Keohane (Ithaca: Cornell University Press, 2006), 129–56.

Chapter 2 begins with evidence on general appraisals of the United States, starting with surveys undertaken prior to the September 11, 2001, terrorist attacks on New York and Washington and continuing through the end of 2007. Key events of the period include the invasion of Afghanistan, controversies before and during the war in Iraq, and the insurgencies that have brought Iraq to the brink of civil war. It then turns to survey data on specific American policies, including not only in Iraq but also regarding the "war on terrorism," the extent to which Washington is sensitive to the interests of other countries, and the proper conditions for uses of force abroad.

Chapter 3 continues the presentation and analysis of survey data, starting with judgments of the American people and continuing with evidence on how publics abroad judge aspects of American society and its major institutions, among them American democracy and its appropriateness as a model for others to emulate; science and technology; such entertainment products as movies, television, and music; business and the practices of firms that operate outside the United States; the role of religion in American life; the quality of life for those who emigrate to America; and the role of values and policies in differences between their countries and the United States.

As noted, even meticulously generated public opinion responses cannot answer crucial questions about the sources of public views of the United States and the extent to which public opinion may have entered into foreign policymaking processes. Chapter 4 undertakes seven brief country studies that attempt to assess whether and how the views of publics abroad may have had any impact on their governments. In the absence of extensive interviews and archival research it is not possible to deal definitively with the issue of causality. If government policies fly in the face of strong public opinions to the contrary, that would raise significant doubts about the impact of public opinion on issues in question. Even if public preferences and policies are essentially identical, that concordance would not be sufficient to establish beyond doubt that the former caused the latter, but the country studies can at least serve as plausibility probes on the question of impact. These studies of Australia, Canada, Indonesia, Mexico, Morocco, South Korea, and Turkey include predominantly Muslim countries (Turkey, Indonesia, and Morocco) and non-Muslim ones (Australia, Canada, Mexico, and South Korea); those that sent troops to Iraq (Australia, South Korea) and the five that refused to do so (Canada, Mexico, and the three predominantly Muslim countries); and members of NATO (Turkey and Canada) as well as five countries that are not members of that alliance.

The data in chapters 2 and 3 reveal that, on balance, critical views of the United States have increased since the initial outpouring of support and sympathy following the September 11, 2001, terrorist attacks, and especially following the invasion of Iraq in March 2003. Chapter 5 examines seven schools of thought that purport to explain anti-American sentiments abroad: the end of the Cold War; globalization; American virtues and values; irrational hatred and envy; strategic scapegoating by elites abroad who prefer to blame the United States for their own failings; ignorance about the United States and its policies, arising in part from ineffective public diplomacy by the State Department; and, finally, American policies. The discussion addresses some policy implications of these seven explanations for growing disaffection for the United States.

Chapter 6 picks up on the last of these explanations by undertaking a brief description and assessment of some recent American policies that appear to have contributed to anti-American views abroad. The discussion includes occasional comparisons with U.S. diplomacy during what was arguably the most productive and innovative period of American foreign policy—the decade following the 1941 Japanese attack on Pearl Harbor that, in the words of Republican senator Arthur Vandenberg, "ended isolationism for any realist."[20]

Before proceeding to the surveys and other evidence, it is worth emphasizing that this study does *not* attempt to analyze or describe the full range of appraisals of the United States over the course of its existence by foreign leaders, intellectuals, artists, and other elites who have made known their views. The literature on those subjects is already immense. Rather, the focus here is on how publics abroad have appraised the United States and its policies in recent years, whether and how and why those views have changed during recent years, and the policy implications of those opinions.

---

20. Arthur H. Vandenberg, Jr., ed., *The Public Papers of Senator Vandenberg* (Boston: Houghton-Mifflin, 1952), 1.

CHAPTER 2

How Publics Abroad View the
United States and Its Foreign Policies

Following the September 11 terrorist attacks on New York and
Washington, President Bush appointed a committee of distinguished experts
headed by former ambassador Edward Djerejian to assess the extent, nature,
and sources of anti-American views abroad, especially in the Middle East and
South Asia. When he presented the report of his committee in October 2003,
Djerejian asserted that "[t]he bottom has indeed fallen out of support for the
United States."[1]

HOW THE UNITED STATES IS VIEWED ABROAD

Concern for how the United States is viewed abroad long predates the September 11 attacks. The U.S. Information Agency actively participated in public
diplomacy efforts ranging from Voice of America and Radio Free Europe
broadcasts to establishing libraries abroad that featured books by American au-
thors and about many aspects of American history, culture, and institutions.
While these efforts were not free of controversy at home—for example, Senator
Joseph McCarthy sent members of his staff to determine whether USIA library
holdings met his standard of true-blue Americanism—many have regarded
these years as the golden era of American public diplomacy. The USIA also conducted regular surveys that attempted to assess how publics abroad judged the

---

1. Edward P. Djerejian, "Briefing on the Report on Public Diplomacy for the Arab and Muslim World," Washington Foreign Press Center, October 3, 2003.

United States, and Eurobarometer studies provided additional evidence on the question. These surveys were largely confined to allied countries in Western Europe, and it was, of course, impossible to conduct such studies in countries aligned with the Soviet Union. We will return to the Cold War–era USIA surveys later, in chapter 6, as they may provide some clues, albeit imperfectly, about the extent to which assessments of the United States by publics abroad are reactions to American policies.

The end of the Cold War and disintegration of the Soviet Union led to curtailment of USIA budgets and activities and, ultimately, in the loss of its status as an independent agency when it was merged within the State Department. In 1990–2000 the State Department undertook surveys in more than thirty countries, spanning all regions of the world, but with a heavier focus on Europe and the Americas, and less attention to countries in Africa and the Middle East. Despite their uneven coverage, the State Department surveys provide at least a partial baseline against which to view results from later polls.

The September 11 attacks stimulated an unprecedented amount of polling activity, much of which centered on views of the United States, American society, and the administration in Washington and its foreign policies. It includes surveys conducted during the past decade by such notable organizations as the Gallup Organization, the Pew Research Center for the People and the Press, and the British Broadcasting Corporation (table 2.1).

The 1999–2000 State Department surveys reveal that, with some notable exceptions, publics abroad generally shared a favorable view of the United States. That was especially true in Europe among traditional NATO allies (Great Britain, France, Germany, Italy) as well as among countries that had recently been invited to join that alliance (Poland, Czech Republic) or that aspired to become members of NATO (Bulgaria, Slovakia). Russia was a very important exception to the overall picture of European publics who viewed the United States in quite favorable terms. Although the Cold War had ended during the early 1990s, that decade also included a number of major issues that roiled relations between Washington and Moscow. The civil wars that erupted in the aftermath of the disintegration of the former Yugoslavia often found the United States and Russia in strong disagreement with how to deal with Serbia, a traditional Russian ally dating back to the prerevolutionary era.[2] The American-led NATO air war against Serbia arising from its policies toward the province of

---

2. Russia's strong support for Serbia during the weeks following the assassination in Sarajevo of Archduke Franz Ferdinand and his wife by Serbian nationalists in June 1914 contributed to that incident escalating to the outbreak of general war in Europe.

TABLE 2.1. Opinions about the United States, 1999–2007

"Please tell me if you have a very favorable, somewhat favorable, somewhat unfavorable or very unfavorable opinion of the United States."

Percent "Very Favorable" Plus "Somewhat Favorable"

	1999– 2000	2001–2	July– Oct. 2002	March 2003	April– May 2003	June 2003	Feb.– March 2004	April– May 2005	April– May 2006	April– May 2007
NATO allies										
Great Britain	83	—	75	48	70	75	58	55	56	51
France	62	—	63	31	43	41	37	43	39	39
Germany	78	—	61	25	45	—	38	41	37	30
Italy	76	—	70	34	60	—	—	—	—	53
Poland	86	—	79	50	—	—	—	62	—	61
Czech Republic	77	—	71	—	—	—	—	—	—	45
Spain	50	—	—	14	38	—	—	41	23	34
Turkey	52	40	30	12	15	—	30	23	12	9
Canada	71	—	72	—	63	81	—	59	—	55
Netherlands	—	—	—	—	—	—	—	45	—	—
Other key countries										
Mexico	68	—	64	—	—	—	—	—	—	56
Brazil	56	—	52	—	34	24	—	—	—	44
Russia	37	—	61	28	36	48	47	52	43	41
Japan	77	—	72	—	—	—	—	—	63	61
Australia	76	—	—	—	60	63	—	—	—	—
South Korea	58	—	53	—	46	49	—	—	—	58
Indonesia	75	21	61	—	15	31	—	38	30	29
India	—	—	54	—	—	—	—	71	56	59
Pakistan	23	5	10	—	13	—	21	23	27	15
Kuwait	—	28	—	—	63	—	—	—	—	46
Jordan	—	24	25	—	1	19	5	21	15	20
Egypt	—	—	6	—	—	—	—	—	30	21
Morocco	77	22	—	—	27	—	27	49	—	15
Nigeria	46	—	77	—	61	—	—	—	62	70
Lebanon	—	—	35	—	27	—	—	42	—	47
China	—	—	—	—	—	—	—	42	47	34
Israel	—	—	—	—	—	—	—	—	—	78

Source: 1999–2000—U.S. Department of State, Office of Research, *The U.S. Image 2000: Global Attitudes toward the U.S. in the New Millennium,* November 2000. 2001–2—Gallup Organization, *International End of the Year Terrorism Poll 2001.* July–October 2002—Pew Research Center, *What the World Thinks in 2002* (Washington, DC: Global Attitudes Project, 2002). March 2003—Pew Research Center, *Views of a Changing World* (June 2003). April–May 2003—Pew Research Center, *America's Image Further Erodes, Europeans Want Weaker Ties.* June 2003—ICM Research, *Survey for the British Broadcasting Corporation,* May–June 2003. February–March 2004—Pew Research Center, *A Year after Iraq War: Mistrust of America in Europe Ever Higher, Muslim Anger Persists,* 2004. April–May 2005—Pew Research Center, *U.S Image Up Slightly, but Still Negative,* 2005. April–May 2006—Pew Research Center, *Conflicting Views in a Divided World,* 2006. April–May 2007—Pew Research Center, *Global Unease with Major World Powers,* 2007.

Kosovo in 1998 no doubt contributed to the low esteem (37 percent favorable) accorded the United States by Russians in the 1999–2000 survey.

Most of those outside Europe who took part in the State Department surveys also generally judged the United States favorably, though with varying levels of enthusiasm. About three-fourths of publics in Japan, Morocco, Australia, and Indonesia provided favorable ratings, followed by those in Mexico, South Korea, and Brazil. The United States has security agreements with all of the countries except for Morocco and Indonesia.

In contrast, publics in countries with substantial Muslim populations presented decidedly mixed responses. America fared exceptionally well in Morocco (77 percent favorable) and Indonesia (75 percent favorable), nonaligned countries with which the United States has generally enjoyed at least moderately good relations. In longtime NATO ally Turkey, a Muslim country with a well-established tradition of secular rule since the Ataturk revolution of the 1920s, vigilantly enforced by the military, the results were mixed: 52 percent offered a favorable judgment of the United States. In contrast, only minorities in Nigeria (46 percent) and Pakistan (23 percent) did so. At least in the pre-9/11 period, the wide range of views in countries with substantial Muslim populations raises at least a question or two about the thesis of solid anti-Americanism among Muslims and Arabs, or about the theory that the end of the Cold War has given rise to a "clash of civilizations."[3]

The first of the post–September 11 polls reported in table 2.1 was a nine-nation study of countries with substantial Muslim populations by the Gallup Organization. At the time of the study—late 2001 and early 2002—U.S. and allied troops had invaded Afghanistan to capture leaders of the al Qaeda terrorist organization that took credit for the 9/11 attacks, and to remove the Taliban regime in Kabul, which had provided a base for various al Qaeda operations, including terrorist training camps. The Gallup surveys revealed a precipitous decline in favorable appraisals of the United States among the four Muslim countries that had also been surveyed by the State Department in 1999–2000. In NATO ally Turkey, positive opinions fell 12 percent to 40 percent. In Pakistan, a neighbor of Afghanistan that also provided a haven for radical anti-Western radical Islamic groups, only a minuscule 5 percent of those polled expressed a positive view of the United States. The figures for Saudi Arabia, another longtime ally that was also the country of origin of fifteen of the nineteen September 11 hijackers, were scarcely better, as only one respondent in six assessed the

---

3. Samuel P. Huntington, *The Clash of Civilizations and the Remaking of World Order* (New York: Simon and Schuster, 1996).

United States favorably.[4] Even in countries geographically more removed from the war in Afghanistan, notably Morocco (22 percent favorable) and Indonesia (21 percent favorable), the overwhelmingly positive views found in the State Department surveys had been completely reversed.

Table 2.1 includes seven surveys conducted by the Pew Research Center for the People and the Press between 2002 and 2007. The first of the seven surveys, about a year after the September 11 attacks, revealed that, with some exceptions, publics abroad accorded the United States favorable ratings. With the notable exception of Turkey, publics in all NATO allies judged the United States in highly favorable terms. Even French and German publics, who later would express much more critical views, joined those in other NATO countries in expressing very favorable judgments. The strong verbal and material support offered by Russian president Vladimir Putin to the military campaign against the Taliban and al Qaeda illustrated the kind of cooperation between Moscow and Washington that had been notably absent during the latter part of the 1990s. Public appraisals of the United States and Americans followed suit, rising sharply from the levels recorded two years earlier in the State Department survey. The Bush administration reciprocated by toning down or eliminating rhetoric about Russian human rights abuses in its campaign against separatists in the province of Chechnya. Aside from countries in the Middle East and Pakistan, the United States enjoyed a favorable image throughout most of the countries surveyed by Pew in 2002. That was the case even in Nigeria and Indonesia, both of which are home to large Muslim populations.[5] The figures for Indonesia reveal an especially impressive improvement, almost tripling from the 21 percent in the Gallup survey.

The Bush administration's rhetorical campaign against the Saddam Hussein regime was initiated in the president's 2002 State of the Union Address, in which Iraq, Iran, and North Korea were labeled as the international "axis of evil."[6] It picked up considerable momentum in early September because the

---

4. Responses from the three Gallup surveys not included in table 2.1 were Lebanon (41 percent favorable), Saudi Arabia (16 percent favorable), and Iran (14 percent favorable).

5. The overall assessments of the United States in the Nigerian surveys fail to reveal the very substantial differences between Christian and Muslim respondents in that country. For example, in the April–May 2003 and 2006 surveys, the United States was rated favorably by 61 percent and 62 percent of the Nigerian sample, but favorable ratings by Christians (85 percent and 89 percent) were far higher than those by Muslim respondents (38 percent and 32 percent).

6. A number of recent memoirs by former Bush administration officials indicate that removal of the Saddam Hussein regime was a top priority well before the September 11 terrorist attacks. The "Secret Downing Street Memo," dated July 23, 2002, indicates that British foreign policy officials were convinced that the Bush administration had already decided on war to oust Saddam Hussein and was searching for intelligence to support that decision. David Manning, "The Secret Downing Street Memo," *Times* (London), www.timesonline.co.uk, May 1, 2005.

anti-Iraq campaign was timed to coincide with the traditional beginning of
U.S. election campaigns and the first anniversary of the terrorist attacks on
New York and Washington. Although high administration officials were appar-
ently divided on the wisdom of taking the issue to the United Nations, the
United States ultimately did so, and it was able to gain unanimous support for
Security Council Resolution 1441, requiring Iraq to conform to commitments
made at the end of the 1991 Gulf War not to acquire weapons of mass destruction, and to admit UN inspectors to verify that it had no such weapons. The
Bush administration was also able to gain congressional approval for the use of
force against Iraq. By votes of 296–133 and 77–23 the House and Senate authorized President Bush to attack Iraq if Saddam refused to give up his weapons of
mass destruction, as required by several Security Council resolutions.

Iraq was the dominant international issue during winter–spring 2003, when
the Pew Research Center undertook two additional surveys. The March study,
which preceded the U.S. invasion of Iraq by just days, surveyed publics in eight
countries—seven NATO members (Great Britain, France, Germany, Italy,
Poland, Spain, Turkey) and Russia. The broader April–May 2003 surveys were
conducted in twenty-one countries, including the United States, and also in areas controlled by the Palestinian Authority.

As revealed in the fourth column of table 2.1, the extended debates about
Iraq in the Security Council and in many other venues did little to enhance
America's image among NATO allies. The contrast between the Pew survey results during the summer of 2002 and in March 2003 is striking. Even in Great
Britain and Poland, countries that contributed military units to the invasion of
Iraq, favorable assessments of the United States fell precipitously. Whereas
three-quarters of the British public had expressed a favorable view less than a
year earlier, that figure fell to less than a majority. Responses in Poland were
quite similar. The results in Spain, which later contributed a small contingent of
1,300 troops, police, and civilians, were even more dismal as only one respondent in seven expressed a favorable view of the United States. The results were
very similar in the other five countries involved in the March 2003 Pew surveys,
as favorable ratings declined by an average of more than 30 percent.

The figures for Turkey are especially telling. The Turkish parliament elected
in November 2002 was under intense pressure, involving both inducements
and threats, to permit the U.S. Fourth Infantry Division to be stationed in
Turkey, with a view to launching a second-front attack from the north against
Iraq. By a very close vote the Grand National Assembly in Ankara rejected the

U.S. request, reflecting faithfully the overwhelming opposition of the Turkish public against the deployment. A more detailed analysis of Turkish public views about the United States and its policies appears in chapter 4.

The Pew international surveys of April–May 2003 took place very shortly after invading American military forces took control of Baghdad and ousted the Saddam Hussein regime. The predictably rapid victory over the poorly equipped and abysmally led Iraqi forces, with losses of military and civilian lives that fell short of the most pessimistic prewar scenarios, resulted in a wide-spread rebound in assessment of the United States in most countries.[7] Only in one case, however, did the favorable responses match or exceed those of the Pew surveys in the previous summer: only in Pakistan was there an increase, but that was from 10 percent in 2002 to a still-abysmal 13 percent. Five of the six NATO countries that Pew had surveyed just prior to the Iraq war saw double-digit increases in favorable assessments of the United States—Turkey was the exception—and the average rose from 27 percent to 45 percent. Most of the other countries surveyed after the Iraq war by Pew had not been included in prewar studies, thus precluding pre- and postwar comparisons.

Shortly after the fall of Baghdad, the British Broadcasting Corporation also conducted a nine-country survey that included an item asking respondents to assess the United States. In four instances (Great Britain, France, Australia, South Korea) the results, reported in the sixth column of table 2.1, were strikingly similar to those of the Pew studies of the previous month; in four countries (Canada, Russia, Indonesia, Jordan) favorable assessments increased significantly, whereas the trend toward increasingly critical views of the United States among Brazilian respondents continued.

The four most recent Pew surveys, conducted annually between 2004 and 2007, revealed a mixed pattern of responses. Among NATO allies, Great Britain, Italy, Canada, and Poland stood out as the only countries in which a majority maintained a favorable view of the United States, and as in previous studies, Turkey stood out at the other end of the spectrum. By 2007, fewer than one in ten Turkish respondents expressed a positive judgment about the United States, an even worse result than in the Pew survey on the eve of the invasion of Iraq.

---

7. According to one careful study, Iraq had suffered some 12,950 fatalities during the war; about 29 percent of them were Iraqi noncombatants. The author indicates that the upper and lower limits of his estimates are 11,000 and 13,000. Carl Conetta, "The Wages of War: Iraqi Combatant and Noncombatant Fatalities in the 2003 Conflict," Commonwealth Institute, Project on Defense Alternatives, Research Monograph 8, Cambridge, MA, October 20, 2003. Other analyses have estimated that Iraqi deaths were much higher, perhaps exceeding 100,000.

There were, however, some encouraging signs elsewhere. Because China was included only in the three most recent Pew surveys, it is not possible to assess the immediate impact of the September 11 terrorist attacks and the invasion of Iraq on Chinese public opinion. The 2005 and 2006 results indicate, however, that the Chinese views of the United States were improving, to the point that in the latter survey virtually half of the respondents expressed favorable opinions, but that figure fell sharply to about one in three the following year.

Until the invasion of Afghanistan, Indonesians stood out among Muslim countries for their warm appraisals of the United States, but those feelings eroded rapidly thereafter, falling to a low of 15 percent in 2003. In 2005, the comparable figure had risen to 38 percent, almost surely as a result of American aid following the devastating tsunami disaster that struck Indonesia at the end of 2004. The most recent Pew surveys in 2006 and 2007 revealed small retreats in favorable appraisals. A fuller discussion of the sources and possible policy consequences of Indonesian views of the United States appears in chapter 4.

Publics in Nigeria, Japan, and Israel expressed favorable judgments of the United States, with the latter two countries counted among Washington's oldest allies. But good news also emerged from Pew surveys in India, where strong majorities of those taking part in the three most recent Pew surveys expressed a favorable view of the United States. The Indian appraisal in 2005 was by far the highest among the sixteen countries taking part in that study. Partial explanations for these results may be a shared concern about China's military buildup and the steady outsourcing of American technology jobs to India.[8] The 2006 and 2007 studies revealed some cooling of Indian enthusiasm for the United States. The controversy in Washington created by President Bush's agreement to exempt India from important features of the Nuclear Nonproliferation Treaty may have been a contributing factor. The sharp 2006 stock market decline in India might also have served to dampen support for U.S.-led globalization policies.

The Pew and most of the other surveys described throughout this book use a Likert scale, in which respondents are offered a series of options, usually rang-

---

8. For example, on June 24, 2005, two major American corporations announced that they were moving technology work to India. IBM stated that they would hire fourteen thousand workers in India, while cutting thirteen thousand jobs in Europe, and Wachovia, a large bank, made a similar announcement, without specifying how many jobs the shift would entail. "IBM to Boost Staff in India by 14,000" and "Wachovia Moving Tech Work to India," both in *Raleigh News and Observer*, June 25, 2005.

ing from "agree strongly" to "disagree strongly," or "approve strongly" to "disapprove strongly," and the like. A thermometer scale asks those taking part in the survey to use a scale of 0 ("very cold feelings") to 100 ("very warm feelings"). Feelings about the United States in five German Marshall Fund surveys are summarized in table 2.2. The results are generally in line with those reported in table 2.1, with a trend of declining favorable opinions during the 2002 to 2006 period. Rank-order correlations between responses to the five Pew and five GMF surveys during those same years are 0.81, 0.76, 1.00, 0.90, and 0.90. That surveys by two organizations using different question formats nevertheless yield quite similar results enhances confidence in the findings.

AMERICA'S INTERNATIONAL ROLE

The evidence cited in the preceding indicates that the widespread expressions of sympathy and support following the 9/11 terrorist attacks have eroded, as most publics abroad have become increasingly critical of the United States. In an initial effort to identify the reasons for the changes, this section examines reactions to various aspects of America's international role and the ways that the United States has exercised its leadership.

TABLE 2.2. Views of the United States, 2002–6

"I'd like you to rate your feelings toward some countries, institutions, and people, with 100 meaning a very warm, favourable feeling, 0 meaning a very cold, unfavourable feeling, and 50 meaning not particularly warm or cold. You can use any number from 0 to 100."

	Mean Scores on a Thermometer Scale of 0 to 100				
	2002	2003	2004	2005	2006
United States	—	92	89	86	84
France	60	50	51	50	46
Germany	63	56	55	51	53
Great Britain	68	61	62	57	54
Italy	68	61	61	57	55
Netherlands	59	55	55	54	52
Poland	65	61	56	56	58
Portugal	—	54	50	51	45
Spain	—	—	42	42	37
Slovakia	—	—	50	55	51
Turkey	—	—	28	28	20
Bulgaria	—	—	—	—	52
Romania	—	—	—	—	73

Source: German Marshall Fund, *Transatlantic Trends, 2006.*

Broad assessments of America's role emerged from year-end surveys in 2003, 2004, 2005, and 2006 by the Program on International Policy Attitudes (PIPA), which asked respondents whether "the United States is having a mainly positive influence in the world." As indicated in table 2.3, American respondents gave the United States a good report card in the 2003–4 survey, they gave an even better one in the following year, and by a still-favorable margin of about two to one they judged that the United States is having a mainly positive role in the world in the two most recent surveys.

These favorable appraisals were not widely shared abroad, as even British respondents leaned slightly toward the negative side of the question in the first of the surveys and responded with increasingly critical opinions in the following three polls. Interestingly, in the earliest of the four studies the United States received favorable ratings in five countries that declined to join the "coalition of the willing" for the invasion of Iraq—Mexico, Brazil, India, Nigeria, and South Africa—and negative judgments from those that deployed forces to Iraq, including NATO allies Great Britain, Italy, and Spain.

Responses to the most recent of the four surveys revealed that, among NATO allies, only in Poland was the United States judged to be having a positive influence in the world, but even there those with a positive opinion declined sharply—from 62 percent to 38 percent—between 2005 and 2006. The well-known critical views of the French and German were only moderately more negative than those of Spaniards and Canadians in the 2005–6 survey. Turkish respondents were most critical of all in the 2006–7 survey, as only 7 percent gave the United States a positive rating. The picture elsewhere is much the same as it had been in the earlier studies. Favorable judgments about the United States persisted in India, Nigeria, and the Philippines, but not among respondents in Latin America (Argentina, Brazil, Mexico, Chile), in Asian/Pacific area countries other than India (South Korea, Indonesia, China, Australia), or in Russia and Egypt. Overwhelmingly critical appraisals of 60 percent or more were especially notable in Indonesia, Argentina, and Australia.

Even prior to the September 11 terrorist attacks, State Department surveys included questions about the desirability of American global leadership. Post–September 11 polls by the German Marshall Fund posed the issue to publics in America's four most important European NATO allies—Germany, France, Italy, and Great Britain—and less frequently in Spain and Turkey. The early 2001 State Department study included the same question, with results that were very much in line with previous studies (table 2.4). The September 11 terrorist attacks stimulated another State Department survey that again asked about the desirability of American global leadership. Publics in the four major NATO allies responded by expressing dramatically greater support for U.S. leadership, ranging from an increase of 5 percent in France to 20 percent in Germany. When the same question was posed in the 2003 GMF surveys, which took place after the invasion of Iraq in March of that year, the results revealed strikingly diminished support for American leadership, ranging from declines of 17 percent in Great Britain and Italy to well over 20 percent in France and Germany. The 2004 GMF surveys coincided with increasing doubts about the existence of evidence that would sustain the stated reasons for the Iraq war—Iraqi weapons of mass destruction and links between the Saddam Hussein regime and the al Qaeda terrorist group responsible for the September 11 attacks. Those doubts, combined with the bloody insurgency in Iraq, probably contributed to further declines in support for American leadership among its key NATO allies.

Additional GMF surveys in 2005 and 2006 indicate continued erosion of enthusiasm for U.S. leadership in world affairs, including steep declines since 2002 of more than 20 percent among publics in four countries—Great Britain, the Netherlands, Italy, and Poland—that had previously been strong supporters of the United States and had joined the "coalition of the willing" in Iraq. The figures from other NATO allies, including Spain, Turkey, and Slovakia, were even worse, as no more than one respondent in five expressed support for U.S. leadership.

A more specific question about America's international role asked respondents in ten countries whether the U.S. military presence has "helped to bring peace and stability" to their regions (table 2.5). Responses varied widely. Eighty percent of Americans agreed, and pluralities in long-time allies Canada, Great Britain, and Australia also stated that the American military presence has had a favorable impact. However, strong majorities in support of the proposition emerged only in Israel and South Korea. As noted earlier (table 2.1), South Koreans often have been lukewarm in their views of the United States, but they also appear to appreciate the stabilizing role played by U.S. troops who have been stationed in their country for more than fifty years. Respondents in two predominantly Muslim countries—Indonesia and Jordan—joined those in France and Russia in expressing strong disagreement on the proposition that the American military presence has helped to bring peace and stability to their widely separated regions of the world.

A closely linked question, posed in 2003 by an ICM/BBC survey, asked respondents whether American military superiority made the world a safer or

TABLE 2.3. U.S. Influence in the World, 2003–7

"Do you agree or disagree that the United States is having a mainly positive influence in the world?" (2003–4 and 2004–5)

"Would you please tell me if you think the United States is having mainly a positive influence or mainly a negative influence in the world?" (2005–6 and 2006–7)

	November 2003–January 2004			November 2004–January 2005			October 2005–January 2006			November 2006–January 2007		
	% Agree	% Disagree	Net[a]	% Agree	% Disagree	Net[a]	% Positive	% Negative	Net[a]	% Positive	% Negative	Net[a]
United States	67	29	38	71	25	46	63	30	33	57	28	29
NATO allies												
Great Britain	47	49	-2	44	50	-6	36	57	-21	33	57	-24
France	21	74	-53	38	54	-16	25	65	-40	24	69	-45
Germany	16	82	-66	27	64	-37	21	65	-44	16	74	-58
Italy	35	56	-21	49	40	9	34	46	-12	35	47	-12
Poland	—	—	—	52	21	31	62	15	47	38	24	14
Spain	33	61	-28	29	51	-22	33	53	-20	—	—	—
Turkey	11	69	-58	18	62	-44	15	49	-34	7	69	-62
Canada	41	56	-15	34	60	-26	30	60	-30	—	—	—

Other key countries

Mexico	46	42	4	11	57	-46	10	55	-45	12	53	-41
Brazil	53	44	9	42	51	-9	33	60	-27	29	57	-28
Russia	14	54	-40	16	63	-47	22	52	-30	19	59	-40
Japan	—	—	—	24	31	-7	—	—	—	—	60	-31
Australia	—	—	—	40	52	-12	29	60	-31	29	60	-31
South Korea	—	—	—	52	45	7	44	53	-9	35	54	-19
Indonesia	39	58	-19	38	51	-13	40	47	-7	21	71	-50
India	70	24	46	54	30	24	44	17	27	30	28	2
Egypt	—	—	—	—	—	—	—	—	—	11	59	-48
Nigeria	57	38	19	—	—	—	76	17	59	72	20	52
China	38	48	-10	40	42	-2	22	62	-40	28	52	-24
South Africa	51	38	13	56	35	21	49	18	31	—	—	—
Argentina	15	72	-57	19	65	-46	19	62	-43	13	64	-51
Chile	31	62	-31	29	50	-21	—	—	—	33	51	-18
Uruguay	23	66	-43	—	—	—	—	—	—	—	—	—
Philippines	—	—	—	88	9	79	85	10	75	73	11	62

Source: PIPA/Globescan, *19 Nation Poll on Global Issues*, 2003–4; PIPA/Globescan, *World Public Opinion Says World Not Going in Right Direction*, 2004–5; PIPA/Globescan, *In 20 of 23 Countries Polled Citizens Want Europe to Be More Influential Than U.S.*, 2005–6; PIPA/Globescan, *World View of U.S. Role Goes from Bad to Worse*, 2006–7.

[a] Net = percent "agree" minus percent "disagree" in the 2003–4 and 2004–5 surveys and percent "positive" minus percent "negative" in the 2005–6 and 2006–7 surveys.

TABLE 2.4   Views of U.S. Leadership in World Affairs, 1982–2006

"How desirable is it that the United States exert strong leadership in world affairs? Very desirable, somewhat desirable, somewhat undesirable, or very undesirable?"

Percent "Very Desirable" Plus "Somewhat Desirable"

	1982	1993	1997	1998	1999	2000	Spring 2001	Fall 2001	2002	2003	2004	2005	2006
United States	—	—	—	—	—	—	—	—	83	—	—	84	83
France	23	37	44	53	45	43	46	51	48	27	24	28	30
Germany	56	70	47	64	50	51	52	72	68	45	37	39	43
Great Britain	75	65	72	77	69	68	68	82	72	55	54	54	48
Italy	61	47	53	65	36	40	44	62	63	46	41	38	34
Netherlands	—	—	—	—	—	—	—	—	75	57	59	56	49
Poland	—	—	—	—	—	—	—	—	64	53	39	42	40
Portugal	—	—	—	—	—	—	—	—	—	43	32	43	38
Spain	—	25	24	29	—	27	—	—	—	—	18	23	20
Slovakia	—	—	—	—	—	—	—	—	—	—	21	33	19
Turkey	—	—	36	—	—	—	—	33	—	—	16	17	13
Bulgaria	—	—	—	—	—	—	—	—	—	—	—	—	21
Romania	—	—	—	—	—	—	—	—	—	—	—	—	48

Source: 1982–2001: *Europeans and Anti-Americanism: Fact vs. Fiction; A Study of Public Attitudes toward the U.S.,* U.S. Department of State, Office of Research, September 2002. 2002–6: German Marshall Fund, *Transatlantic Trends, 2006.*

TABLE 2.5.   Impact of the American Military Presence, 2003

"Thinking about the American military presence in this part of the world, do you agree or disagree that it has helped to bring peace and stability to the area?"

	% Agree	% Disagree	Net[b]
United States[a]	80	18	62
Australia	50	40	10
Brazil		— Not asked —	
Canada	48	43	5
France	34	60	−26
Indonesia	16	74	−58
Israel	60	33	27
Jordan	12	87	−75
S. Korea	63	31	32
Russia	11	78	−67
Great Britain	49	41	8

Source: ICM Research, *Survey for the British Broadcasting Corporation,* May–June 2003.

[a]U.S. wording: "Do you agree or disagree that America's military presence around the world helps bring international peace and stability?"

[b]Net = percent "agree" minus percent "disagree." "Don't know" responses excluded.

more dangerous place (table 2.6). Although the survey included a number of America's major allies, only in the United States and Israel did a majority of the publics select the "safer place" option. Pluralities in Australia, Canada, and Great Britain expressed the same opinion, but strong majorities in Brazil, Indonesia, Jordan, South Korea, and Russia disagreed. The South Korean judgment seems incongruent in the light of the view that the American military presence has brought peace and stability to North Asia (table 2.5).

One of the more contentious issues among international relations theorists is the relationship between system structure, as measured by the distribution of power, and international stability. The 2002 and 2004 Pew surveys asked respondents to address one facet of this issue: "Do you think the world would be a safer place or a more dangerous place if there was another country that was equal in military power to the United States?" The results are reported in table 2.7.

Not surprisingly, in 2002 more than two-thirds of Americans asserted that the existence of another superpower would make the world more dangerous. This is one issue on which there was almost an international consensus, as respondents in all but a handful of other countries agreed with the U.S. judgment. The Pew survey was conducted at a time when it was already probable that the Iraq issue would divide not only the Security Council but also much of the world. Nevertheless, publics in France, Germany, and Russia were in close

TABLE 2.6. The Effects of America's Superior Military Power, 2003

"George W. Bush has said that 'America has, and intends to keep, military strength beyond challenge.' Does America's superior military power make the world a safer place, a more dangerous place or does it make no difference?"

	% Safer Place	% Makes No Difference	% More Dangerous Place	Net[a]
United States	68	18	12	56
Australia	42	14	39	3
Brazil	12	23	59	−47
Canada	41	19	37	4
France	17	36	45	−28
Indonesia	13	8	72	−59
Israel	56	19	21	35
Jordan	6	14	79	−73
South Korea	20	8	67	−47
Russia	7	16	66	−59
Great Britain	37	26	34	3

Source: ICM Research, *Survey for the British Broadcasting Corporation,* May–June 2003.
[a]Net = percent "safer place" minus percent "more dangerous place." "Don't know" responses excluded.

agreement with Americans, with majorities of better than two to one expressing the view that the existence of a second superpower would be dangerous. Some American critics have accused France of opposing the United States on Iraq in order to erode Washington's international standing and thereby enhance France's drive to play a major leadership role. Whether or not French leaders have been driven by that aspiration, it is not a goal that in 2002 had widespread support among the French public, only 30 percent of whom believed that the emergence of another superpower would make the world a safer

TABLE 2.7. Potential Impact of Another Country Equal to the United States in Military Power, 2002 and 2004

"Do you think the world would be a safer place or a more dangerous place if there was another country that was equal in military power to the United States?"

	July–October 2002			February–March 2004		
	% Safer Place	% More Dangerous	Net[a]	% Safer Place	% More Dangerous	Net[a]
United States	19	69	−50	30	50	−20
NATO allies						
Great Britain	27	60	−33	42	43	−1
France	30	64	−34	54	41	12
Germany	27	63	−36	37	47	−10
Italy	30	54	−24	—	—	—
Poland	26	46	−20	—	—	—
Czech Republic	27	53	−26	—	—	—
Turkey	40	44	−4	41	46	−5
Canada	26	63	−37	—	—	—
Other key countries						
Mexico	20	70	−50	—	—	—
Brazil	37	56	−19	—	—	—
Russia	25	53	−28	37	44	−7
Japan	6	88	−82	—	—	—
South Korea	36	56	−20	—	—	—
Indonesia	23	68	−45	—	—	—
India	45	29	16	—	—	—
Pakistan	19	51	−36	18	61	−43
Jordan	33	63	−30	29	53	−24
Egypt	25	55	−30	—	—	—
Morocco	—	—	—	21	65	−44
Nigeria	47	44	3	—	—	—

Source: Pew Research Center, *What the World Thinks in 2002* (Washington, DC: Global Attitudes Project, 2002); Pew Research Center, *A Year after Iraq War: Mistrust of America in Europe Ever Higher, Muslim Anger Persists,* 2004.

[a]Net = percent "safer place" minus percent "more dangerous place."

place. Given the superpower status of the USSR during the Cold War period, the apparent lack of widespread nostalgia for "the good old days" among Russians is especially interesting.

Respondents in regions other than Europe also generally agreed with Americans on this issue. The question could not be posed in China—an obvious candidate for future superpower status—but among other important regional powers, including Japan, South Korea, Canada, and Brazil, there was at best lukewarm enthusiasm for a bipolar international system. Only in India (another potential future superpower) and Nigeria did a plurality of respondents express the view that a military competitor to the United States would make the world safer. Even in predominantly Muslim countries, where the prevailing view of the United States, as revealed in table 2.1, lies somewhere between disdain and outright hostility, a majority in none of those surveyed by Pew (Turkey, Indonesia, Pakistan, Jordan, and Egypt) judged the possible existence of another superpower as a contribution toward making the world a safer place.

An interesting pattern emerged when the same question was posed by the Pew Research Center in a smaller sample of countries in early 2004. The key intervening international event was, of course, the invasion of Iraq in March 2003, resulting in a regime change in Baghdad. Among NATO countries and in Russia there was a notable movement away from the view that the emergence of another superpower would make the world more dangerous. Only in France did a slight majority (54 percent) welcome that prospect, but in the United States, Great Britain, Germany, and Russia the margin in favor of the "more dangerous" response fell by double digits; even in the United States, presumably the country with least to gain by the emergence of a rival military superpower, those selecting that option declined from 69 percent to 50 percent during the eighteen-month interval between the two Pew surveys.

SENSITIVITY TO THE INTERESTS OF OTHERS

In presenting his committee's 2003 report on declining support for the United States abroad, Ambassador Djerejian pointed to the need for more effective public diplomacy, but he also noted that American policies probably accounted for 80 percent of the critical views of the United States.[9] This section summarizes survey evidence on the question, with a view to assessing the validity of

---

9. Djerejian, "Briefing on the Report on Public Diplomacy."

Djerejian's thesis that American foreign policies are the primary impetus for growing anti-American sentiments abroad.

The "realist" approach to international affairs is rooted in the proposition that countries will pursue their own vital interests. A corollary is that effective statesmen must be sensitive to, if not necessarily sympathetic with, the vital interests of others. As Hans Morgenthau, the dean of American realist theorists, stated:

> Political realism refuses to identify the moral aspirations of a particular nation with the moral laws of the universe. . . . [I]t is exactly the concept of interest defined in terms of power that saves us from both moral excess and political folly. . . . We are able to judge other nations as we judge our own and having judged them in this fashion, we are then capable of pursuing policies that respect the interests of other nations, while protecting and promoting those of our own.[10]

Since the September 11 attacks, the United States has not been reticent about defining its vital interests in dealing with terrorism and in making demands upon others to follow America's lead in foreign affairs. The assertion that "you are with us or you are with the terrorists" has been Washington's position with unmistakable clarity. Bush administration officials have repeatedly claimed that, in contrast to those that preceded them, they are guided by realism rather than the mushy idealism they attributed to the Bill Clinton administration. To what extent have American demands also taken into account the interests of other countries in the manner stipulated by Morgenthau's definition of realism?

The Pew 2002 survey of forty-four countries asked, "In making international policy decisions, to what extent do you think the United States takes into account the interests of countries like [your country]—a great deal, a fair amount, not too much, or not at all?" The question was repeated in the Pew 2003, 2004, 2005, and 2007 studies.

Most Americans believe that the interests of other countries are reasonably well considered in Washington (table 2.8). In all five of the Pew surveys, over two-thirds of Americans selected one of the first two response options, whereas only 30 percent or fewer of them felt that the interests of other countries were largely disregarded. The major intervening event between the first two Pew surveys—the invasion of Iraq—had only minor impact on American responses.

---

10. Hans J. Morgenthau, *Politics among Nations*, 4th edition (New York: Knopf, 1967), 10–11.

That is, Americans continue to believe that officials in Washington are indeed sensitive to the vital interests of other countries, although that does not, of course, imply an answer to the question whether U.S. policies should be affected by the preferences of others.

The American belief that U.S foreign policy decision makers pay adequate attention to the interests of other countries is not widely shared abroad. Rather, two generalizations emerge from responses to the five Pew surveys, summarized in table 2.8. First, the 2002 Pew survey revealed that publics in countries with the closest ties to the United States, including those in NATO members, did not believe that Washington was especially sensitive to their interests. Majorities of various magnitudes, even in staunch ally Great Britain and in neighboring Canada and Mexico, judged that the United States takes their interests into account "not much" or "not at all."

Second, the invasion of Iraq in March 2003 did little to enhance the American reputation for sensitivity to the interests of its allies, much less those of other countries with less intimate ties to the United States. During the intervening year, top officials in the Pentagon and elsewhere in Washington described several NATO allies in less than flattering terms. These barbs were aimed primarily at France, Germany, Belgium, and Luxembourg (the latter two countries were not included in any of the five Pew surveys that posed the question about U.S. sensitivity to others). Not surprisingly, publics in these targets of undiplomatic rhetoric were less inclined to describe the United States as sensitive to their interests. In the light of the anti-France hysteria among some well-placed American officials—including the replacement of French fries by "freedom fries" in the House of Representatives cafeteria—it is worth noting that French responses in 2005 and 2007, while at the low end of the countries listed in table 2.8, were more flattering than those in Turkey, which received some well-publicized verbal spankings for refusing to allow the U.S. Fourth Infantry Division to deploy in Turkey to launch a northern front strike against Iraq, or in Spain, which joined the "coalition of the willing" in Iraq.

Although Great Britain, the Netherlands, Poland, and Australia also sent armed forces to join the invasion of Iraq, respondents in these countries were not impressed that U.S. decision makers are concerned with their national interests. British views on the issue are especially telling because Prime Minister Tony Blair has been an ultraloyal ally, following Washington's lead into Iraq despite lukewarm support for the invasion at home. Other than frequent photo opportunities featuring Blair and President Bush, there is little indication that the latter had responded in kind by offering support on the issues of most in-

TABLE 2.8. U.S. Attention to Interests of Other Countries, 2002–7

"In making international policy decisions, to what extent do you think the United States takes into account the interests of countries like [your country]—a great deal, a fair amount, not too much, or not at all?"

	July–October 2002			April–May 2003			February–March 2004			April–May 2005			April–May 2007		
	% A Great Deal	% Not at All	Net[a]	% A Great Deal	% Not at All	Net[a]	% A Great Deal	% Not at All	Net[a]	% A Great Deal	% Not at All	Net[a]	% A Great Deal	% Not at All	Net[a]
United States	31	3	28	28	6	22	34	6	28	28	7	21	23	8	15
NATO allies															
Great Britain	11	15	–4	7	16	–9	7	18	–11	8	22	–14	7	29	–22
France	4	26	–22	1	41	–40	3	33	–30	2	31	–29	1	40	–39
Germany	9	10	–1	3	24	–21	3	22	–19	3	15	–12	3	22	–19
Italy	6	17	–11	6	21	–15	—	—	—	—	—	—	3	17	–14
Poland	4	20	–16	—	—	—	—	—	—	2	28	–26	2	22	–20
Czech Republic	3	18	–15	—	—	—	—	—	—	—	—	—	2	27	–25
Spain	—	—	—	7	34	–27	—	—	—	7	47	–40	3	44	–41
Turkey	5	47	–42	3	58	–55	5	44	–39	3	50	–47	5	56	–51
Canada	7	26	–19	5	28	–23	—	—	—	4	25	–21	2	33	–31
Netherlands	—	—	—	—	—	—	—	—	—	4	28	–24	—	—	—

Other key countries

Mexico	12	27	-15	—	—	—	—	—	—	—	—	—	13	24	-11
Brazil	13	28	-15	13	29	-16	—	—	—	—	—	—	21	27	-6
Russia	3	25	-22	7	33	-26	5	30	-25	—	—	-23	4	31	-27
Japan	4	10	-6	—	—	—	—	—	—	—	—	—	3	9	-6
Australia	—	—	—	8	21	-13	—	—	—	—	—	—	—	—	—
South Korea	5	19	-14	5	19	-14	—	—	—	13	4	9	5	21	-16
Indonesia	12	10	2	5	17	-12	—	—	—	21	10	11	9	9	0
India	13	14	-1	—	—	—	—	—	—	12	21	-9	16	8	8
Pakistan	5	27	-22	4	40	-36	3	32	-29	—	—	—	5	35	-30
Israel	—	—	—	25	5	20	—	—	—	—	—	—	24	6	18
Kuwait	—	—	—	27	15	12	—	—	—	—	—	—	8	42	-34
Jordan	7	36	-29	3	36	-33	1	39	-38	5	41	-36	8	32	-24
Morocco	—	—	—	13	46	-33	9	41	-32	—	—	—	3	57	-54
Nigeria	49	6	43	29	16	13	—	—	—	—	—	—	30	8	22
Lebanon	—	—	—	5	45	-40	—	—	—	13	30	-17	6	33	-27
Palestinian territories	—	—	—	1	61	-60	—	—	—	12	10	2	5	57	-52
China	—	—	—	—	—	—	—	—	—	—	—	—	10	11	-1

Source: Pew Research Center, *What the World Thinks in 2002* (Washington, DC: Global Attitudes Project, 2002); Pew Research Center, *Views of a Changing World,* June 2003; Pew Research Center, *A Year after Iraq War: Mistrust of America in Europe Ever Higher, Muslim Anger Persists,* 2004. Pew Research Center, *U.S. Image Up Slightly, but Still Negative,* 2005; Pew Research Center, *Global Unease with Major World Powers,* 2007.

[a]Net = percent "a great deal" minus percent "not at all."

terest to the British, including trade, environmental issues, the International Criminal Court, increased aid to Africa, and the like.[11] The Blair Labor government survived the 2005 parliamentary election, but it did so while losing most of its majority even though it was pitted against Tory and Social Democrat parties that were hamstrung by rather weak and ineffective leaders.

Finally, the responses of South Koreans are of special interest because North Korea was identified as a member of the "axis of evil" in President Bush's 2002 State of the Union address and because of the heightened tensions between Washington and Pyongyang over the latter's open boast and demonstration that it has an active nuclear weapons program. The United States has stationed troops in South Korea for decades and is pledged by the Mutual Security Treaty of 1954 to protect that country against another incursion from the north. It is nevertheless clear that few South Koreans believe that their concerns play much of a role in American decision making. Additional analyses of South Korean views appear in chapter 4.

The 2005 and 2007 Pew surveys confirmed, once again, that publics in America's closest allies do not believe that Washington pays much attention to their vital interests. The response option "a great deal" never reached even 10 percent in any NATO country, whereas "not at all" was chosen by a low 15 percent in Germany to a high of 56 percent in Turkey. However, in some other countries the United States revealed a somewhat more favorable scorecard on sensitivity to their interests, notably in Indonesia, India, Israel, and Nigeria. In each case, those selecting "a great deal," while constituting a small minority, nevertheless matched or outnumbered those choosing the "not at all" response option. American aid following the tsunami tragedy in the waning days of 2004 no doubt accounted for at least part of the higher sensitivity ratings in Indonesia.

On balance, then, the belief that the administration in Washington is largely indifferent to the vital interests of others is quite widespread, and it is especially deeply felt among publics in members of NATO, America's most important alliance since its inception more than a half century ago.

THE USES OF FORCE

In September 2002, one year after the September 11 terrorist attacks on New York and Washington, the Bush administration released the document *The Na-*

---

11. For a brief summary of the many policy humiliations inflicted by the Bush administration on Great Britain, see Alex Massie, "Dog Days: Breaking the Special Relationship," *New Republic* (April 3, 2006): 18–19.

tional Security Strategy of the United States of America.[12] The core of the national security strategy (NSS) was that in the post-9/11 global environment, the Cold War policies of deterrence and containment can no longer ensure security and thus the United States has a self-justified right to undertake military action against any adversary that might pose a serious future national security threat. The right of self-defense has long been accepted in international law and it is, in fact, embedded within the United Nations Charter in Article 51, but in order to undertake preemptive use of military force, the threat must be massive, imminent, and permit no time for alternative responses.[13]

The Pew Global Attitudes survey undertaken in the spring of 2003, soon after the overthrow of the Saddam Hussein regime in Iraq, asked respondents whether "using military force against countries that may seriously threaten our country" would be justified. That is, the question asked those taking part to assess an action such as that contemplated in the NSS. Results from the Pew survey are summarized in table 2.9.

A majority of respondents in the United States, Great Britain, and Australia—three of the four countries that contributed personnel to the 2003 invasion of Iraq—judged that preemptive use of military force in such circumstances was either "often" or "sometimes" justified. Turks were almost evenly divided on the issue, but the 27 percent who stated that such action was "often" justified was the highest among NATO members. In contrast, although Spain subsequently sent a token military unit to Iraq, Spaniards taking part in the survey were second only to Jordanians in their opposition to such action, as a majority asserted that it was "never" justified.

Respondents elsewhere also expressed varying degrees of approval of preemptive military action. Canadians were almost evenly split on the question, with 51 percent asserting that it was "often" or "sometimes" justified and 45 percent judging that preemption was "rarely" or "never" acceptable. The most pronounced expressions of support for preemption emerged from responses in Pakistan (70 percent) and Israel (66 percent), two countries that exist in volatile regions, have frequently gone to war with their neighbors, continue to have unresolved territorial disputes in Kashmir and Palestine, respectively, and also

---

12. White House, *The National Security Strategy of the United States of America,* http://www.whitehouse.gov/nsc/nss.pdf.
13. Michael Byers, "Preemptive Self-Defense: Hegemony, Equality, and Strategies of Legal Change," *Journal of Political Philosophy* 11 (June 2003): 171–90. For an extended analysis by an expert on military affairs, see Jeffrey Record, "The Bush Doctrine and the War with Iraq," *Parameters: U.S. Army War College Quarterly* (spring 2003): 4–21.

possess nuclear weapons. Israel has long acted on principles similar to those articulated in the NSS—witness the attack in 1981 on an Iraqi nuclear plant as it was nearing completion as well as more limited preemptive strikes against organizations and individuals deemed to pose a terrorist threat to Israel. Perhaps more worrying is the fact that such a large majority of Pakistanis were willing to sanction preemptive use of force at least "sometimes." It seems clear that these respondents did not have in mind an attack against Iraq inasmuch as a huge majority of those taking part in the survey also approved of Pakistan's decision *not* to take part in the invasion to remove the Saddam Hussein regime (see table 2.14). Rather they almost surely responded with India in mind; Pak-

TABLE 2.9. Attitudes about Preemptive Military Force against Potential Threats, 2003

"Do you think that using military force against countries that may seriously threaten our country, but have not attacked us, can often be justified, sometimes be justified, rarely be justified, or never be justified?"

	% Often Justified	% Sometimes Justified	% Rarely Justified	% Never Justified	% Don't Know/ Refused
United States	22	44	17	13	3
NATO allies					
Great Britain	15	50	20	13	2
France	7	35	26	30	2
Germany	7	24	31	35	3
Italy	8	30	19	40	3
Spain	9	19	18	51	3
Turkey	27	19	11	37	6
Canada	10	41	29	16	4
Other key countries					
Brazil	8	17	21	43	11
Russia	11	16	21	42	11
Australia	12	41	30	15	2
South Korea	10	32	30	25	3
Indonesia	9	21	36	29	5
Pakistan	44	26	11	12	7
Israel	35	31	13	18	3
Kuwait	27	18	9	43	4
Jordan	1	5	28	65	[a]
Morocco	8	16	19	42	15
Nigeria	20	26	18	31	5

Source: Pew Research Center, *Views of a Changing World*, June 2003.
[a]Fewer than 0.5 percent.

istan has lost three wars to its larger neighbor since independence, has a serious territorial grievance—Kashmir—against India, and has gone to the brink of war against India several times in recent years. Because India was not included in the 2003 Pew survey, it is impossible to determine whether the views about preemptive action expressed in Pakistan could also be found in India; it seems a reasonable guess that they would.

Publics in the other NATO countries expressed only modest approval of preemptive action, including France (42 percent), Italy (38 percent), and Germany (31 percent), and Russians were even less likely to support preemptive action. Although South Korea is faced with a hostile northern neighbor that has embarked on a nuclear weapons program and conducted a successful atomic bomb test in 2006, only a minority of respondents (42 percent) in that country felt that preemptive military action is justified.

At the other end of the spectrum, at least 40 percent of those taking part in the Pew surveys in Italy, Spain, Brazil, Russia, Kuwait, Jordan, and Morocco answered "never" to the question about when preemptive military action might be justified.

THE WAR ON TERRORISM

Many countries have been the targets of terrorist activities in which nonstate actors employ violence against civilians with a view to gaining international attention and achieving political goals. The hostage-taking events and murder of Israeli athletes at the 1972 Munich Olympic Games took place before the highest concentrations of media persons in history, and thus, they were played out before a huge global audience. The United States has suffered losses in several such events, but until the attacks of September 11, 2001, the worst terrorist attack on U.S. territory—the Oklahoma City bombing—was perpetrated by a homegrown decorated veteran of the Persian Gulf War and some of his right-wing confederates. The attacks on the World Trade Center towers and the Pentagon tragically illustrated the point that it is virtually impossible for any country to provide absolute security against well-organized plotters who are prepared to commit suicide to make a dramatic political statement.

The initial reaction abroad to the 9/11 attacks was one of overwhelming sympathy and support for the United States. For the first time in its history, NATO members invoked Article 5, "An attack on one is an attack on all," but the administration's response to offers of allied support was distinctly lukewarm as it preferred to go it alone rather than having to coordinate and possibly having to compromise with allies. Despite U.S. disdain for NATO's action, the military campaign in Afghanistan that overthrew the Taliban regime benefited from many contributions of many countries, ranging from deployment of troops, basing rights, and overflight rights in nearby countries to intelligence about terrorist networks.

Even before the September 11 attacks there was an active debate on the causes of terrorism and the most effective means of combating it. When publics were asked by a German Marshall Fund survey whether military action is the most appropriate way to eliminate terrorist organizations, responses ranged from 42 percent in Germany to 74 percent in Turkey (table 2.10). Differences among American, British, French, Polish, Dutch, and Portuguese publics, all of whom expressed support for the proposition on the utility of military force against terrorists, were rather small. These findings offer little support for the cliché that Americans are from Mars whereas Europeans are from Venus.

In six annual surveys conducted between 2002 and 2007, the Pew Research

TABLE 2.10. Military Action to Eliminate Terrorist Organizations Is the Most Appropriate Way to Fight Terrorism, 2004

"Please tell me whether you agree or disagree with each of the following: Military action to eliminate terrorist organizations is the most appropriate way to fight terrorism."

	% Agree
United States	63[a]
Great Britain	56
France	55
Germany	42
Italy	43
Poland	57
Spain	44
Turkey	74
Netherlands	58
Portugal	54
Slovakia	45

Source: German Marshall Fund, *Transatlantic Trends,* 2004.

[a]U.S. responses by party: Republicans 86%, Democrats 51%, independents 61%.

Center asked a more specific question about support for the "the U.S.-led efforts to fight terrorism." The results, presented in table 2.11, can be summarized in two broad generalizations. The range of views expressed by respondents in the participating countries was quite wide in all six surveys, and with a few exceptions, assessments of the U.S. effort were generally less favorable in 2007 than they had been five years earlier. The latter finding may have arisen at least in part because some respondents drew a distinction between the military campaigns in Afghanistan and Iraq; that is, they may have viewed the invasion of Afghanistan as a legitimate response to the September 11 attacks, but they regarded the invasion of Iraq as, at best, a diversion rather than a central part of the fight against terrorists.

Publics in eight of the nine NATO countries surveyed by Pew in 2002 (including the United States) expressed strong support for American antiterrorism policies. Aside from Turkey, where the opponents of U.S. policies outnumbered the supporters by almost two to one, in none of the other countries did as many as one-third of the respondents state that they were opposed. Interestingly, expressions of support for American antiterrorism policies in France, Germany, and Russia—all 70 percent or higher—exceeded those in Great Britain. The five post-Iraq-war surveys undertaken by Pew (2003–7) revealed a steady erosion of support among many NATO allies for American antiterrorism efforts. The 2005 survey found strong support for U.S. policy in Poland and the Netherlands, and that approval persisted in Poland and the Czech Republic through 2007. In contrast, by 2007 49 percent of British respondents opposed policies pursued by Washington, while majorities among publics in France, Germany, Spain, Canada, and Turkey also opposed them. It might be noted that Madrid (March 2004) and London (July 2005) suffered bloody terrorist bombings in recent years.

Support and opposition for U.S. efforts against terrorism among countries other than NATO allies were very mixed. Respondents in Russia, where the government has sought to gain legitimacy for its actions against Chechen rebels by defining them as part of a broader fight against global terrorism, have been among the strongest supporters. Israel, Nigeria, and India, also the victims of several terrorist bombings, have consistently favored U.S. efforts, whereas South Korea has not.

The finding of variability in support of American counterterrorism policies emerged most clearly in countries with significant Muslim populations; they have generally opposed the U.S. efforts. With the exception of Nigeria, expressions of opposition vastly outnumbered those in favor of U.S. policies across all

TABLE 2.11. Assessments of the U.S.-Led Efforts to Fight Terrorism, 2002–7

"And which comes closer to describing your view? I favor the U.S.-led efforts to fight terrorism, or, I oppose the U.S.-led efforts to fight terrorism."

	July–October 2002			April–May 2003			February–March 2004			April–May 2005			April–May 2006			April–May 2007		
	% Favor	% Oppose	Net[a]	% Favor	% Oppose	Net[a]	% Favor	% Oppose	Net[a]	% Favor	% Oppose	Net[a]	% Favor	% Oppose	Net[a]	% Favor	% Oppose	Net[a]
United States	89	8	81	—	—	—	81	13	68	76	18	58	73	19	54	70	23	47
NATO allies																		
Great Britain	69	23	46	63	30	33	63	30	33	51	40	11	49	42	7	38	49	-11
France	75	23	52	60	39	21	50	47	3	51	48	3	43	57	-14	43	57	-14
Germany	70	25	45	60	35	25	55	43	12	50	45	5	47	50	-3	42	51	-9
Italy	67	22	45	70	27	43	—	—	—	—	—	—	—	—	—	40	41	-1
Poland	81	11	70	—	—	—	—	—	—	61	29	32	—	—	—	52	36	16
Czech Republic	82	17	65	—	—	—	—	—	—	—	—	—	—	—	—	57	38	19
Spain	—	—	—	63	32	31	—	—	—	26	67	-41	19	76	-57	21	67	-46
Turkey	30	58	-28	22	71	-49	37	56	-19	17	71	-54	14	77	-63	9	79	-70
Canada	68	27	41	68	26	42	—	—	—	45	47	-2	—	—	—	37	56	-19
Netherlands	—	—	—	—	—	—	—	—	—	71	26	45	—	—	—	—	—	—

Other key countries

Mexico	52	37	15	—	—	—	—	—	—	—	—	—	—	—	—	31	61	-30
Brazil	57	35	22	42	53	-11	—	—	—	—	—	—	—	—	—	41	53	-12
Russia	73	16	57	51	28	23	73	20	53	55	34	21	52	35	17	50	33	17
Japan	61	32	29	—	—	—	—	—	—	—	—	—	—	—	—	40	47	-7
Australia	—	—	—	68	28	40	—	—	—	—	—	—	—	—	—	10	86	-76
South Korea	24	72	-48	24	71	-47	—	—	—	—	—	—	—	—	—	32	56	-24
Indonesia	31	64	-33	23	72	-49	—	—	—	50	42	8	39	57	-18	49	42	7
India	65	10	55	—	—	—	16	60	-44	52	41	11	65	30	35	13	59	-46
Pakistan	20	45	-25	16	74	-58	—	—	—	22	52	-30	30	50	-20	78	16	62
Israel	—	—	—	85	13	72	—	—	—	—	—	—	—	—	—	37	54	-17
Kuwait	—	—	—	56	35	21	—	—	—	—	—	—	—	—	—	18	77	-59
Jordan	13	85	-72	2	97	-95	12	78	-66	12	86	-74	16	74	-58	26	67	-41
Egypt	5	79	-74	—	—	—	28	66	-38	—	—	—	10	82	-72	16	64	-48
Morocco	—	—	—	9	84	-75	—	—	—	—	—	—	—	—	—	34	63	-29
Lebanon	38	56	-18	30	67	-37	—	—	—	31	65	-34	—	—	—	—	—	—
Palestinian territories	—	—	—	2	94	-92	—	—	—	—	—	—	—	—	—	6	79	-73
Nigeria	75	20	55	60	36	24	—	—	—	—	—	—	49	47	2	63	33	30
China	—	—	—	—	—	—	—	—	—	—	—	—	19	63	-44	26	55	-29

Source: Pew Research Center, *What the World Thinks in 2002* (Washington, DC: Global Attitudes Project, 2002); Pew Research Center, *Views of a Changing World*, June 2003; Pew Research Center, *A Year after Iraq War: Mistrust of America in Europe Ever Higher, Muslim Anger Persists*, 2004; Pew Research Center, *U.S. Image Up Slightly, but Still Negative*, 2005; Pew Research Center, *Conflicting Views in a Divided World*, 2006; Pew Research Center, *Global Unease with Major World Powers*, 2007.

[a]Net = percent "favor" minus percent "oppose." "Don't know" and "refused" responses excluded.

the Pew surveys. The United States has generally maintained good relations with Egypt (the recipient of the second-largest annual U.S. foreign aid package since the Camp David Accords), Pakistan, Jordan, Lebanon, and Turkey (a NATO member). Nevertheless, in 2002 and 2003 public support for U.S. policies in these countries ranged from moderate (56 percent in Kuwait) to abysmal (5 percent in Egypt and even lower in Jordan and in the Palestinian territories), and the subsequent surveys did not unearth substantial changes for the better.

The absence of consistent support for U.S. policies extended not only to Middle Eastern countries but also to those in more geographically removed areas, including Morocco and Indonesia, both countries that, like Egypt, have experienced bloody terrorist bombings. Whereas Indonesians also expressed critical appraisal of the U.S. policy in the first two Pew surveys, in 2005 half of them stated that they favored the American effort, but that support fell again during the following two years. Indonesia was the site of suicide bombings in Bali, most likely by the Jemaah Islamiyah organization, in October 2002 and October 2005, resulting in 202 and 23 deaths, respectively. In each case, the subsequent Pew surveys revealed a sharp *decline* in support for the American effort to fight terrorism.

The overall pattern of declining international support for the U.S.-led efforts to combat terrorism during the interval between the six Pew surveys suggests that the invasion of Iraq in March 2003 was a contributing factor. The Bush administration was long on rhetoric that linked al Qaeda and other international terrorists to the regime in Iraq, but it was somewhat shorter on any evidence of a connection. More than four years after the capture of Baghdad, information of a linkage eluded the American and British occupation forces despite the best American efforts to find corroborating evidence. The same period has witnessed a violent insurgency in Iraq that continues to take a high toll.

IRAQ

The question of how best to cope with Iraq and allegations of Baghdad's weapons of mass destruction and ties to al Qaeda dominated international politics during the seven-month period leading to the American invasion in March 2003, and thus it is not surprising that the issue has been at the center of numerous surveys in the United States and abroad. Because the Iraq issue has been so controversial, the analysis here draws on multiple surveys in order to identify findings that are not dependent on a single polling organization or question format.

The more thoughtful surveys went beyond a simple "support-oppose" question on whether force should be used to effect a regime change in Baghdad; respondents were typically asked about the conditions under which they were willing to support such an undertaking. In 1991 President George H. W. Bush gained the approval of the UN Security Council to use force, and he assembled a broad coalition of twenty-six countries, including important regional powers Egypt and Turkey, to drive Iraqi invaders from Kuwait. Many of the questions in 2002–4 surveys asked respondents whether similar support from the Security Council should, in their judgment, be a necessary condition for an invasion of Iraq.

The 2002 Chicago Council on Foreign Relations/German Marshall Fund (CCFR/GMF) posed that question in the United States and six NATO allies: Great Britain, France, Germany, the Netherlands, Italy, and Poland. The results, summarized in table 2.12, indicate a strong convergence of views on both sides of the Atlantic. Majorities ranging between 53 and 70 percent indicated that they would approve an American invasion of Iraq only "with UN approval and the support of its allies." American respondents stood in the middle of the range, with just under two respondents in three (65 percent) conditioning their approval of an invasion on UN and allied support. Only in the U.S. survey did as many as one-fifth of the participants agree that "[t]he U.S. should invade Iraq even if they have to do it alone."

Many NATO allies have sent troops to Afghanistan following removal of the Taliban regime in Kabul, but several of them, notably France, Germany and

TABLE 2.12. Preferences on a U.S. Invasion of Iraq to Overthrow Saddam Hussein, 2002

"There has been some discussion about whether the U.S. should use its troops to invade Iraq and overthrow the government of Saddam Hussein. Which of the following positions is closest to yours?"

	U.S. (%)	Great Britain (%)	France (%)	Germany (%)	Netherlands (%)	Italy (%)	Poland (%)
The United States should not invade Iraq.	13	20	27	28	18	33	26
The United States should only invade Iraq with UN approval and the support of its allies.	65	69	63	56	70	54	53
The United States should invade Iraq even if they have to do it alone.	20	10	6	12	11	10	10
Don't know/other	2	1	3	4	2	4	11

Source: Chicago Council on Foreign Relations and German Marshall Fund, *Worldviews 2002: American and European Public Opinion and Foreign Policy* (Chicago, 2004).

Turkey, were among the most visible critics of the U.S.-led invasion of Iraq. When asked by a German Marshall Fund survey in late 2004 whether they approved of the decisions of their governments on troop deployments to Afghanistan and Iraq, many publics expressed their support, but there were also some notable exceptions (table 2.13).

Support for sending troops to Afghanistan elicited majorities in France, Germany, Great Britain, Italy, and the Netherlands; split verdicts in Portugal, Spain, and Turkey; and overwhelming opposition in Poland. In the light of the vitriolic criticism in this country, especially among right-wing media cheerleaders for the administration, that the French and Germans have virtually suc-

TABLE 2.13. Support for Deployment of Troops in Afghanistan and Iraq, 2004

"As you may know, [your country] troops are currently stationed in Afghanistan/Iraq. Do you approve or disapprove of the presence of [your country] troops in Afghanistan/Iraq?"

	Afghanistan		Iraq	
	% Approve	% Disapprove	% Approve	% Disapprove
United States	69	26	57	40
France	55	35	—	—
Germany	59	38	—	—
Great Britain	50	41	50	47
Italy	56	39	47	50
Netherlands	66	29	58	40
Poland	24	67	24	73
Portugal	41	49	28	65
Spain	48	44	—	—
Turkey	41	52	—	—
Slovakia	—	—	21	71

"As you may know, [your country] decided not to send troops to Iraq. Do you approve or disapprove of this decision?"

	% Approve	% Disapprove
France	93	6
Germany	89	10
Turkey	71	23

"As you may know, Spain decided to remove its troops stationed in Iraq. Do you approve or disapprove of this decision?"

	% Approve	% Disapprove
Spain	74	23

Source: German Marshall Fund, *Transatlantic Trends,* 2004.
Note: "Don't know" and "refused" responses excluded.

cumbed to thoughtless pacifism, it may be worth noting that their support for troops in Afghanistan exceeded that of the British.

American, British, and Dutch respondents to the German Marshall Fund surveys approved of having troops in Iraq, but those in Italy, Poland, Portugal, and Slovakia did not. Publics in France, Germany, and Turkey overwhelmingly supported the decisions of their governments not to send troops to Iraq, and the Spanish expressed equally strong support for the decision of the government that came to power following the March 2004 election to withdraw their small contingent from Iraq.

Shortly after the fall of Baghdad an ICM poll undertaken for the British Broadcasting Corporation asked publics in a dozen countries whether "America was right or wrong to invade Iraq." The survey took place after the predictably rapid military defeat of Iraqi forces, but before the onset of an insurgency that has shown few signs of abating more than four years later. That context of military success against Iraq might be expected to maximize favorable judgments about the war.

More than 70 percent of Americans and Israelis judged that the U.S. invasion was the right thing to do. Great Britain and Australia also contributed troops to the invasion, and by identical margins of 54 percent to 38 percent their publics agreed with their governments. Canadians were almost evenly split on the issue, but overwhelming majorities in excess of 70 percent of respondents in other countries judged that the war against Iraq was "wrong." Those negative views were especially pronounced in Brazil, Jordan, Indonesia, South Korea, and Russia.

Several months later a Eurobarometer poll posed essentially the same question, though the response options were "justified" and "not justified" rather than "right" and "wrong." The fifteen European Union countries in the survey, most of which are also members of NATO, included six that had deployed armed forces to Iraq. The judgment that the intervention was justified garnered a majority only in Denmark. Dutch and British respondents were almost evenly divided on the issue, and elsewhere majorities ranging from 59 percent to 96 percent judged that the Iraq intervention was not justified. Although Italy (3,000 troops), Portugal (127), and Spain (1,300) deployed small contingents of personnel to Iraq, they did so in the absence of much public enthusiasm for the invasion.

The issue of participation in the Iraq intervention was also probed in a Pew Research Center twenty-country study shortly after the fall of Baghdad in 2003 and again in surveys undertaken in each of the next two years. Respondents

were asked to express their views on the policy choices of the respective governments on the use of force against Iraq. As the 2003 survey was undertaken
after the militarily successful campaign and before the onset of the bloody in-
surrection, any response bias would likely be in the direction of supporting the
use of force, in the same way that postelection surveys typically show a higher
vote for the winning candidate than he or she had actually received on election
day.

The results summarized in table 2.14 indicate a close concordance between
government policy and public opinion in the initial 2003 survey. That is not, of
course, sufficient to demonstrate a causal relationship wherein government
policies are guided by public opinion. The only exception to this generalization
is Spain, where by a margin of two to one the public responded that its government had made the wrong decision in sending a small military contingent to
Iraq after the fall of Baghdad.[14] A majority of respondents in the United States,
Great Britain, and Australia judged that their governments had made the right
choice in joining the "coalition of the willing" in invading Iraq.

The same question was posed in fifteen countries that did not take part in
the military action against Iraq. Those governments varied in the vehemence
with which they expressed their disapproval prior to the March 2003 invasion;
the notable exception in this respect was support for U.S. policy from the
Berlusconi government in Italy. Although 83 percent of Italian respondents
supported Rome's initial decision not to join the "coalition of the willing," Italy
later deployed a contingent of three thousand troops and policemen to Iraq.
The surveys uncovered overwhelming approval for the refusal of those governments to join in the action to overthrow the Saddam Hussein regime. The margin of approval ranged from about two to one in Canada to well over ten to one
in Brazil, Russia, Jordan, Morocco, and Israel.

The two most recent Pew surveys found some erosion of American, British,
and Spanish support for decisions to take part in the invasion of Iraq, and a
concurrent firming of favorable judgments about choices made by governments that declined to join in the American-led military campaign against the
Saddam Hussein regime. Even in the United States, those expressing the views
that the invasion was the "right decision" fell from 74 percent to a bare major-

---

14. Spain withdrew its personnel from Iraq in 2004 following an election that resulted in the unexpected ouster
of the incumbent government, largely because the Madrid administration was perceived as falsely blaming the
bombing on Basque separatists.

TABLE 2.14. Postwar Attitudes on the Use or Nonuse of Military Force against Iraq, 2003–5

"On the subject of Iraq, did [your country] make the right decision or the wrong decision to use military force against Iraq?"

	2003		2004		2005	
	% Right Decision	% Wrong Decision	% Right Decision	% Wrong Decision	% Right Decision	% Wrong Decision
United States	74	20	60	32	54	42
Great Britain	61	34	43	47	39	53
Spain	31	62	—	—	24	69
Australia	59	37	—	—	—	—
Netherlands	—	—	—	—	59	39
Poland	—	—	—	—	24	67

"On the question of Iraq, did (your country) make the right or wrong decision to allow the U.S. and its allies to use bases for military action in Iraq?"

	2003	
	% Right Decision	% Wrong Decision
Kuwait	83	9

"On the subject of Iraq, did [your country] make the right decision or the wrong decision not to use military force against Iraq?"

	2003		2004		2005	
	% Right Decision	% Wrong Decision	% Right Decision	% Wrong Decision	% Right Decision	% Wrong Decision
Canada	65	31	—	—	80	17
Brazil	96	3	—	—	—	—
France	83	16	88	11	92	8
Germany	80	19	86	11	87	11
Italy	83	13	—	—	—	—
Russia	89	7	83	10	88	6
South Korea	74	22	—	—	—	—
Indonesia	78	19	—	—	70	14
Nigeria	84	12	—	—	—	—
Pakistan	73	21	68	12	63	21
India	—	—	—	—	75	16
Lebanon	86	9	—	—	85	7
Jordan	95	4	87	3	89	8
Morocco	88	7	84	9	—	—
Israel	92	6	—	—	—	—
Turkey	52	37	72	22	81	13

Source: Pew Research Center, *Views of a Changing World*, June 2003; Pew Research Center, *A Year after Iraq War: Mistrust of America in Europe Ever Higher, Muslim Anger Persists*, 2004; Pew Research Center, *U.S. Image Up Slightly, but Still Negative*, 2005.

ity in 2005 and still further to 40 percent in 2007.[15] Almost three-fifths of the Dutch taking part in the survey agreed that their government had made a correct decision to send a military contingent to Iraq, but publics in Great Britain, Spain, and Poland took the opposite position on the question. Respondents in countries that chose not to join the Iraq war expressed overwhelming support in 2004 for the decision to abstain, and they confirmed those judgments even more strongly a year later. In the 2005 study, majorities describing the abstention as the "right decision" ranged between 63 percent in Pakistan to over 80 percent or more in seven other countries, including NATO allies Canada, France, Germany, and Turkey.

A follow-up question asked respondents, "Were you happy that the Iraqi military put up so little resistance to the U.S. and its allies, or were you disappointed about that?" Publics in some countries that opposed the invasion also expressed considerable pleasure in the lack of effective Iraqi resistance: Canada (79 percent), France (59 percent), Germany (81 percent), Italy (83 percent), Spain (68 percent), Nigeria (54 percent), and Israel (77 percent). But that view was not universally shared, as only minorities in several countries expressed happiness about the predictably abysmal performance of Iraq's military: Brazil (40 percent), Russia (24 percent), Turkey (13 percent), South Korea (26 percent), Indonesia (15 percent), Pakistan (12 percent), Lebanon (11 percent), Jordan (8 percent), and Morocco (3 percent).

Global Market Insite (GMI) undertook another probe on the Iraq issue in a 2004 survey among publics in the "Group of Eight" countries (table 2.15). Among American respondents, about two in five judged that the Iraq intervention was a mistake, but only about the same number felt that military strikes against al Qaeda and Iraq have decreased global terrorism, or that the recently revealed prisoner abuses in Abu Ghraib prison were isolated events.

Judgments in the other seven countries included in the GMI study were considerably more critical. Even in Great Britain, America's most important ally in the Iraq war, a solid 57 percent described the intervention as a mistake, and overwhelming majorities expressed negative views about the war on terrorism and the Abu Ghraib issues. Canadian assessments on these issues closely

---

15. Several subsequent polls in the United States found that by mid-2005, a majority of Americans judged the invasion of Iraq to have been a mistake, and by early 2007, majorities in all major polls (Gallup, Pew, CBS/*New York Times*, ABC/*Washington Post*, etc.) reveal that majorities believe the Iraq invasion was a mistake.

TABLE 2.15. Views of the United States and American Policies: GMI Survey of Publics in the Group of Eight Countries, June 2004

	United States	China	Canada	Britain	France	Russia	Germany	Japan
Do you believe the United States made a mistake by sending troops into Iraq? (% "yes")	42	83	58	57	79	88	78	60
Do you view George W. Bush as an effective global leader? (% "yes")	49	37	26	19	7	15	11	14
Do you think the United States strikes against al Qaeda and Iraq have decreased global terrorism? (% "yes")	39	22	22	17	11	9	9	5
Do you believe that the recent abuse in Iraq at Abu Ghraib prison, by the U.S. military, is an isolated event? (% "yes")	37	16	17	20	9	15	15	9

Source: Global Market Insite (GMI), *World Poll Survey*, June 2004.

mirrored those of the British, and those in China, France, Russia, Germany, and Japan were even more critical.[16]

Although the Bush administration has refused access to the media at Dover Air Force Base, the first stop for remains of military personnel killed in Afghanistan or Iraq, several American newspapers provide daily or weekly updates on these deaths. Much less is known about war-related deaths among Afghan and Iraqi civilians. Estimates range widely and even if accurate figures were available, given the brutal methods employed by insurgents in Iraq, it would be hard to pinpoint the sources of all civilian casualties.[17]

Two surveys conducted in 2003 asked respondents whether the United States and its allies do enough to minimize civilian casualties. The Pew survey (table 2.16) found that public reactions to the issue divided in fairly predictable ways. Great Britain and Australia joined the United States in the "coalition of the willing," and publics in all three countries judged that their forces "tried very hard" to avoid civilian casualties. Those in Israel and Kuwait rendered the same verdict.

At the other end of the spectrum of views on the issue, publics in predominantly Muslim countries—Turkey, Indonesia, Pakistan, Lebanon, Jordan, and Morocco—overwhelmingly expressed the opinion that the United States and its allies "didn't try hard enough." Most of the respondents appear to have accepted the thesis that the invasions of Afghanistan and Iraq were part of a "clash of civilizations"—a wider war against Islam. Responses in Nigeria, which were almost evenly divided on the question, represented the exception to the pattern.

An ICM/BBC survey, also conducted shortly after the fall of Baghdad, posed a similar question about civilian casualties but with some important differences. Whereas the Pew study asked about actions of "the U.S. and its allies," the ICM/BBC question centered on "American military." Moreover, the response options in the latter study were different and, arguably, so poorly phrased as to virtually invite the selection of the second one: "does enough" and "could do more." The American public responded similarly to the two surveys, with good marks for the efforts of the military, but responses in Great Britain

16. The GMI survey included a question about George W. Bush's global leadership. The analyses in this study exclude any questions that refer explicitly to the president in order to avoid conflating judgments about the president with broader assessments of the United States and its policies.

17. According to a more recent report based on mortuary records, at least fifty thousand Iraqi civilians have died. Louise Roug and Doug Smith, "War's Iraqi Death Toll Tops 50,000," *Los Angeles Times*, June 25, 2006. A somewhat controversial study by the Johns Hopkins School of Public Health estimated that more than a half million Iraqi civilians have been killed since the 2003 invasion.

and Australia varied sharply. In contrast to the favorable judgments expressed in the Pew survey, strong majorities in both countries—as well as the other countries—selected the "could do more" option.

Assessments of the Iraq war in the light of its costs in blood and treasure also emerged from German Marshall Fund surveys conducted in the United States and among European countries in mid-2003 and mid-2004. Although the earlier study took place just weeks following the ouster of the regime in Baghdad—after Iraqi armed forces had been crushed but before the insurgency that gave lie to the rather optimistic belief that United States and allied forces would be greeted as liberators—only American respondents agreed that the invasion was worth its costs (table 2.17). Even the British public was divided on

TABLE 2.16. Avoidance of Civilian Casualties in Iraq, 2003

"Did the U.S. and its allies try very hard to avoid civilian casualties, or didn't they try hard enough?"

	% Tried Very Hard	% Didn't Try Hard Enough	Net[a]
United States	82	14	68
NATO allies			
Great Britain	64	32	32
France	25	74	−49
Germany	41	52	−11
Italy	50	44	6
Spain	25	67	−42
Turkey	9	88	−79
Canada	—	—	—
Other key countries			
Russia	14	72	−58
Australia	61	34	27
South Korea	22	74	−52
Indonesia	11	83	−72
Pakistan	9	81	−72
Israel	69	26	43
Lebanon	23	74	−51
Kuwait	59	35	24
Jordan	3	97	−94
Morocco	4	91	−87
Nigeria	49	43	6

Source: Pew Research Center, *Views of a Changing World,* June 2003.
[a]Net = percent "tried very hard" minus "didn't try hard enough."
"Don't know" and "refused" responses excluded.

the question, with a very small majority disagreeing with the proposition that the war was worth it, and elsewhere the judgments were even more negative.

The GMF posed two versions of the same question a year later. The first was identical to the 2003 wording, whereas the second added the phrase "to liberate the Iraqi people," thus highlighting the goal emphasized by the Bush administration after its claims that the Saddam Hussein regime possessed weapons of mass destruction and had ties to al Qaeda became increasingly suspect if not totally discredited. Judgments about the worth of the war fell without exception during the interval between the two GMF surveys—even among Americans. Although question wording is often a crucial variable in surveys, in this case adding the phrase "to liberate the Iraqi people" had a relatively minor effect—an increase in positive answers of less than 4 percent on average—and none among American respondents. Polish and Portuguese publics did respond more favorably to the revised question wording, by 9 and 7 percent, respectively, but in neither case were affirmative opinions forthcoming from as many as one in four of those taking part in the survey.

Overall, the results of the GMF surveys, which included a number of coun-

TABLE 2.17. Assessments of the War against Iraq, 2003–4

A. "Do you think the war in Iraq was worth the loss of life and the other costs of attacking Iraq or not?" (2003 and 2004 surveys)

B. "Do you think the war in Iraq to liberate the Iraqi people was worth the loss of life and other costs of attacking Iraq or not?" (2004 survey)

	2003: Wording A			2004: Wording A			2004: Wording B		
	% Yes	% No	% Don't Know/ Refused	% Yes	% No	% Don't Know/ Refused	% Yes	% No	% Don't Know/ Refused
United States	55	36	9	44	50	6	44	50	6
France	13	84	3	8	89	3	13	85	3
Germany	15	81	4	8	89	3	11	85	4
Great Britain	42	51	7	29	65	6	35	58	8
Italy	26	68	6	17	77	5	22	74	5
Netherlands	38	55	7	31	64	5	37	57	6
Poland	30	62	8	14	79	7	23	70	7
Portugal	24	71	5	12	79	9	19	69	12
Spain	—	—	—	11	87	2	9	86	6
Slovakia	—	—	—	16	73	11	16	67	17
Turkey	—	—	—	7	88	6	5	91	4
Europe average	27	67	6	16	79	6	19	74	7

Source: German Marshall Fund, Transatlantic Trends, 2003; German Marshall Fund, Transatlantic Trends, 2004.

tries that made at least a token contribution to the "coalition of the willing," reveal that the well-known French and German opposition to the Iraq war was rather widely shared right after the fall of Baghdad, and even more emphatically a year later.

The heinous nature of the Saddam Hussein regime lent plausibility to repeated assertions from Washington that the U.S.-led invasion would give rise to an improved quality of life for average Iraqis. Pew surveys conducted soon after the fall of Baghdad and ten months later asked how well the United States and its allies were doing in "taking into account the needs and interests of the Iraqi people." The results summarized in table 2.18 reveal very mixed judgments in the earlier survey, as only Americans, Kuwaitis, and Nigerians judged that, on balance, the occupying forces were doing at least a "good" job in this respect. Publics in alliance partners Great Britain, Spain, Italy, and Australia disagreed. As in so many surveys that included predominantly Muslim countries, respondents in Turkey, Indonesia, Jordan, Morocco, Lebanon, and areas controlled by the Palestinian Authority were overwhelmingly critical, as were those in Russia and South Korea. Perhaps the most surprising finding was the highly critical judgment of Israeli respondents, only 29 percent of whom judged that the needs of the Iraqi people were adequately met.

In the ten months between the two Pew surveys, various insurgent groups, using tactics of unusual brutality, including suicide bombings and beheading of hostages, were able to disrupt life in Iraq, especially in the "Sunni triangle" in and around Baghdad. Despite the very modest successes in restoring electric power, reopening hospitals, and increasing oil production, respondents to the 2004 Pew survey continued to be highly critical of the manner in which the United States and its allies took into account the needs and interests of the Iraqi people. Moroccans and Jordanians were a bit less harsh than they had been in 2003, but about two-thirds of them still rated attention to the interests of the Iraqi people as no better than "fair." Some corroboration for these views emerged from CNN/*USA Today*/Gallup surveys conducted in Iraq. Immediately after the fall of Baghdad in 2003, equal numbers of Iraqis (43 percent) described the coalition forces as "occupiers" and "liberators." When the same question was posed in March–April 2004, by a margin of 71 percent–29 percent, Iraqis described the coalition forces as "occupiers."[18]

Reputation, a significant element of "soft power," matters in international affairs. All other things being equal, everyone would prefer his or her country

---

18. CNN/*USA Today*/Gallup survey, March 22–April 9, 2004; Pew Research Center poll, January 10–15, 2007.

to be viewed internationally as trustworthy and one in which others can have a high degree of confidence. The Pew survey conducted a year after the fall of Baghdad posed two questions that asked respondents in nine countries to appraise the impact of the Iraq war on whether the conflict increased or decreased their faith in American trustworthiness and their confidence in the many proclamations from Washington that its policies promote democracy all around the world.

TABLE 2.18. Attention to Needs and Interests of the Iraqi People in Rebuilding Iraq, 2003 and 2004

"In rebuilding Iraq, how good a job are the U.S. and its allies doing in taking into account the needs and interests of the Iraqi people? Is the coalition doing an excellent job, a good job, only a fair job, or a poor job in taking into consideration the interests and needs of the Iraqi people?"

	April–May 2003			February–March 2004		
	% Excellent or Good	% Fair or Poor	Net[a]	% Excellent or Good	% Fair or Poor	Net[a]
United States	59	32	27	50	40	10
NATO allies						
Great Britain	41	50	−9	30	63	−33
France	45	54	−9	35	60	−25
Germany	23	70	−47	16	80	−64
Italy	36	52	−16	—	—	—
Spain	26	64	−38	—	—	—
Turkey	23	63	−40	16	69	−53
Canada	41	46	−5	—	—	—
Other key countries						
Brazil	31	54	−23	—	—	—
Russia	10	78	−68	13	75	−62
Australia	40	53	−13	—	—	—
South Korea	10	84	−74	—	—	—
Indonesia	12	83	−71	—	—	—
Pakistan	14	60	−46	10	52	−42
Israel	29	60	−31	—	—	—
Kuwait	53	40	13	—	—	—
Jordan	17	80	−63	27	65	−38
Morocco	11	67	−56	16	68	−52
Nigeria	59	34	25	—	—	—
Lebanon	25	70	−55	—	—	—
Palestinian territories	7	87	−80	—	—	—

Source: Pew Research Center, *Views of a Changing World,* June 2003; Pew Research Center, *A Year after Iraq War: Mistrust of America in Europe Ever Higher, Muslim Anger Persists,* 2004.

[a]Net = percent "excellent" or "good" minus "fair" or "poor." "Don't know" and "refused" responses excluded.

By majorities of two to one or better, Americans taking part in the Pew survey clearly judged that the Iraq war had rendered the United States more trustworthy and more deserving of confidence (table 2.19). Those views were not shared abroad, not even in America's most important partner in the war—Great Britain. Publics in the other seven countries were even less inclined to assert that the war had enhanced America's reputation. As has been the case in so many questions concerning U.S. policy during the post-9/11 era, respondents in countries with substantial Muslim populations overwhelmingly expressed the view that the Iraq war had rendered the United States less trustworthy, including with respect to its professed goal of promoting democracy. These judg-

TABLE 2.19. Consequences of the War in Iraq, 2004

"As a consequence of the war [in Iraq], do you have more confidence or less confidence that the U.S. is trustworthy?"

	% More	% Less	% Same (volunteered)
United States	58	29	6
Great Britain	24	58	12
France	14	78	6
Germany	10	82	5
Russia	8	63	21
Turkey	8	74	11
Pakistan	5	64	7
Jordan	4	50	38
Morocco	12	72	7

"As a consequence of the war [in Iraq], do you have more confidence or less confidence that the U.S. wants to promote democracy all around the world?"

	% More	% Less	% Same (volunteered)
United States	69	21	3
Great Britain	41	45	5
France	16	78	3
Germany	24	70	3
Russia	14	53	21
Turkey	9	73	9
Pakistan	5	57	5
Jordan	7	56	28
Morocco	15	66	8

Source: Pew Research Center, *A Year after the Iraq War: Mistrust of America in Europe Ever Higher, Muslim Anger Persists,* 2004.
Note: "Don't know" and "refused" responses excluded.

ments suggest that the costs of the Iraq war should be measured not only in blood and treasure but also in reputation.

A central theme in the Bush administration's defense of the war in Iraq is that the overthrow of the regime in Baghdad has had important payoffs beyond those in Iraq: ridding the region of a serial aggressor that attacked neighbors Iran and Kuwait will, according to administration officials, bring greater stability to the Middle East, and even in the absence of clear evidence linking the Saddam Hussein regime to al Qaeda, victory in Iraq has nevertheless made an important contribution in the war against terrorism.

Shortly after the fall of the Saddam Hussein regime, a Pew survey asked respondents whether "U.S. policies in the Middle East make the region more stable or less stable." Two-thirds of Americans selected the "more stable" option (table 2.20). Slightly under half of those taking part in the Pew survey in Great Britain, France, Germany, Italy and Canada—the most important NATO allies—agreed, whereas in Spain and Turkey, only 29 percent and 15 percent, respectively, agreed with the American appraisal. Judgments elsewhere varied sharply, as 70 percent of Israelis judged that U.S. policies had contributed to greater stability, but fewer than 10 percent of Indonesians, Jordanians, and those living in areas controlled by the Palestinian Authority expressed the same view.

The 2004 Pew survey posed a question on the putative connection between the invasion of Iraq and the war on terrorism. As revealed at the top of table 2.21, Americans taking part in the study agreed by a margin of more than two to one that "the war in Iraq has helped the war on terrorism," but respondents elsewhere disagreed sharply.[19] About one-third of respondents in NATO allies Great Britain, France, and Germany expressed the opinion that the Iraq war has made a useful contribution in dealing with terrorism, but in the other five countries similar judgments ranged from 24 percent in Turkey to only 8 percent in Pakistan.

A German Marshall Fund survey in 2004 posed a somewhat similar question about the effects of the Iraq war on the threat of terrorism. The results summarized in the bottom half of table 2.21 show that few respondents in eleven NATO countries agreed that the military action in Iraq had "decreased

---

19. By September 2004, only 45 percent of those responding to a *Newsweek*/Princeton Research Associates survey agreed that "the war with Iraq has made the U.S. safer from terrorism," and several 2005 surveys also reveal growing doubts among Americans about whether the Iraq war has contributed to national security. A year later, polls by CNN/*USA Today*/Gallup, Harris, and Pew revealed that 34 percent, 38 percent, and 43 percent, respectively, stated that the Iraq war has helped in protecting the United States from terrorism, and by January 2007 that figure had fallen to 31 percent according to a *Newsweek* poll.

the threat of terrorism around the world." Only about one in four American respondents stated that the war had reduced the threat of terrorism, and in none of the other countries did as many as 10 percent render a favorable judgment about the impact of the Iraq war.

CONCLUSION

The evidence reviewed here clearly indicates that America's reputation among publics abroad had declined in many parts of the world during the period since

TABLE 2.20. The Effects of U.S. Policies in the Middle East, 2003

"Do you think U.S. policies in the Middle East make the region more stable or less stable?"

	% More Stable	% Less Stable	% No Difference (volunteered)	Net[a]
United States	66	24	2	42
NATO allies				
Great Britain	43	45	3	−2
France	46	49	4	−3
Germany	44	46	2	−2
Italy	47	34	10	13
Spain	29	49	8	−20
Turkey	15	61	5	−46
Canada	48	39	2	9
Other key countries				
Brazil	35	39	11	−4
Russia	16	39	21	−23
Australia	47	44	3	3
South Korea	39	47	5	−8
Indonesia	7	74	9	−67
Pakistan	14	43	12	−29
Israel	70	20	7	50
Kuwait	48	40	5	8
Jordan	4	91	4	−87
Morocco	10	63	9	−53
Nigeria	44	37	11	7
Lebanon	25	56	13	−31
Palestinian territories	3	85	10	−82

Source: Pew Research Center, *Views of a Changing World*, June 2003.

[a]Net = percent "more stable" minus "less stable." "Don't know" and "refused" responses excluded.

TABLE 2.21. The Iraq War and the War on Terrorism, 2004

A. *"Do you think the war in Iraq has helped the war on terrorism, or has it hurt the war on terrorism?"*

	% Helped	% Hurt	% No Effect (volunteered)
United States[a]	62	28	3
Great Britain[a]	36	50	5
France	33	55	10
Germany	30	58	5
Russia	22	50	18
Turkey	24	56	8
Pakistan	8	57	6
Jordan	12	36	37
Morocco	16	67	8

B. *"According to you, has the military action in Iraq increased the threat of terrorism around the world, decreased the threat of terrorism around the world, or has it had no effect on the threat of terrorism?"*

	% Increased	% Decreased	% No Effect
United States[a]	49	26	20
Great Britain[a]	68	5	23
France	75	4	20
Germany	72	5	22
Italy[a]	76	5	18
Netherlands[a]	60	6	32
Poland[a]	74	8	11
Portugal[a]	73	6	15
Spain[a]	76	2	19
Slovakia[a]	74	6	12
Turkey	68	7	11

Source: A. Pew Research Center, *A Year after the Iraq War: Mistrust of America in Europe Ever Higher, Muslim Anger Persists,* 2004; B. German Marshall Fund, *Transatlantic Trends,* 2004.

Note: "Don't know" and "refused" responses omitted.

[a]Sent troops to Iraq; subsequently withdrawn by Italy, Netherlands, Portugal, and Spain.

the September 11 terrorist attacks. Owing to the unprecedented volume of international polling by a broad array of survey organizations based in the United States and abroad, that conclusion cannot be casually dismissed as an artifact of methodologically flawed or ideologically driven studies that seek to blacken this country's reputation.

An initial effort to identify possible sources of anti-Americanism examined a wide array of data on how publics abroad have viewed the U.S. role in the world, such as controversial foreign policy undertakings as the war in Iraq and, more broadly, the effort to deal with terrorism. Evidence on the latter issue may be especially telling because, since the September 11 attacks, deadly terrorist bombing have also taken place in Spain, Indonesia, Egypt, Morocco, and Great Britain, all countries where respondents have been asked not only their general views of the United States but also their judgments about the American effort to deal with the global problem of terrorism. The evidence suggests that, among other things, the U.S.-led invasion of Iraq is often viewed as a distraction from rather than a contribution to dealing with that issue. More generally, there appears to be a close correlation between how publics abroad view the United States, on the one hand, and, on the other, their judgments about American foreign policies.

Given the widespread critical views of the United States and its policies, it remains to be seen whether and how these opinions have also affected the manner in which publics abroad view other aspects of this country, including the American people, society, and major American institutions. These questions will be addressed in the next chapter.

CHAPTER 3

How Publics Abroad View Americans
and American Society

The evidence presented and analyzed in chapter 2 reveals that publics abroad have indeed become increasingly critical of the United States and some of its major foreign policy undertakings during the years since the September 11 terrorist attacks. For many of those taking part in the international surveys, the U.S.-led invasion of Iraq in March 2003 appears to have been a major catalyst for unleashing anti-American opinions.

An unanswered question is whether the critical views are largely confined to the U.S. government and its foreign policies. Are anti-American judgments largely focused on what the United States *does*? Alternatively, do such negative opinions of this country extend much further to include the American people and important features of American society and its major institutions—what the United States *is*? Effective policy analysis depends on information about both what a country is and what it does. Sole reliance on the latter may leave one's assessment excessively dependent on the zigs and zags of recent events. Focusing exclusively on what a country is tends to cast the analysis in concrete, with little room for considering the possibilities of genuine change rather than merely tactical maneuvers. Cognitive dissonance theory suggests that there may be a tendency for negative judgments about American foreign policy to spill over and color other aspects of the United States. Alternatively, are publics abroad able and willing to make more-nuanced judgments in which they can simultaneously hold both negative and positive opinions about the United States?

The discussion that follows probes polling evidence in four broad categories. The first examines judgments about the American people and some rather general descriptions of American society (tables 3.1–3.4). The following section examines how publics abroad rate some specific American institutions such as democracy, religion, science, popular culture, and business (tables 3.5–3.9). Tables 3.10–3.12 focus on the extent to which publics abroad would welcome the spread of American ideas and institutions to their own countries and whether those who immigrate to this country experience an improvement in their lives. An underlying question in this and the previous chapter is to what extent publics abroad judge this country on the basis of what the United States *is* and what it *does*. A Pew survey in 2002 asked respondents whether differences between their countries and the United States arise from different values or policy differences. The findings presented in table 3.13 bring the chapter to a conclusion.

THE AMERICAN PEOPLE AND SOCIETY

The results summarized in chapter 2 indicate a fairly clear but not universal pattern of increasingly critical judgments of the United States by publics abroad, especially after the issue of Iraq took center stage in world politics, but it remains an open question whether such views extend to all aspects of this country. There are presumably some respondents who, having expressed critical views of the United States and its foreign policy, also believe that the American people and its institutions are without any redeeming features, just as there are Americans who hold similar beliefs about China, Iran, Cuba, or any number of other countries. Do they constitute majorities or at least significant minorities, or are most publics abroad able and willing to make significant distinctions among the many and varied features of the United States?

Those taking part in six of the seven Pew Research Center international surveys were asked to express their opinions not only about the United States and its foreign policy undertakings but also about "Americans." The results, summarized in table 3.1, reveal a widespread tendency for favorable assessments of the American people to outstrip those of the country as a whole. To be sure, in many cases positive views of the American people declined somewhat during the five years spanning the Pew surveys, but the magnitude of the decline paled in comparison with the trends revealed in table 2.1. Among NATO allies, solid majorities exceeding 60 percent of the publics in Great Britain, France, Germany, Poland, Canada, and the Netherlands consistently expressed favorable views of Americans, even in the three most recent studies (2005, 2006, and

2007). Recall that these same surveys revealed growing disenchantment with the United States and many of its foreign policies. The responses of the French and German publics are especially telling because the governments in Paris and Berlin have been outspokenly critical of American policy, especially on the issue of Iraq. Nevertheless, strong majorities in France and Germany have consistently expressed favorable judgments about the American people.

These results are consistent with other studies showing that the public is capable of making judgments that do not necessarily reflect those of the government.[1] One possible explanation for these findings is that many Europeans, including French and Germans, have had direct contact with American tourists and students, as well as a broader cross section of Americans in their own travels to the United States. To the extent that this is so, it may make them less dependent on opinion leaders and the media for their information about the United States. Perhaps there was also recognition that, prior to the war, the American public in fact expressed preferences in a multitude of surveys about the Iraq situation that did not differ much from those among European publics. Most notably, virtually every survey revealed the existence among Americans of a steady majority in favor of military action against Iraq conditioned upon the support of the United Nations and major allies.[2] How much this thinking may have influenced responses to the Pew surveys abroad is, of course, impossible to determine from the existing data and thus must be considered highly speculative.

The pattern of responses elsewhere is rather mixed. Mexicans, Russians, Japanese, Australians, South Koreans, Indians, and Nigerians have quite consistently seen Americans in a favorable light, but in many predominantly Muslim countries, other than Kuwait and Lebanon, the picture is much less benign. Although Turkey is a longtime member of NATO and the government in Pakistan claims to be a faithful ally in the fight against al Qaeda and other terrorist groups, publics in those countries are the most critical of Americans, with favorable ratings of only 13 percent and 19 percent, respectively, in the most recent Pew survey.

On balance, these results should put to rest some of the most pessimistic diagnoses of rampant anti-Americanism abroad. That Americans are generally viewed in a favorable light in most of Europe, Russia, Japan, and India suggests

1. For example, Maxine Isaacs, "Two Different Worlds: The Relationship between Elite and Mass Opinions on American Foreign Policy," *Political Communication* 15 (June 1998): 323–45.
2. The evidence is summarized in Ole R. Holsti, *Public Opinion and American Foreign Policy,* 2nd edition (Ann Arbor: University of Michigan Press, 2004), chap. 6. See especially tables 6.4, 6.7, and 6.8.

TABLE 3.1. Opinions about "Americans," 2002–7

"Please tell me if you have a very favorable, somewhat favorable, somewhat unfavorable, or very unfavorable view of Americans."

	Percent "Very Favorable" or "Somewhat Favorable"					
	July–Oct. 2002	April–May 2003	Feb.–March 2004	April–May 2005	April–May 2006	April–May 2007
NATO allies						
Great Britain	83	80	73	70	69	70
France	71	58	53	64	65	61
Germany	70	67	68	65	66	63
Italy	74	77	—	—	—	62
Poland	77	—	—	68	—	63
Czech Republic	70	—	—	—	—	56
Spain	—	47	—	55	37	46
Turkey	31	32	32	23	17	13
Canada	78	77	—	66	—	76
Netherlands	—	—	—	66	—	—
Other key countries						
Mexico	56	—	—	—	—	52
Brazil	54	43	—	—	—	45
Russia	67	65	64	61	57	54
Japan	73	—	—	—	82	75
Australia	—	74	—	—	—	—
South Korea	61	74	—	—	—	70
Indonesia	65	56	—	46	36	42
India	58	—	—	71	67	58
Pakistan	17	38	25	22	27	19
Kuwait	—	71	—	—	—	62
Jordan	53	18	21	34	38	36
Egypt	13	—	—	—	36	31
Morocco	—	54	37	—	—	25
Nigeria	74	67	—	—	56	66
Lebanon	47	62	—	66	—	69
China	—	—	—	43	49	38

Source: July–October 2002—Pew Research Center, *What the World Thinks in 2002* (Washington, DC: Global Attitudes Project, 2002); April–May 2003—Pew Research Center, *America's Image Further Erodes, Europeans Want Weaker Ties,* April–May 2003; February–March 2004—Pew Research Center, *A Year after Iraq War: Mistrust of America in Europe Ever Higher, Muslim Anger Persists,* 2004; April–May 2005—Pew Research Center, *U.S. Image Up Slightly, but Still Negative,* 2005; April–May 2006—Pew Research Center, *Conflicting Views in a Divided World,* 2006; April–May 2007—Pew Research Center, *Global Unease with Major World Powers,* 2007.

that, at least in this respect, globalization is having a positive impact. The most recent Pew survey also indicates that despite decades of Cold War hostility and such important unresolved issues as the status of Taiwan, about half of the Chinese public has a favorable view of the American people in 2006, but that figure fell somewhat the following year.

Aside from Africans who were forcibly brought to the United States and sold into slavery, many immigrants to this country braved daunting hazards in a search for freedom from various kinds of religious and other kinds of persecutions, and for better economic opportunities than existed in their lands of birth. Consequently, an important and enduring part of the American self-image—including John Winthrop's 1630 description of the colonies as a "city on

TABLE 3.2. Assessments of America as a Beacon of Hope and a Force for Good, 2003

"America is a beacon of hope and opportunity."

	% Agree		% Disagree		
	Strongly	Slightly	Slightly	Strongly	Net[a]
United States	70	23	4	3	86
Australia	22	34	23	19	14
Brazil	16	17	43	17	−27
Canada	39	33	15	11	46
France	11	33	28	24	−8
Indonesia	19	27	25	21	0
Israel	52	23	10	14	51
Jordan	9	12	9	71	−59
South Korea	5	35	45	10	−15
Russia	4	14	17	56	−55
Great Britain	20	37	22	15	10

"America is a force for good in the world."

United States	62	27	6	3	79
Australia	25	33	21	17	20
Brazil	10	13	51	21	−50
Canada	31	35	19	13	34
France	8	27	35	23	−28
Indonesia	12	19	34	31	−34
Israel	43	29	11	16	44
Jordan	4	6	5	85	−79
South Korea	5	38	42	11	−10
Russia	4	11	15	62	−63
Great Britain	20	36	22	14	20

Source: ICM Research, *Survey for the British Broadcasting Corporation,* May–June 2003.
[a]Net = percent "agree" minus "disagree." "Don't know" responses excluded.

the hill," Abraham Lincoln's assertion that the United States is "the last best hope for mankind," and Emma Lazarus's inspiring words on the Statue of Liberty—is that the country represents a model for the world community.

A 2003 ICM survey for the British Broadcasting Corporation, undertaken soon after the ouster of the Saddam Hussein regime in Baghdad, asked respondents in eleven countries to judge whether and how strongly they agreed that the United States is indeed a "beacon of hope and opportunity" and a "force for good" in the world. The results, summarized in table 3.2, reveal that virtually all Americans taking part in the study agreed with both propositions.

Respondents in the other ten countries expressed a very wide range of opinions on both questions. Canadians and Israelis led the way with agreement by strong majorities, followed by the Australians and British. Both of the latter two countries joined the U.S.-led "coalition of the willing" against Iraq. In contrast, Russians, French, Brazilians, South Koreans, and Jordanians expressed varying degrees of dissent from both items. As noted in chapter 2, publics in none of these countries supported the invasion of Iraq. Jordan's preferential trade agreement with the United States appears to have had little impact on responses to these questions. It seems likely that American relations with Israel are a more important consideration in how Jordanians appraised the United States. Indonesians rendered a split verdict, splitting evenly on the "beacon" question, but stating strong disagreement with the proposition that the United States is a "force for good." A more detailed analysis of Indonesian opinions of the United States and their possible impact on policy appears in the next chapter.

A 2004 Harris Interactive survey asked respondents to assess ten aspects of the United States and its foreign policies. Table 3.3 presents the net assessments—percent positive minus percent negative—for the six major NATO allies. The most striking feature of the responses is the ability and willingness of those taking part in the study to make discriminating rather than blanket judgments. For example, the uniformly favorable views of the "American people" largely confirm the results presented in table 3.1. Opinions about the quality of life in America, as well as of films and television, were also positive. U.S. business practices also received favorable judgments, except in Canada, America's leading trade partner.[3]

---

3. Canadian opinions about American business practices almost surely stem in part from repeated violations of the North American Free Trade Agreement, signed by the United States, Canada, and Mexico in 1994, especially with respect to softwood lumber. U.S. tariffs have cost upward of twenty thousand jobs in the province of British Columbia. For further details, see chapter 4.

In contrast, publics in all six countries were overwhelmingly critical of American foreign policy, as well as of American policies in Afghanistan and Iraq. Respondents in Great Britain and Italy, countries that joined the "coalition of the willing" in Iraq, were somewhat more restrained in their opposition, but the deployment of Spanish forces to Iraq did not mute the strongly critical opinions of Spaniards taking part in the study.

Assessments of American values and system of government varied sharply, with strongly positive appraisals from Italian respondents, mixed results from Canadians and Brits, and negative ones from the other three countries in the study—Spain, France, and Germany. It seems likely that the somewhat mixed, though on balance negative, views of American courts and the justice system were colored by the capital punishment issue—all European countries have abolished the death sentence—and the revelations about U.S. abuse of prisoners and detainees in Iraq and the Guantanamo Bay facilities in Cuba. If we examine responses by country, Italians clearly rendered the most favorable assessments of the United States, whereas the French and Germans were most inclined to be critical. Canadians and Spaniards expressed the most favorable views of the American people and American popular culture, but were otherwise rather critical.

The ICM/BBC 2003 survey undertaken shortly after the fall of Baghdad asked respondents in eleven countries to rate the United States on several pairs of descriptors, including humble/arrogant, friendly/antagonistic, religious/not

TABLE 3.3. Rating Aspects of the United States, 2004

"For each of the following please indicate how positively or negatively you feel."

	% Positive Minus % Negative									
	A	B	C	D	E	F	G	H	I	J
Canada	45	27	1	−4	−12	42	−7	−45	−25	−44
Great Britain	41	48	6	−10	2	35	6	−31	−35	−37
Germany	21	16	−32	−21	−37	12	8	−62	−65	−71
France	23	1	−13	−36	−40	7	9	−68	−39	−70
Italy	42	32	21	30	21	36	36	−18	−20	−31
Spain	45	21	−1	−33	−23	40	6	−63	−54	−71
Average	36	24	−3	−12	−15	29	10	−48	−40	−54

Source: Harris Interactive, *What Do Europeans Like and Dislike about the United States?* March 2004.
Note: Key to column headings—A = American people; B = Quality of life in America; C = American values; D = American system of government; E = American courts and system of justice; F = American films and TV programs; G = How Americans do business; H = American foreign policy since 2000; I = Policies of the American government in Afghanistan; J = Policies of the American government in Iraq.

religious, united/divided, and free/unfree. As revealed in table 3.4, once again publics abroad revealed a tendency to express mixed judgments rather than uniformly negative or positive ones. For example, the predominant view in every country, notably including the United States, was that America is arrogant rather than humble and free rather than unfree, but there were striking differences on the other pairs of descriptors. Respondents in most countries described America as "friendly," rather than "antagonistic," but those in Indonesia, Brazil, and Jordan did not, and publics in the latter three countries were also the least inclined to view the United States as "united." Majorities among Americans, Canadians, Australians, and the French stated that America is a religious country, an assessment that ran strongly counter to those expressed by Israelis, Brazilians, and Jordanians. Interestingly, publics in the latter three countries, all of which described the United States as, on balance, "not religious," represent three quite different faiths: Jewish, Catholic, and Muslim.

AMERICAN INSTITUTIONS AND VALUES

Some of the most useful surveys of international public opinion have been conducted by the Pew Research Center as part of its Global Attitudes Project. The 2002, 2003, and 2007 studies included questions asking respondents to appraise several American values and institutions. The results, summarized in tables 3.5

TABLE 3.4. **Descriptions of the United States, 2003**

"Which of the following best describes America?"

	Percent Responses				
	Humble/ Arrogant	Friendly/ Antagonistic	Religious/ Not Religious	United/ Divided	Free/ Unfree
United States	35/54	75/19	70/24	67/30	87/10
Canada	12/68	54/37	63/22	67/26	77/16
Great Britain	14/66	63/23	56/27	65/25	74/16
Israel	19/63	72/15	25/59	67/23	79/14
Australia	11/72	61/27	64/24	64/27	72/22
South Korea	8/67	40/31	52/32	58/26	86/8
Russia	10/67	33/32	58/22	54/27	71/15
France	11/81	45/44	78/15	56/39	62/33
Indonesia	10/69	31/48	47/40	44/39	87/8
Brazil	14/68	18/50	29/49	31/55	47/35
Jordan	26/41	23/35	10/57	26/53	54/30

Source: ICM Research, Survey for the British Broadcasting Corporation, May–June 2003.
Note: "Neither" responses excluded.

through 3.9, highlight not only some differences across countries but also the ability and willingness of respondents to distinguish between those features of America that they like and dislike. Moreover, as the surveys straddle the American-led invasion of Iraq in March 2003, they provide an opportunity to assess whether and how that undertaking may have affected responses.

Table 3.5 reveals that "American ideas about democracy" received very mixed appraisals in the 2002 survey, even from NATO allies, all of which are democracies. Except in France and Turkey, slight pluralities stated that they

TABLE 3.5. American Ideas about Democracy, 2002–7

"Which of these comes closer to your view? I like American ideas about democracy, OR I dislike American ideas about democracy."

	July–October 2002			April–May 2003			April–May 2007		
	% Like	% Dislike	Net[a]	% Like	% Dislike	Net[a]	% Like	% Dislike	Net[a]
NATO allies									
Great Britain	43	42	1	45	45	0	36	47	−11
France	42	53	−11	33	65	−32	23	76	−53
Germany	47	45	2	39	55	−16	31	65	−34
Italy	45	37	8	59	33	26	38	42	−4
Spain	—	—	—	30	61	−31	19	66	−47
Turkey	33	50	−17	22	71	−49	8	81	−73
Canada	50	40	10	59	33	26	37	51	−14
Other key countries									
Mexico	—	—	—	—	—	—	29	60	−31
Brazil	35	51	−16	27	65	−38	26	67	−41
Russia	28	46	−18	31	41	−10	21	62	−41
Australia	—	—	—	56	36	20	—	—	—
South Korea	58	37	21	59	31	28	59	33	26
Indonesia	52	40	12	26	65	−39	28	57	−29
Pakistan	9	60	−51	17	73	−56	6	72	−66
China	—	—	—	—	—	—	48	36	12
India	—	—	—	—	—	—	41	49	−8
Japan	—	—	—	—	—	—	57	25	32
Israel	—	—	—	68	25	43	61	29	32
Kuwait	—	—	—	53	39	14	37	56	−19
Jordan	29	69	−40	38	60	−22	42	55	−13
Morocco	—	—	—	43	48	−5	30	51	−21
Nigeria	86	8	78	76	20	56	75	21	54
Lebanon	49	45	4	46	50	−4	39	56	−17
Palestinian territories	—	—	—	13	83	−70	16	71	−55

Source: Pew Research Center, *What the World Thinks in 2002* (Washington, DC: Global Attitudes Project, 2002); Pew Research Center, *Views of a Changing World,* June 2003; Pew Research Center, *Global Unease with Major World Powers,* 2007.

[a]Net = percent "like" minus "dislike." "Don't know" and "refused" responses excluded.

"like" American ideas about democracy, but only in Canada did as many as half of the respondents express that view. Elsewhere the results were also mixed, even among countries with substantial Muslim populations. Opinions in Indonesia, Nigeria, and Lebanon were on balance favorable, as were those in South Korea, whereas responses in Brazil, Russia, Pakistan, and Jordan were strongly negative.

The 2003 Pew survey revealed that opinions about American democracy turned sharply more negative in several countries, including among NATO allies France, Germany, and Turkey, as well as in Brazil and Indonesia. The most dramatic change occurred in the last case, as the 52 percent majority that liked American democracy in 2002 was cut in half during the interval between the two surveys. These results were offset by more favorable judgments in Italy, Canada, Russia, South Korea, and Jordan, as well as positive responses in several countries that had not been included in the previous Pew study: Australia, Israel, and Kuwait. Although the survey data do not provide evidence on why support for American ideas about democracy was less than overwhelming, it is possible that the 2000 election, wherein the clear winner of the popular vote lost the election, may have had an impact inasmuch as the historical rationale and workings of the U.S. Electoral College may be unfamiliar for many.

The 2007 Pew surveys revealed a very marked deterioration in opinions on American ideas and democracy. The average decline among seven NATO allies was a startling 23 percent. Publics in South Korea, China, Japan, Israel, and Nigeria maintained favorable views, but in other important countries, including Mexico, Brazil, Russia, Indonesia, and Pakistan, responses were on balance very negative.

Many observers of American society, including Alexis de Tocqueville, have noted that religion plays an important part in the life of this country. Among the more obvious reasons is that for four centuries many immigrant groups came to these shores to escape religious persecution in Europe. From the Puritans who left England in the seventeenth century to Jews who emigrated, first to escape pogroms in Russia and then to flee Nazi persecution, the United States has promised the opportunity to exercise the freedom of worship.

The importance of religion in public life has waxed and waned, reaching high points during the pre–Civil War era on the issue of slavery, during the Progressive era on questions of prohibition and women's suffrage, and in recent years on a broad agenda of concerns, ranging from civil rights and the teaching of evolution to abortion and capital punishment. To be sure, anti-Catholic and anti-Semitic sentiments have also played an important role in American public life. In 1938, the ship *Saint Louis,* loaded with Jews seeking refuge from Nazi Germany, was not allowed to disembark its passengers in this country even though sending them back was virtually tantamount to a death sentence. And as recently as the 1960 presidential election, John F. Kennedy's Catholicism presented a major hurdle on his journey to the White House.

The 2003 Pew Research Center asked respondents in twenty countries and in areas controlled by the Palestinian Authority, "Is the U.S. too religious a country or not religious enough?" The results, summarized in table 3.6, reveal a near consensus on the latter option. About two-thirds of respondents in France, a country with a strong anticlerical tradition dating back to the French Revolution, stated that the United States is "too religious," and by the narrowest of margins, a plurality (35 percent to 32 percent) of Australians agreed with

TABLE 3.6. Religion in the United States, 2003

"What's your opinion: Is the U.S. too religious a country or not religious enough?"

	% Too Religious	% Not Religious Enough	% About Right	Net[a]
United States	19	62	11	−43
NATO allies				
Great Britain	33	35	11	−2
France	65	22	7	43
Germany	36	42	3	−6
Italy	14	50	24	−36
Spain	18	45	8	−27
Turkey	19	55	13	−36
Canada	25	39	11	−14
Other key countries				
Brazil	15	73	3	−58
Russia	25	41	17	−16
Australia	35	32	11	3
South Korea	25	61	8	−36
Indonesia	7	81	10	−74
Pakistan	11	72	6	−61
Israel	13	46	28	−33
Kuwait	7	73	6	−67
Jordan	2	81	15	−79
Lebanon	11	72	8	−61
Morocco	31	52	3	−21
Nigeria	23	64	6	−41
Palestinian territories	2	79	3	−77

Source: Pew Research Center, *Views of a Changing World,* June 2003.
[a]Net = "too religious" minus "not religious enough." "Don't know" and "refused" responses excluded.

the French. Respondents elsewhere, including a strong majority in this country, stated that the United States is "not religious enough." That judgment was especially strong among respondents in countries with large Muslim populations, reaching over 70 percent in Pakistan, Indonesia, Kuwait, Jordan, Lebanon, and the Palestinian Authority. Brazilians, South Koreans, Nigerians, and Turks held similar views, although by somewhat smaller majorities.

As with most survey questions it is impossible to pin down the reasons that lie behind the answers about religion in American life. Is it because many respondents abroad find a yawning gap between American ideals, many of which are deeply rooted in the Christian faith, and policies on such issues as capital punishment, the growing gap between the rich and poor, or the war in Iraq, which was repeatedly and publicly opposed by a venerated Pope?

At this point it is appropriate to recall that an ICM/BBC survey, undertaken at precisely the same time (June 2003), yielded somewhat different assessments of American religiosity (table 3.4). In both surveys, respondents in Brazil, Israel, and Jordan agreed that the United States is not religious, but there were some striking differences in the judgments rendered by Americans, Canadians, Brits, South Koreans, Indonesians, and Russians, pluralities of whom described the United States as "religious" in the ICM/BBC study and "not religious enough" in the Pew survey.

The Bush administration appears to be of two minds about American science and technology, providing strong support in some cases while acquiescing—and in some cases even leading the charge—in attacks on some aspects of science that have been targeted by some of the administration's most vocal and well-funded core support groups.

Since, more than two decades ago, President Ronald Reagan announced plans to develop a missile defense system that would render missiles "impotent and obsolete," vast research and development funds have gone into efforts to develop and deploy such a system. Despite repeated test failures, the administration, convinced that the science and engineering problems for a national missile defense system can be resolved, has continued exceptionally generous funding for the program. The North Korean nuclear explosion in October 2006 will no doubt be cited repeatedly by missile defense system proponents as adding urgency to the success of the program.

Other aspects of American science have fared less well. In the face of mounting evidence that global warming is in fact taking place, that polar icecaps are melting, with potentially significant risks for those living in low-lying coastal areas, the president and his advisers continue to assert that even if global warming is a fact, most proposals to deal with it are too costly. As Vice President Cheney stated, energy conservation is a "personal virtue," not an appropriate target of government action. Consequently the administration has opposed the Kyoto Protocol, as well as any international negotiations to modify it in ways that would meet American objections; and it has repeatedly asserted further research is needed before any actions can be undertaken to deal with the problem.

The life sciences provide other examples. An overwhelming majority of biologists consider evolution as a core concept in the field, but that view is vigorously opposed by a number of religious leaders who dismiss evolution because it is antithetical to biblical explanations of the origins and development of life on earth. Well-funded groups such as the Discovery Institute in Seattle, the Creation Studies Institute in Fort Lauderdale, and Answers in Genesis in Kentucky have flexed their political muscles to the point that policymakers in nineteen states are weighing various proposals that question the teaching of evolution. They also had a powerful champion in Senator Rick Santorum (R-PA) until his electoral defeat in 2006. These efforts resemble the edict of the Soviet Central Committee in 1948 stipulating the official status of Lysenko's genetics. As organized challenges to evolution increase in number and intensity, publishers may become increasingly sensitive to demands that alternative explanations appear in science texts. Those who take a less rigid stance on biblical "inerrancy" nevertheless urge that biology students be offered both evolution and "intelligent design" as theories so that they can come to their own conclusions about the relative merits of each. President Bush has publicly supported the latter position, urging that it is better to give students a choice. Other aspects of science that are under official attack include proposals to expand the scope of stem cell research in the hopes of finding cures for some of mankind's worst afflictions. Indeed, President Bush's only veto in the first six years of his presidency was on stem cell legislation.

Against this background of controversy, the 2002, 2003, and 2007 Pew surveys asked respondents whether they do or do not "admire the U.S. for its technological and scientific advances." In a world of sharply conflicting opinions on just about every important issue, the favorable scorecard for American science and technology, summarized in table 3.7, probably comes as close to an international consensus as we are ever likely to see. Publics just about everywhere, save in Russia, expressed overwhelming admiration for these important achievements of American society in 2002, and there is no indication that the widespread disagreements with U.S. policy on the Iraq issue affected appraisals of science and technology. Judgments about science and technology in 2003 were, on average, slightly a bit more favorable (74.8 percent) than those in the previous Pew study (71.3 percent). Even in predominantly Muslim countries, whose populations have not been reticent about expressing disagreement about almost all aspects of the United States and its foreign policies, admiration for American science and technology was almost universal, and it actually reached a slightly higher level than in the other countries surveyed by Pew.

TABLE 3.7. American Technology and Science, 2002–7

"Which of the following phrases comes closer to your view? I admire the U.S. for its technological and scientific advances, OR I do not admire the U.S. for its technological and scientific advances."

	July–October 2002			April–May 2003			April–May 2007		
	% Admire	% Not Admire	Net[a]	% Admire	% Not Admire	Net[a]	% Admire	% Not Admire	Net[a]
NATO allies									
Great Britain	77	17	60	78	17	61	74	16	58
France	65	33	32	64	35	29	71	29	42
Germany	64	34	30	72	25	47	65	33	32
Italy	79	12	67	87	10	77	74	14	60
Spain	—	—	—	73	24	49	61	35	26
Turkey	67	24	43	67	29	38	37	51	−14
Canada	76	19	57	83	14	69	74	21	53
Other key countries									
Mexico	—	—	—	—	—	—	62	33	29
Brazil	78	17	61	77	21	56	74	24	50
Russia	41	44	−3	40	44	−4	32	53	−21
Australia	—	—	—	79	16	63	—	—	—
South Korea	81	16	65	86	11	75	85	11	74
Indonesia	92	7	85	81	16	65	84	12	72
Pakistan	42	22	20	72	21	51	36	37	−1
China	—	—	—	—	—	—	80	11	69
India	—	—	—	—	—	—	64	26	38
Japan	—	—	—	—	—	—	81	9	72
Israel	—	—	—	76	22	54	73	19	54
Kuwait	—	—	—	94	5	89	88	10	78
Jordan	59	39	20	64	36	28	68	27	41
Morocco	—	—	—	85	14	71	55	26	29
Nigeria	93	5	88	90	9	81	86	13	73
Lebanon	84	13	71	86	13	73	74	22	52
Palestinian territories	—	—	—	62	32	30	67	25	42

Source: Pew Research Center, *What the World Thinks in 2002* (Washington, DC: Global Attitudes Project, 2002); Pew Research Center, *Views of a Changing World,* June 2003; Pew Research Center, *Global Unease with Major World Powers,* 2007.

[a]Net = percent "admire" minus "do not admire." "Don't know" and "refused" responses excluded.

With a few exceptions—Turkey, Pakistan, and Russia—admiration for American science and technology persisted through 2007. That was notably true in South Korea, China, Japan, India, and Israel, countries that have made significant technological progress in recent years and that in some respects are competitors in markets for high technology products and services. Even among Islamic publics that have been highly critical of the United States and Washington's foreign policies—including Indonesia, Kuwait, Jordan, Morocco, and Lebanon—American science and technology are still viewed very favorably. The widespread admiration for its science and technology would appear to open interesting avenues for American efforts to "win the hearts and minds" of publics abroad.

A 2004 Harris Interactive survey (table 3.3) revealed strongly favorable assessments of American films and television programs among respondents in six NATO countries. Pew studies undertaken in 2002, 2003, and 2007 phrased a rather similar question that included American music as well as movies and television. The results summarized in table 3.8 reinforce those of the Harris survey: except in the case of Turkey, publics among NATO allies expressed strongly favorable judgments about these aspects of American popular culture, and there is little evidence, except perhaps in Great Britain, that these favorable opinions were eroded by the invasion of Iraq that took place between the three surveys. Canadian leaders have often expressed concerns about American dominance of popular culture north of the 49th parallel, but those views were not evident in the overwhelmingly favorable appraisals of U.S. music, movies, and television. Moreover, there is little evidence that French, German, Italian, Spanish, Mexican, and Brazilian opposition to the American-led invasion of Iraq spilled over into their judgments about entertainment products from the United States. Only in Russia, China, and India, and some predominantly Muslim countries, including Pakistan, Jordan, Turkey, and the area controlled by the Palestinian Authority, were assessments of American entertainment predominantly negative, but those opinions were offset somewhat by favorable assessments in Indonesia, Nigeria, and Lebanon. Publics in China, India, and Japan, not included in the first two Pew studies, expressed mixed assessments of American entertainment products in 2007, with strongly favorable opinions in Japan, a split verdict in China, and strongly negative views in India.

Many multinational corporations based in the United States have a truly global reach. Coca Cola, Microsoft, IBM, Colgate, Procter and Gamble, Nike, Exxon, Citicorp, McDonalds, Starbucks, and American International Group are but a few of the major firms that operate not only on every continent but also in a majority of the globe's almost two hundred countries. Thus, many respondents to the Pew surveys who were asked whether they like or dislike "the American way of doing business" (table 3.9) have had at least some opportunity to use U.S. products or services.

According to the figures in table 3.9, respondents in NATO allies were, on balance, quite critical and the trend between 2002 and 2007 was toward in-

TABLE 3.8. American Music, Movies, and Television, 2002–7

"Which of the following phrases comes closer to your view? I like American music, movies and television, OR I dislike American music, movies and television."

	July–October 2002			April–May 2003			April–May 2007		
	% Like	% Dislike	Net[a]	% Like	% Dislike	Net[a]	% Like	% Dislike	Net[a]
NATO allies									
Great Britain	76	19	57	62	30	32	63	28	35
France	66	32	34	65	34	31	65	35	30
Germany	66	29	37	67	29	38	62	34	28
Italy	63	29	34	69	28	41	66	23	43
Spain	—	—	—	73	24	49	72	25	47
Turkey	44	46	–2	44	53	–9	22	68	–46
Canada	77	17	60	76	18	58	73	19	54
Other key countries									
Mexico	—	—	—	—	—	—	53	41	12
Brazil	69	29	40	67	32	35	69	30	39
Russia	42	50	–8	40	47	–7	38	54	–16
Australia	—	—	—	66	28	38	—	—	—
South Korea	53	38	15	49	39	10	49	42	7
Indonesia	59	40	19	58	40	18	50	46	4
Pakistan	4	79	–75	10	88	–78	4	80	–76
China	—	—	—	—	—	—	42	46	–4
India	—	—	—	—	—	—	23	68	–45
Japan	—	—	—	—	—	—	70	22	48
Israel	—	—	—	62	32	30	72	22	50
Kuwait	—	—	—	42	52	–10	53	44	9
Jordan	30	67	–37	42	57	–15	40	59	–19
Morocco	—	—	—	57	41	16	42	52	–10
Nigeria	76	19	57	70	27	43	59	39	20
Lebanon	65	34	31	66	33	33	71	28	43
Palestinian territories	—	—	—	21	77	–56	23	68	–45

Source: Pew Research Center, *What the World Thinks in 2002* (Washington, DC: Global Attitudes Project, 2002); Pew Research Center, *Views of a Changing World,* June 2003; Pew Research Center, *Global Unease with Major World Powers,* 2007.

[a]Net = percent "like" minus "dislike." "Don't know" and "refused" responses excluded.

creasingly negative opinions. That was clearly the judgment of a majority in Canada, America's top trade partner. Economic relations between the United States and Canada will be revisited in chapter 4.

In contrast, the opinions about American business practices elsewhere were much more mixed, and they did not follow the pattern of responses on many other issues. For example, Australians who disliked American business practices outnumbered those who liked them by a margin of more than two to one.

TABLE 3.9. The American Way of Business, 2002–7

"Which of the following phrases comes closer to your view? I like the American way of doing business, OR I dislike the American way of doing business."

	July–October 2002			April–May 2003			April–May 2007		
	% Like	% Dislike	Net[a]	% Like	% Dislike	Net[a]	% Like	% Dislike	Net[a]
NATO allies									
Great Britain	37	44	−7	37	44	−7	24	53	−29
France	23	73	−50	23	74	−51	25	75	−50
Germany	32	58	−26	34	57	−23	27	64	−37
Italy	39	43	−4	45	43	2	32	46	−14
Spain	—	—	—	30	54	−24	25	52	−27
Turkey	27	59	−32	19	75	−56	6	83	−77
Canada	34	56	−22	37	52	−15	29	59	−30
Other key countries									
Mexico	—	—	—	—	—	—	38	53	−15
Brazil	34	51	−17	34	59	−25	31	61	−30
Russia	41	30	11	34	35	−1	32	41	−9
Australia	—	—	—	27	62	−35	—	—	—
South Korea	59	32	27	57	31	26	61	28	33
Indonesia	54	38	16	56	35	21	42	46	−4
Pakistan	14	53	−39	29	53	−24	16	56	−40
China	—	—	—	—	—	—	49	25	24
India	—	—	—	—	—	—	51	38	13
Japan	—	—	—	—	—	—	40	36	4
Israel	—	—	—	62	21	41	70	19	51
Kuwait	—	—	—	75	19	56	71	23	48
Jordan	44	52	−8	56	43	13	51	47	4
Lebanon	65	28	37	69	28	41	63	33	30
Morocco	—	—	—	64	30	34	44	39	5
Nigeria	85	7	78	77	18	59	78	19	59
Palestinian territories	—	—	—	34	59	−25	40	46	−6

Source: Pew Research Center, *What the World Thinks in 2002* (Washington, DC: Global Attitudes Project, 2002); Pew Research Center, *Views of a Changing World,* June 2003; Pew Research Center, *Global Unease with Major World Powers,* 2007.

[a]Net = percent "like" minus "dislike." "Don't know" and "refused" responses excluded.

But frequently critical publics in Kuwait, Lebanon, Jordan, Morocco, and South Korea were among those who expressed strong approval for American business practices. The latter group of respondents were probably reacting to the perceived benefits of job-creating American investments in their countries. In addition, publics in China, India, and Japan (major Asian trade partners) were also on balance favorably disposed toward American business practices.

International trade and the reach of multinational corporations have

TABLE 3.10. The Spread of American Ideas and Customs, 2002–7

"Which of the following phrases comes closer to your view? It's good that American ideas and customs are spreading here, OR it's bad that American ideas and customs are spreading here."

	July–October 2002			April–May 2003			April–May 2007		
	% Good	% Bad	Net[a]	% Good	% Bad	Net[a]	% Good	% Bad	Net[a]
NATO allies									
Great Britain	39	50	−11	33	56	−23	21	67	−46
France	25	71	−46	27	72	−45	18	81	−63
Germany	28	67	−39	24	70	−46	17	80	−63
Italy	29	58	−29	43	45	−2	25	59	−34
Spain	—	—	—	18	76	−58	16	76	−60
Turkey	11	78	−67	9	86	−77	4	86	−82
Canada	37	54	−17	40	50	−10	22	67	−45
Other key countries									
Mexico	—	—	—	—	—	—	23	68	−45
Brazil	30	62	−32	24	72	−48	23	73	−50
Russia	16	68	−52	20	65	−45	14	76	−62
Australia	—	—	—	28	64	−36	—	—	—
South Korea	30	62	−32	42	45	−3	38	48	−10
Indonesia	20	73	−53	11	83	−72	11	76	−65
Pakistan	2	81	−79	4	93	−89	4	84	−80
China	—	—	—	—	—	—	38	39	−1
India	—	—	—	—	—	—	29	62	−33
Japan	—	—	—	—	—	—	57	25	32
Israel	—	—	—	48	43	5	56	32	24
Kuwait	—	—	—	13	79	−66	10	85	−75
Jordan	13	82	−69	5	93	−88	12	81	−69
Morocco	—	—	—	16	80	−64	12	77	−65
Nigeria	64	31	33	61	35	26	51	44	7
Lebanon	26	67	−41	31	65	−34	38	58	−20
Palestinian territories	—	—	—	4	94	−90	3	90	−87

Source: Pew Research Center, *What the World Thinks in 2002* (Washington, DC: Global Attitudes Project, 2002); Pew Research Center, *Views of a Changing World*, June 2003; Pew Research Center, *Global Unease with Major World Powers*, 2007.

[a]Net = percent "good" minus "bad." "Don't know" and "refused" responses excluded.

clearly increased during the past several decades, but they are not the only features of globalization. The previously cited data on appraisals of American cultural products, including music, movies, and television, indicate that the globalization of entertainment has, with some exceptions in India, Russia, and several Muslim countries, generally been well received by publics abroad. Three Pew surveys also included an item that deals with broader issues of globalization, asking respondents whether it is "good" or "bad" that "American ideas and customs are spreading here."

The results summarized in table 3.10 reveal a gaping chasm between the generally favorable assessments of American entertainment products and the overwhelmingly negative reaction to the globalization of "ideas and customs." With the notable exception of Nigerians, those taking part in the 2002 Pew study expressed little if any enthusiasm for the Americanization of their countries. In none of the predominantly Muslim countries—Turkey, Indonesia, Pakistan, Jordan, and Lebanon—did as many as one-third of the respondents select the "good" option.

The 2003 survey added several countries—Spain, Morocco, Israel, Australia, Kuwait, and the Palestinian Authority—but the results differed only marginally from those of the earlier study. Of the added countries, all except respondents in Israel lamented Americanization. Italians, Canadians, Russians, and South Koreans were somewhat less inclined to judge the spread of American ideas and customs as bad, but those changes were offset by opinions emanating from Great Britain, Turkey, Brazil, Indonesia, Pakistan, and Jordan. The results in both Pew studies were so one-sided that it would be hard to ascribe the negative 2003 responses to the Iraq war.

The negative trend persisted in responses to the most recent Pew survey in 2007. Among publics in the seven NATO allies, the average ratio of "bad" to "good" judgments about Americanization was more than four to one (74 percent to 18 percent). The verdict in predominantly Muslim countries, even those with which the United States has generally maintained cordial relations—Indonesia, Pakistan, Kuwait, Jordan, and Lebanon—was even more negative. Responses elsewhere were slightly more varied as publics in Japan, Israel, and Nigeria expressed more favorable opinions about American ideas and customs and, interestingly, those in China were almost evenly divided on the question.

The 2003 ICM/BBC survey gave respondents in eleven countries another opportunity for a multidimensional evaluation of the United States when it asked, "Which of the following things about America do you think your own country should aspire to achieve?" The results in table 3.11 provide still further evidence that most publics abroad are inclined to make discriminating rather than blanket judgments about the United States.

Once again, American science and technology received high ratings in most countries, including in two predominantly Muslim ones—Indonesia and Jordan—that have in many other respects been quite critical of the United States. Assessments about "economic opportunities" were also, on balance, quite favorable, whereas judgments about "freedom of expression" and "democratic institutions" were mixed at best. The uniformly negative judgments about "American popular culture" give rise to a puzzle because other surveys (tables 3.3 and 3.8) indicated American movies, television, and music have found considerable favor abroad. The contradictory results may arise in part from the wording of the question; perhaps the term "popular culture" has wider, or at least different, connotations than references to music, movies and other specific forms of entertainment.

A striking feature of the responses is the consistency with which Americans overestimated the extent to which others aspire to match this country's achievements. Table 3.11 includes ten other countries and six areas of U.S.

TABLE 3.11. Aspirations to Achieve American Qualities, 2003

"Which of the following things about America do you think your own country should aspire to achieve?"

	Percent Responses						
	A	B	C	D	E	F	G
United States[a]	91	92	84	71	81	61	0
Canada	75	62	41	39	36	20	9
Great Britain	76	66	55	45	26	21	8
Israel	72	77	57	62	45	24	3
Australia	69	44	41	33	20	8	14
South Korea	43	33	28	29	18	11	1
Russia	46	54	22	27	29	4	14
France	59	19	19	6	10	2	11
Indonesia	80	55	54	27	28	8	3
Brazil	55	72	37	35	35	23	5
Jordan	90	80	51	65	68	15	5

Source: ICM Research, *Survey for the British Broadcasting Corporation,* May–June 2003.

Note: Key to column headings—A = Scientific and technological innovation; B = Economic opportunities for people; C = American standards of freedom of expression; D = Democratic institutions; E = Military power; F = American popular culture; G = None of these.

[a]U.S. respondents were asked "Which of the following things about America do you think other countries want to aspire to achieve?"

achievement; all sixty of the responses by publics abroad are lower than the corresponding American estimates. The gap is especially evident in column E—military power. More than four out of five Americans believe that others aspire to match the United States, whereas only in Jordan did as many as half identify that as an appropriate goal for their own county. In France that figure was only 10 percent.

Another measure of how American society is viewed abroad emerges from the 2004 Pew survey that asked, "Do people who move to the United States have a better or worse life there?" Although the question was not restricted to respondents with family or friends who have in fact moved to the United States, a surprisingly large number of them were prepared to offer an opinion. Unfortunately the survey did not include Mexico, home country of by far the largest number of recent immigrants to the United States.

As shown in table 3.12, respondents in all countries except Germany stated that, on balance, those immigrating to the United States had a better rather than worse life. British, Russian, Turkish, and Moroccan participants in the survey were especially inclined to select the "better" option. Given American immigration laws, British, French, and German respondents were probably more likely than those from countries outside Western Europe to have known persons who made such a move; many of them also judged that those who moved

TABLE 3.12. Life in the United States for Those Who Move There, 2004

"Do people who move to the United States have a better or worse life there?"

	% Better	% Worse	% Neither
United States	88	1	6
Great Britain	41	6	35
France	24	12	57
Germany	14	16	58
Russia	53	10	17
Turkey	50	19	14
Pakistan	30	28	19
Jordan	31	21	28
Morocco	47	27	17

Source: Pew Research Center, *A Year after the Iraq War: Mistrust of America Ever Higher, Muslim Anger Persists,* 2004.

Note: "Know of no one who has moved there," "don't know," and "refused" responses excluded.

to the United States had a mixed experience—neither better nor worse. Presumably the high standards of living in Western Europe would lead respondents to believe that immigrants would find a comparable life in the United States.

CONCLUSION

Among the goals of this and the previous chapter is to determine the extent to which assessments of this country among publics abroad are driven by opinions about what the United States *is* versus what the United States *does*. The evidence to this point suggests that the latter, American policy, is more important. A closely related question posed by Pew after the September 11 attacks but before the invasion of Iraq asked, "When there are differences between our country and the United States, do you think these differences occur because we have different values than the United States or because we have different policies than the United States?" Even though the survey was conducted prior to the most contentious issue in relations between the United States and other countries—the invasion of Iraq—respondents in most countries identified divergent policies rather than values as the primary source of conflict between their countries and the United States.

The question, as worded, cannot point to specific areas of disagreement, but it does provide some insight into the perceived permanence of any divergences with the United States. Those who select the "policies" response option presumably have in mind some specific issues; these might be amenable to resolution by compromise, policy shifts by one country or the other, or changes in leadership positions. In contrast, divergences in values are likely to be perceived as more permanent, at least in part because it is usually difficult to find compromises between conflicting value positions. Moreover, changes in values, if they occur, are likely to take place over a longer time span. Although it is not identical, the "values" option on this question bears a slight resemblance to Samuel Huntington's "clash of civilizations" thesis.[4]

As indicated at the top of table 3.13, almost two-thirds of Americans believe that "policies" are the source of differences between the United States and other countries. They seem to believe, in short, that core American values are quite widely shared abroad, or at least that they do not give rise to differences with

---

4. Samuel P. Huntington, *The Clash of Civilizations and the Remaking of World Order* (New York: Simon and Schuster, 1996).

other countries. According to responses to this item, the majority Americans' view is shared by many respondents abroad, especially in areas of traditional U.S. interests, including Europe and the Americas. Perhaps because the survey preceded clear and well-publicized trans-Atlantic disputes over the Iraq issue, clear majorities in Great Britain, France, Germany, Poland, and Canada selected the "policies" response option, and even in Turkey a strong plurality did

TABLE 3.13. Sources of Differences between the United States and Other Countries, 2002

"When there are differences between our country and the United States, do you think these differences occur because we have different values than the United States or because we have different policies than the United States?"

	% Different Values	% Different Policies	% Don't Know/ Refused
United States[a]	28	63	9
NATO allies			
Great Britain	41	55	3
France	33	65	2
Germany	37	58	6
Italy	44	44	12
Poland	27	52	21
Czech Republic	62	34	4
Spain	—	—	—
Turkey	35	47	18
Canada	37	57	7
Other key countries			
Mexico	34	57	9
Brazil	36	53	11
Russia	37	49	14
Japan	61	34	5
South Korea	41	53	6
Indonesia	66	31	3
India	15	46	39
Pakistan	14	38	48
Jordan	35	61	4
Egypt	38	45	17
Nigeria	29	47	3

Source: Pew Research Center, *What the World Thinks in 2002* (Washington, DC: Global Attitudes Project, 2002).

[a]U.S. respondents were asked: "When there are differences between the U.S. and European countries, do you think these differences occur because the U.S. has different values than Europe or because the U.S. has different policies than Europe?"

so. It is also noteworthy that the results in Russia were almost a carbon copy of those in Turkey.

Elsewhere the picture is somewhat more forbidding. Among Asian countries there was a wide divergence of views between, on the one hand, Indonesia and Japan, where the "values" response gained very strong majorities, and India and Pakistan, where fewer than one-fifth of those taking part in the Pew surveys selected that option, although in both of the two South Asian countries a great many respondents were unable or unwilling to answer the question, and thus the results may not be very meaningful.

Aside from Indonesia, in none of the three predominantly Muslim countries (Egypt, Jordan, and Turkey) did as many as 40 percent of the respondents attribute differences with the United States to divergent values. While responses to this question provide no evidence about specific policy differences, the issue of Palestine and the looming war in Iraq were surely at the forefront in the minds of many respondents.

On balance, the evidence summarized in table 3.13 suggests that for many publics abroad, their critical views of the United States may be bounded and perhaps transient rather than deeply embedded in core values. There were three exceptions to the general pattern. More than 60 percent of respondents in the Czech Republic, Japan, and Indonesia stated that values lay at the root of their differences with the United States. To understate the case, this is a very diverse group of countries in many respects, not the least of which include religion and culture. This is not to say that the task of rebuilding—or in many cases establishing—good relations abroad will be easy, or that in all cases it would be wise to "split the differences" on crucial policy issues. It does indicate, however, that thoughtful diplomacy, often lacking since 2001, could be a useful step in bridging avoidable gaps with publics abroad.

The evidence presented in this and the previous chapter has been long on description and much shorter on explanations for critical opinions about the United States. As a partial effort to remedy this shortcoming, chapter 4 undertakes a series of seven brief country studies that attempt to identify more fully the sources and possible policy consequences of these opinions.

The Impact of "How They See Us"

Seven Mini–Case Studies

Because neither democracies nor authoritarian countries conduct foreign policy by plebiscite, the impact of public opinion—much less opinions about a single country, even one as important as the United States—cannot be assumed. The survey data described in chapters 2 and 3 provide a fairly compelling picture of increasingly critical views about the United States and its foreign policies among many publics abroad, including among some of this country's oldest allies, but even a cursory examination of anecdotal evidence reveals that the correlation between public opinion and important policy decisions falls far short of 1. As revealed earlier in this book, Prime Minister Tony Blair's decision to follow the United States into Iraq was taken in the face of very limited public enthusiasm for the undertaking. Although Spanish and Italian contributions to the "coalition of the willing" involved smaller military contingents, decisions by the governments in Madrid and Rome clearly flew in the face of growing public criticism of the United States and, especially, of Washington's policy on the Iraq issue.

In other cases the anecdotal evidence suggests that public views of the United States and its foreign policies may indeed have had policy consequences. As noted earlier, during his very difficult reelection campaign in 2002, Chancellor Gerhard Schroeder publicly pledged that German armed forces, which had been sent to Afghanistan in the wake of the September 11 terrorist attacks to remove the Taliban regime and to hunt down al Qaeda leaders, would not under any circumstances be deployed to Iraq. That pledge, which mirrored the strongly held views of the German public, appears to have been sufficient to fuel a close electoral victory for Schroeder.

In an effort to go beyond such anecdotal evidence, this chapter seeks to shed more light on how public views of the United States may have entered into the policy process in seven countries with which Washington traditionally has had cordial relations: Turkey, Indonesia, Mexico, Canada, Australia, Morocco, and South Korea. Indeed, this country has alliance and other ties with Turkey (NATO), Australia (ANZUS pact), South Korea (bilateral security pact), Canada (NATO and NAFTA), and Mexico (Rio Pact, NAFTA). Even without formal alliance ties, U.S. relations with Indonesia and Morocco have generally been amicable.

There is more to be learned about the sources and impact of anti-American opinions by focusing on countries where such sentiments are not necessarily part of a long tradition of opposition to the United States, its people, its institutions, and its policies. The list thus excludes traditional adversaries whose publics have had to endure long periods of official anti-American propaganda and where, in any case, public opinion polling opportunities are very limited (North Korea, Iran, Cuba, Libya, Syria); some important countries for which there are rather limited data on public views of the United States (China, Japan, Egypt); and three others that have taken strong positions opposing American policies in Iraq, but that have already been the focus of extensive analyses elsewhere (France, Germany, Russia).

The country studies that follow cannot establish beyond reasonable doubt the sources and consequences of public views of the United States. Even elite interviews and archival research, neither of which is available for such recent events, might not yield definitive conclusions. These case studies begin with the assumption that public opinion has at best a limited impact on policy unless there is substantial evidence to the contrary. Thus, the burden of proof is on the thesis that public opinion about the United States and its policies was in fact consequential.

Following a very brief description of pre–September 11, 2001, relations with the United States, each of the country studies examines how the government in question reacted to some of the important events of the subsequent years. These include the September 11, 2001, terrorist attacks, the invasion of Afghanistan in October 2002, the run-up to and invasion of Iraq in March 2003, and events in Iraq since the fall of Baghdad, including insurgency that has brought the country to the brink of civil war. The analyses will also include additional events that may have been important for one, but not necessarily all seven, of the countries; for example, the devastating tsunami that struck Indonesia in December 2004, Mexican immigration issues, and U.S. tariffs imposed on softwood lumber from Canada.

TURKEY

Modern Turkey, which emerged from World War I as the core remnant of the Ottoman Empire, was transformed into a secular republic by the "Ataturk Revolution." The Turkish republic was proclaimed on October 23, 1923, and Kemal Ataturk was unanimously elected president by the assembly. The population is predominantly Muslim, and the army has been among the institutions that enforces the strict separation between church and state that Ataturk deemed essential for modernizing the country. Owing to its size and geographical location—it currently borders on Georgia, Armenia, Iran, Iraq, Syria, Bulgaria, and Greece—Turkey serves as a bridge between Europe and the Middle East. It is also a bridge between Islamic and Western cultures.

Turkey remained neutral during World War II until February 1945 when it declared war on Germany and Japan, thereby earning a place at the San Francisco Conference that drew up the United Nations Charter. It has played an important international role since the end of that conflict. Soviet pressures for Turkish concessions on the Bosporus and in eastern Turkey, combined with a British note to the U.S. State Department in 1947 that it would no longer be able to maintain its traditional security role in the Mediterranean area, led to a package of American aid to Greece and Turkey, as well as a pledge of support for countries facing a direct or indirect Soviet threat, as part of what became known as the "Truman Doctrine." Although Turkey was not a charter member of NATO when that alliance came into existence in 1949, it joined three years later. Turkey was one of sixteen countries that contributed armed forces to the U.S.-led and United Nations–sanctioned intervention to repel the North Korean invasion of its southern neighbor in June 1950. The almost thirty thousand troops in Korea, the first military units deployed outside Turkey's borders, fought with great valor and suffered heavy casualties, including 717 killed and 2,256 wounded.[1] Upon return of the "Koreli," veterans of the Korean War, "Turkey changed forever" according to one observer.[2]

Despite NATO ties and American military assistance, relations between Ankara and Washington have not always been harmonious, largely as a result of threats of war between Turkey and Greece, another member of NATO. Crises over Cyprus, an island inhabited by Greeks and a substantial Turkish minority, erupted in 1963–64 and 1967. Greece precipitated a crisis in 1974 by engineering

---

1. Bruce Kuniholm, "Turkey," in *Encyclopedia of U.S. Foreign Relations,* ed. Bruce W. Jentleson and others (New York: Oxford University Press, 1997), 3:220.
2. Stephen Kinzer, *Crescent and Star: Turkey between Two Worlds* (New York: Farrar, Straus and Giroux, 2001), 158.

a coup that toppled Archbishop Makarios III, the first president of Cyprus, and replaced him with Nicos Sampson. Turkey's 1974 invasion and subsequent partition of Cyprus into Greek and Turkish zones led to a suspension for several years of American military assistance, as well as Turkish reduction of basing rights for U.S. forces. Arms shipments to Turkey resumed in February 1979. During the Cold War, Turkey anchored the southeastern flank of NATO. The disintegration of the Soviet Union in 1991 diminished the significance of that role somewhat, but the 1979 Iranian revolution that brought a fundamentalist Islamic regime to power in Tehran and continuing turmoil in several other parts of the region have added to Turkey's importance.

Iraq's invasion of Kuwait in 1990 further tested relations between the two countries. Although the Kirkuk-Yumurtai oil pipeline that brought Iraqi oil to a Turkish seaport was a major source of revenue, Turkey acceded to Washington's request to shut it down. Turkey also joined the coalition of twenty-six countries that successfully drove the invading Iraqi forces out of Kuwait. President Turgut Ozal shattered precedent by overruling the military, who opposed taking an active role in the conflict.[3] Turkish armed forces did not cross into Iraq, but their presence on the Iraqi frontier tied down some of Saddam Hussein's forces. The United States promised aid to compensate for the serious economic losses suffered by Turkey during the Gulf War—those losses included not only the oil pipeline revenues but also trade with Iraq and drastic reductions in tourism—but in fact little of it was actually delivered.

At the risk of great oversimplification, on the eve of the September 11, 2001, terrorist attacks, some of the most salient features of Turkey and its external relations included the following. First, Turkey is an overwhelmingly Muslim country with a long tradition since the Ataturk revolution, vigilantly maintained by the military, of secularism. It is a multiparty electoral democracy but a somewhat fragile one. Since World War II the military has taken power by coups in 1960, 1971, and 1980, one of which resulted in the execution of President Adnan Menderes and two cabinet ministers in 1961. More recently, although the military did not assume power in 1997, it forced the resignation of an elected pro-Islamic government. According to one observer, "[f]ear of Islamic fundamentalism" grips Turkish elites, but the secularists must recognize that "religion is a strong force in Turkey and they cannot hope ever to suppress it."[4] The Turkish military once again intervened in politics in 2007 to oppose

---

3. Ibid., 166.
4. Ibid., 60 and 81.

the presidential candidacy of foreign minister Abdullah Gul, whose wife wears a headscarf and who is a close associate of Prime Minister Erdogan. Without mentioning Gul by name, the military stated that "an Islamic reactionary mentality" was engaged in "endless efforts to disturb the fundamental values of the republic of Turkey."[5] Prime Minister Erdogan responded by calling for an early election, resulting in large gains for the AKP, fueled at least in part by its economic successes, including a 7 percent annual growth rate. With 47 percent of the popular vote—up from 34 percent in 2002—the AKP controlled 340 seats in the Grand National Assembly, Turkey's parliament. On the third round of voting for the presidency, the GNA elected Gul in August. Members of the military appear to have accepted that outcome but pointedly they did not attend Gul's inauguration ceremony. An additional issue that may roil relations between civilian and military leaders is Erdogan's proposal to lift a constitutional prohibition against university women wearing headscarves at universities.

Second, for many years Turkey was engaged in a bloody civil war against separatist Kurdish organizations in the eastern part of the country. Although the conflict came to a temporary end in 1997, when the Kurdistan Workers Party (Partiya Karkeren Kurdistan) ended its fourteen-year armed insurgency, it did not escape Turkish notice that Kurds in northern Iraq came to enjoy a good deal of autonomy in the aftermath of the Gulf War, igniting fears that demands for creation of an independent Kurdistan might spill over into Turkey, reigniting the civil war. The "no fly zone" authorized by Security Council Resolution 688 and enforced by the U.S. Air Force prevented the Saddam Hussein regime in Baghdad from repeating earlier atrocities against Iraqi Kurds. The PKK ended its unilateral cease-fire in June 2004 but called for a new one in September 2006 at the behest of its imprisoned leader, Abdullah Ocalan. The Turkish military has been eager to take action against PKK militants in Iraq.

Finally, Turkey has applied for membership in the European Union, and it has taken some significant steps to meet EU requirements, including abolition of capital punishment in 2002. A European Commission staff report in October 2004 provided a good summary of Turkey's geopolitical significance. "Turkey is situated at the regional crossroads of strategic importance for Europe: the Balkans, Caucasus, Central Asia, Middle East and Eastern Mediter-

---

5. Vincent Boland, "Generals Throw Down the Gauntlet to Foreign Minister," *Financial Times*, April 30, 2007; and see Boland, "A Tale of Misunderstandings, Snobbery, Bruised Egos and Mutinous Soldiers," *Financial Times*, May 1, 2007.

ranean; its territory is a transit route for land and air transport with Asia, and for sea transport with Russia and Ukraine. Its neighbours provide key energy supplies for Europe, and it has substantial water resources."[6] However, despite U.S. support, unresolved issues concerning Cyprus—combined with opposition from France and Germany arising at least in part from Turkey's size, lower level of economic development, and overwhelmingly Muslim population— cloud the outlook for an invitation to join the EU. Former French president Giscard d'Estaing flatly asserted that EU membership would mean "the end of Europe."[7] His successor as French president, Nicolas Sarkozy, has been equally outspoken in opposing Turkish membership in the EU. The 2006 German Marshall Fund survey found that by a margin of 54 percent to 22 percent, Turkish respondents felt that their country's entry into the European Union would be "a good thing," but that view was not shared among those in France (net score of minus 33 percent), Germany (minus 27 percent), and the Netherlands (minus 18 percent).[8] Tensions involving the Muslim populations residing in the latter three countries no doubt are among the sources of this opposition to Turkish membership.

Immediately following the September 11 terrorist attacks, government officials in Ankara and the Turkish media responded with outpourings of support for America, much in the same way that they had reacted to the assassination of President John F. Kennedy in 1963. All major news media provided extensive coverage of the attacks, while also expressing sympathy. For example, the newspaper *Hurriyet* asserted that as a result of the attacks "Washington DC and New York turned into hell."[9] Prime Minister Bulent Ecevit, speaking on behalf of the government and the Turkish people, stated that the "U.S. is a world state, and the things that happen there affect the whole world."[10]

More importantly, action followed expressions of sympathy. Turkey joined its allies in invoking Article 5 of the NATO Treaty, which effectively stipulates that "an attack on one is an attack on all." The Ankara government also supported UN Security Council Resolution 1373, thereby committing Turkey to the

6. Quoted in Meltem Muftuler-Bac, "Turkey and the European Union: Partners in Security in an Era of Insecurity," *Security Matters, Newsletter of the Centre for European Security Studies* 17 (January 2007): 8.
7. Michael S. Teitelbaum and Philip L. Martin, "Is Turkey Ready for Europe?" *Foreign Affairs* (May/June 2003): 97–111.
8. German Marshall Fund, *Transatlantic Trends 2006.*
9. "Like World War Three," *Hurriyet*, September 12, 2001.
10. "Crisis Desk Ankara," *Milliyett*, September 12, 2001.

international effort to fight terrorism, and it issued a statement that, "in the aftermath of the September 11th attacks, Turkey expressed its unequivocal solidarity with the United States of America and responded favorably to its call to join in an international coalition aiming at bringing to justice the perpetrators and organizers of these attacks."[11] At the same time Turkey opened its airspace to U.S. military transport aircraft participating in the invasion of Afghanistan and issued a blanket clearance for landings and takeoffs at several Turkish airfields. It did so despite public opposition to the U.S. military action in Afghanistan.[12] Some four thousand U.S. flights into Afghanistan originated from the Incirlik base.[13] These actions in support of the U.S.-led incursion into Afghanistan to remove the Taliban regime and to capture al Qaeda leaders triggered relatively limited domestic debate about Turkey's role. Turkish troops in Afghanistan were involved in a variety of missions, including helping with reconnaissance, guiding the Northern Alliance forces that opposed the Taliban regime, supporting humanitarian efforts, and protecting civilians.[14]

Turkish support for the invasion of Afghanistan did not end with the successful removal of the Taliban regime in Kabul in late 2001. Indeed, Turkey took over command of the NATO-led peacekeeping force International Security Assistance Force (ISAF) in 2003, and it served a second term in that role in 2005. Although a few critics raised questions about American reasons for involvement in the region—oil was one purported motive[15]—there are few indications that the U.S.-led invasion of Afghanistan was a major catalyst in sparking or fueling anti-American sentiments among substantial parts of the Turkish public. The Gallup 2001–2 survey revealed that 40 percent of Turkish respondents had a favorable view of the United States, by far the highest among the predominantly Muslim countries in the study.

Among the many official expressions of support for the United States in the aftermath of the September 11 attacks was a statement that

> [t]he Foreign Ministry and the Chief of General Staff decided that Turkey would actively participate in a possible NATO operation against bases of terrorism. . . . Ankara is mainly focusing on an air strike against Afghanistan. . . . Iraq

---

11. "Report to the Security Council Committee Established Pursuant to Resolution 1373," *Turkish Daily News*, January 1, 2002, http://www.turkishnews.com/tr/oldeditions.php?dir=010102.html.

12. Gallup Organization, *Gallup International End of the Year Terrorism Poll 2001*.

13. Ibid.

14. "Full Support from Turkey," *Sabah*, September 15, 2001.

15. "In Turkish Youth's Eyes, a Cynical Ploy by the U.S.," *Turks.US*, January 14, 2003. Turkish student opinions of the United States are also analyzed in Ann Kelleher, Ozlen Kuncek, and Sevilay Kharaman, "Turkish Student Attitudes about the United States," *International Studies Perspective* 4, no. 3 (2003): 250–64.

comes second on the list. .... [I]t will assess the evidence that the United States
has to offer and then support an operation if it finds the evidence convincing.[16]

These prescient words indicated that the burden of proof would be on Washington to demonstrate links between Baghdad and al Qaeda if Turkey were to
be enlisted in military operations against Iraq.

In his State of the Union address in 2002, President Bush identified Iran,
North Korea, and Iraq as "the axis of evil." Although there have been reports
that an invasion to topple the Saddam Hussein regime in Baghdad had been
discussed at the first cabinet meeting of the new administration a year earlier,
this was the first public indication that military action against Iraq was under
serious consideration. During the ensuing months the administration
mounted a full-scale campaign, centered on allegations of Iraqi possession of
weapons of mass destruction and ties to al Qaeda, to gain domestic and international support for military action.

Whereas Turkey had enthusiastically supported military action in neighboring
Afghanistan, the possibility of war against Iraq raised a number of serious
problems for Turkey. One analyst clearly summarized the point: "It thus
seemed that Turkey would have a crucial role in the war on terrorism. However,
this picture greatly altered in 2003 with the crisis between Turkey and the USA
over the war in Iraq."[17] The Kurdish question was clearly the most urgent concern in Ankara. Whatever the many differences between Turkey and Iraq, their
governments shared at least one important goal: to prevent the four million
Kurds in Iraq and eleven million Kurds in Turkey from gaining autonomy
within their home countries and, far worse, from joining forces to create an independent Kurdistan. In 1987 the two countries agreed to allow Turkey to pursue members of the PKK who sought refuge in Iraq following terrorist attacks
in Turkey.

Although the public campaign to garner support for the use of force against
Iraq did not begin until September 2002—as White House Chief of Staff Andrew Card told the *New York Times,* "from a marketing point of view you don't
introduce a new product in August"—on July 14 Paul Wolfowitz and Marc
Grossman visited Ankara to discuss war plans, including permission for the

16. "Full Support from Turkey."
17. For an excellent overview of the Iraq issue in Turkish-American relations, see Meltem Muftuler-Bac, "Turkey
and the USA at Cross Roads: The Impact of the War in Iraq," *International Journal* 61 (winter 2006): 61–82.

United States to station eighty thousand troops in Turkey and to upgrade seaports and airports to accommodate them.[18]

During the autumn of 2002 the Bush administration gained congressional approval for the use of force in Iraq, and the United Nations Security Council passed resolution 1441 demanding that Baghdad readmit United Nations inspection teams to determine whether Iraq was in compliance with prohibitions, dating back to the end of the Gulf War in 1991, against developing weapons of mass destruction. Turkey held elections on November 2, 2002, that brought to power the moderate Islamic Justice and Development Party (AKP in Turkish), led by Recep Tayyip Erdogan, with an unexpectedly large margin. Because parties with fewer than 10 percent of the vote are denied representation, the 34 percent received by the AKP translated into a majority of the seats in the Grand National Assembly (GNA), Turkey's parliament.

Anticipating an attack on Iraq from the southeast in the near future—U.S. forces would undertake the invasion from Kuwait—the Bush administration entered into negotiations with Ankara about stationing the Fourth Infantry Division in Turkey, with a view to launching a second-front attack on Iraq from the north. Wolfowitz and Grossman returned to Ankara in early December for further discussions to confirm the war plans that had been outlined in July. They met with members of the Turkish armed forces (TAF) and with Erdogan, leader of the AKP. Erdogan was not eligible to become prime minister until a special election on March 9 gave him a seat in parliament. Shortly after the Wolfowitz-Grossman meeting, Erdogan made a brief visit to Washington.

Discussions between Washington and Ankara were complicated by the position of the TAF. The military, strongly secular by long tradition, were wary of the AKP. They were also suspicious of American war aims. The sometimes difficult negotiations involved a number of issues, including the possibility of a $26 billion American aid package. At least one view in Washington was that Turkey was engaging in blackmail by demanding too much of its ally, including a written financial commitment, signed by President Bush. The Turks were not amused that they were sometimes depicted in the United States as a "checkbook ally" or as "corrupt merchants, horse traders or worse."[19] Given the American failure to deliver promised economic aid after the Gulf War, Ankara's bargaining position was understandable. After his visit to Ankara, Deputy Secretary of

---

18. Elizabeth Bumiller, "Traces of Terror: The Strategy; Bush Aides Set Strategy to Sell Policy on Iraq," *New York Times*, September 7, 2002; and Robert Olson, "Views from Turkey: Reasons for the United States War against Iraq," *Journal of Third World Studies* (fall 2005): 141–60.

19. Olson, "Views from Turkey."

Defense Paul Wolfowitz left with the impression that Turkish military leaders supported the plan.

The proposed deployment of U.S. troops went to the newly elected 533-member Grand National Assembly for a vote at the beginning of March. A Pew survey, undertaken in December 2002, had revealed that 83 percent of Turkish respondents opposed the plan, and other surveys yielded similarly one-sided sentiments against it.[20] Although Erdogan supported the proposal, other Turkish officials were divided. President Ahmed Necdet Sezer raised a broader concern about the Iraq issue, asserting that "I do not find it right that the USA is behaving unilaterally before the UN process has ended."[21] The Turkish constitution stipulates that proposals involving foreign armed forces on home territory must be approved by an absolute majority of the total membership. The parliamentary vote was exceptionally close, with 264 approving the deployment of U.S. forces, 250 opposing it, and 19 abstaining. It thus fell only 3 votes short of the required 267 favorable votes.

Although there was scant reason to believe that a second-front attack would materially affect the outcome of the war—Baghdad fell less than three weeks after the start of the invasion as the poorly equipped and poorly led Iraqi forces put up only token resistance—Washington reacted with fury to the parliamentary vote. Ten days after the GNA vote, President Bush asked Prime Minister-elect Erdogan to reintroduce the issue. The conversation took an ugly turn when Erdogan refused to do so.[22] Not surprisingly, the United States then withdrew its offer of $6 billion in aid to Turkey.

In an effort to repair relations with Washington, shortly before the fall of Baghdad Turkey agreed to allow the United States to use its territory for overland supplies of food, water, fuel, and nonlethal necessities, but during a trip to Ankara, Secretary of State Powell expressed "lingering disappointment" over the earlier GNA decision on the Fourth Infantry Division.

Paul Wolfowitz then threw gasoline on the smoldering relations between Washington and Ankara. In an interview with CNN Turk, he publicly asserted that, in order to maintain good relations with the United States, the Turkish government would have to admit the error of its ways and apologize for denying American forces the use of its territory as a staging ground for the invasion. Further, he stated that the Turkish military should have taken a more active

---

20. Matthew Rothschild, "Democracy for Iraq, Not Turks," *Turks.US*, May 9, 2003.
21. Muftuler-Bac, "Turkey and the USA at Cross Roads."
22. Eric Schmitt and Dexter Filkins, "Erdogan Turkish Party Leader, to Form Government as U.S. Presses for Use of Bases," *New York Times*, March 11, 2003.

leadership role on the issue.[23] Assuming that Wolfowitz, a University of Chicago political science Ph.D., had at least the most rudimentary acquaintance with the role of the military in post–World War II Turkish history, he appeared to be regretting that the military had not once again come out of the barracks to take command of the government. Perhaps there are other instances in which a top official of one country has seemingly wished for a military coup against a democratically elected government of an allied country, but one does not immediately come to mind. Some administration cheerleaders in the American media, notably *New York Times* syndicated columnist William Safire, a longtime vocal advocate of Kurdish independence, were equally outspoken in their condemnation of Turkey. After a series of virulent attacks, Safire magnanimously suggested that the United States should "forgive, but don't forget."[24] In contrast, the decision of the Turkish parliament was described by one analyst as "a rare victory for democracy."[25]

Turkish public reactions to the events surrounding the invasion of Iraq in March 2003 were fairly predictable. Even prior to the parliamentary vote a massive rally had opposed basing of U.S. troops in Turkey.[26] Turkish media did not allow Wolfowitz's undiplomatic comments to go unnoticed, and spirited commentaries followed. In addition to widespread support for Turkey's Fourth Infantry Division–basing decision, the discussion revealed strong disapproval of the entire U.S. operation in Iraq.[27] Although broad anti-American attitudes have only infrequently marked coverage of the United States in the Turkish media, the events surrounding the March 2003 invasion of Iraq provided ample material for critical views, with a special focus on the Kurdish question. There is scant evidence that, despite the long alliance relationship with Turkey, American leaders had an adequate appreciation for the depth of Ankara's concern with the Kurdish issue and how an invasion of Iraq from the north might be viewed in Turkey as primarily a political, rather than military, issue.

---

23. These statements were made on CNN Turk, a CNN-Turkish media conglomerate joint venture. "Interview with CNN Turk," May 6, 2003, http://www.defenselink.mil/transcripts/2003/tr20030506-depsecdef0156.html; and Josh Marshall, "On Democracy: One Step Forward, Two Steps Back." *Hill*, May 14, 2004. A Turkish poll revealed that 9.5 percent approved of Wolfowitz's statement, 59.1 percent disapproved, and 31.1 percent expressed no opinion. Nasuh Uslu, Metin Toprak, Ibrahim Dalmis, and Ertan Aydin, "Turkish Public Opinion Toward the United States in the Context of the Iraq Question," *Middle East Review of International Affairs* 9, no. 3 (2005): 75–107, table 26.
24. William Safire, "Let Turks Grovel: We Can Forgive Them Later," *New York Times*, June 1, 2003.
25. Christopher Deliso, "An Improbable War and Turkey's New Opportunities," March 29, 2005, http://www .balkanalysis.com.
26. "The Turkish People Have Spoken," *Turks.US*, March 3, 2003.
27. Derya Sazak, "Wolfowitz and the United States' 'Democratic' Side," *Turks.US*, May 8, 2003.

As late as 2005, Secretary of Defense Donald Rumsfeld blamed Turkey for the persisting insurgency in Iraq, asserting that it would have been nipped in the bud had the United States been able to open a northern front in 2003.[28] Earlier Rumsfeld had echoed President Bush's dismissal of the insurgents—"bring 'em on" the president boasted in July 2003—as a few inconsequential "dead enders."[29] Two years later it was more convenient to blame Turkey for post-Saddam difficulties that Rumsfeld and his colleagues had repeatedly dismissed and refused to consider during the run-up to the invasion. According to the secretary of defense, "Given the level of the insurgency today, two years later, clear, if we had been able to get the Fourth Infantry Division in from the north through Turkey, more of the Iraqi Saddam Hussein Baathist regime would have been captured or killed." When asked whether the United States should have sent more troops into Iraq in the beginning to better secure the post-Saddam regime, he replied that doing so would have created an image of "occupation" rather than "liberation."[30] The Fox News interviewer did not ask Rumsfeld how the decision to disband the entire Iraqi army soon after the fall of Baghdad, removing thousands of trained and armed young men from the payroll, might have contributed to the insurgency.

The invasion of Iraq gave rise to several other issues that roiled relations between the United States and Turkey. The arrest in Sulaymaniyah on July 4, 2003, of eleven Turkish Special Forces troops who had been on a special mission, with full knowledge of the Pentagon and the Turkish chief of staff, was one such event. They were suspected of plotting to assassinate a Kurdish leader. In the light of the background of previous differences on Iraq, reactions in the Turkish government and media were predictably very critical. One leading Turk compared the plight of the soldiers to American diplomats who had been blindfolded while being held captive by Iranian militants in 1979.[31] The Turkish chief of staff described the incident as "the worst crisis of confidence" between the two countries.[32]

On October 6, 2003, the Turkish GNA voted to allow the deployment of ten thousand Turkish peacekeepers to help deal with the growing insurgency in

---

28. Tom Rogan, "Turkey, U.S. Relations Hit New Rough Spot," *Christian Science Monitor*, March 21, 2005.

29. On June 18, 2003, the secretary of defense stated, "In those regions where pockets of dead-ends are trying to reconstitute, General Franks and his team are rooting them out. In short, the coalition is making good progress." Quoted in Patrick Cockburn, "The Path to Peace: Allies Face a Tough Battle to Bring Normality," http://www.globalpolicy.org/security/issues/iraq/occupation/2003/0625path.htm.

30. "Turkey, US Relations Hit New Rough Spot."

31. Muftuler-Bac, "Turkey and the USA at Cross Roads."

32. Dexter Filkins, "U.S. Frees Turkish Soldiers, but Relations Remain Strained," *New York Times*, July 7, 2003.

Iraq, but the plan fell through when the provisional government in Baghdad expressed its opposition. Once again the Kurdish issue entered the picture. Iraqi Kurds opposed the presence of Turkish troops on the grounds that they might stand in the way of Kurdish autonomy. Moreover, L. Paul Bremer, chief of the Coalition Provisional Authority, furious at reprimands for the Sulaymaniyah episode, asked Washington to refuse the offer.

In the face of growing tensions between Ankara and Washington, President Bush and Prime Minister Erdogan met in January 2004. Bush reiterated American support for Turkish entry into the European Union and repeated a pledge that "Iraq's territorial integrity will be protected in a federal structure and the Turcomen minority's rights will be protected."[33]

Subsequent events in Iraq did little to temper Turkish criticism of American policies in that occupied country. Revelations of abuse at Abu Ghraib prison of Iraqi detainees were dismissed by many American officials as isolated and unauthorized actions by a few low-ranking enlisted personnel, but few Turks were persuaded. Rather, they perceived such behavior as not consistent with America's stated goal of promoting democracy in the Middle East. The several elections that led, by the end of 2005, to adoption of a constitution and a parliament in Baghdad and, in 2006, to a multiparty cabinet were not sufficient to assuage all Turkish concerns about U.S. policy in Iraq.

Turks have also been displeased by the manner in which their country was depicted in the American print media and television stories—for example, an article in the *Wall Street Journal* in which visiting journalist Robert Pollock described their country as a hotbed of viciously anti-American attitudes.[34] On the other hand, some Americans have expressed dismay at the growing sales in Turkey of Hitler's *Mein Kampf* and of a novel, *Metal Storm*, that depicts the U.S. invasion of Turkey and the hero's subsequent act of revenge—the destruction of Washington with a nuclear device.[35]

Sales of *Mein Kampf* aside, Turkey has a history of cordial dealings with Jews. The Ottoman Empire welcomed Jewish refugees from persecution in Europe as far back as the Spanish Inquisition in 1492, modern Turkey has maintained good relations with Israel, and trade between the two countries is currently valued at $2.5 billion annually.

---

33. Soli Ozel, "The Future of Turkish Politics," *Sabah*, February 5, 2004, quoted in Muftuler-Bac, "Turkey and the European Union." The Turcomen ethnic group, related to Turks, constitutes a small minority of about 5 percent of Iraq's population.

34. Robert L. Pollock, "The Sick Man of Europe—Again," *Wall Street Journal*, February 16, 2005.

35. "Turkey Shrugs Off Success of Hitler's Mein Kampf." Reuters, March 28, 2005.

While the Kurdish situation is clearly of most concern to Turks, an older question—the allegation that Turkey massacred up to 1.5 million Armenians in 1915—has occasionally served as an irritant in relations between Ankara and Washington. A strong Armenian lobby in Washington has pushed for a congressional resolution commemorating the alleged genocide. In 2000 President Clinton acted to have the resolution pulled off the floor of the House of Representatives in order not to offend a good ally, but in the light of recent rough bumps in relations with Turkey, the issue is likely to come up again. Foreign Minister Abdullah Gul visited Washington in February 2007 with a view to heading off a resolution on Armenia but came away empty-handed; House Speaker Nancy Pelosi refused even to meet with Gul.[36]

Some writers who have had the temerity to discuss the events in Armenia have been arrested, underscoring the point that Turkish sensitivities on the allegations have remained alive almost a century later. French president Jacques Chirac used the issue in an effort to achieve his goal of excluding Turkey from the European Union by demanding that Ankara issue a statement of guilt for the alleged genocide. Whatever the truth about the fate of the Armenians, Chirac's demand has deliberately placed Ankara between a rock and hard place because it seems unlikely that any Turkish government could accept an admission of guilt. As a clear part of a campaign to keep Turkey out of the European Union, the French National Assembly passed legislation making it illegal to deny Turkey's role in the alleged genocide against Armenians. It may also have its desired effect in reducing public support in Turkey for membership in the EU.

The assassination in 2007 of Hrant Dink, a Turkish editor and columnist of Armenian descent, underscores the passions still aroused by the genocide issue. Although Dink was a moderate who favored Turkey's application for entry into the European Union, his death may amplify the voice of those who oppose Turkey's application.[37]

This brief overview of American relations with Turkey since the September 11 attacks must necessarily focus on the most salient events rather than the full range of issues involving the two countries, but the evidence clearly seems to point to policies rather than preexisting biases as the major source of critical public views of the United States. The invasion of Afghanistan to remove the

---

36. Guy Dinmore and Vincent Boland, "US-Turkey Relations Set to Worsen over Iraq and Armenia 'Genocide,'" *Financial Times*, February 9, 2007.

37. Sebnem Arsu, "Editor Who Spoke for Turkey's Ethnic Armenians Is Slain," *New York Times*, January 20, 2007.

Taliban regime and hunt down al Qaeda leaders gained the full support of the Turkish government. The evidence presented in table 2.1 revealed that the moderately favorable views of the United States prior to the September 11 attacks rapidly eroded as the Iraq issue took center stage in world politics. Surveys since 2002 indicate that Edward Djerejian might well have been speaking of Turkey when he asserted that the "bottom has indeed fallen out of support for the United States."[38]

The Iraq war was clearly the major irritant in relations between the two NATO allies. As shown in table 2.8, few Turks believe that Washington pays much attention to the vital interests of others. After repeated betrayals of Kurdish nationalists dating back to the post–World War I peace settlement, perhaps a reasonable case could be made for creation of an independent Kurdistan. The United States hoped to use Kurds as allies to weaken the Shiite-dominated Saddam Hussein regime. From Ankara's perspective, however, the Kurdish question topped the agenda in virtually all of its calculations. At minimum, there was a threat of a renewed civil war in eastern Turkey; the worst-case scenario threatened the Turkish territorial integrity because an independent Kurdistan would almost surely include at least some parts of Turkey. In September 2007 Prime Minister Erdogan refused to rule out military action against Kurdish separatists who had taken refuge in northern Iraq.[39]

Two surveys conducted by the International Strategic Research Organization (ISRO) in March and August 2005 provide some additional insight into Turkish public opinion. The earlier survey posed several questions about the United States and its policies.[40] The results revealed that 74 percent described the United States and Turkey as "allies," only 16 percent considered themselves to be "anti-American," only 4 percent "hate the American people," and only 14 percent believe that "the Turkish people are anti-American." However, fewer than 1 percent approve of the Bush administration's global policies, 75 percent stated that the PKK in northern Iraq was the major obstacle to Turkish-American relations, and an additional 9 percent located the problem in the "U.S. Kurdish policy." Only 4 percent blamed Turkish policies. These results clearly indicate that opposition to the United States arises from differences in policy rather than deep-seated anti-Americanism. According to a veteran analyst of

---

38. Edward P. Djerejian, presenting *Changing Minds, Winning Peace*, a report submitted to the Committee on Appropriations, House of Representatives, October 1, 2003.

39. Sebnem Arsu, "Turkey Keeps Options Open along Iraqi Border," *New York Times*, September 19, 2007.

40. International Strategic Research Organization (ISRO), "Turkey-USA Relations Survey Results," Ankara, March 12, 2005.

Middle East politics, "Right now, opposition to U.S. policies is the nearest thing to a national consensus in Turkey."[41]

The August ISRO survey of 2,500 Turks on questions of terrorism supplemented those of the earlier study.[42] Respondents were highly critical of Osama bin Laden, as 91 percent described him as a "terrorist." They were equally critical of al Qaeda, as 0 percent stated that it was "defending the rights of Muslims" and 75 percent denied that al Qaeda represented Muslims. Moreover, the terrorist attacks on New York and Washington, London, Madrid, and Egypt were opposed by 86 percent, 90 percent, 90 percent, and 90 percent, respectively; 66 percent identified U.S. Middle East policies as "the reason for global terrorism," and an additional 5 percent blamed the occupation of Iraq; and only 7 percent asserted that to combat global terrorism, the West and the United States "must maintain existing policies."

Two years after the decision on the Fourth Infantry Division, a Turkish observer wrote, "Turkey should stay away from becoming entangled with U.S. war plans in the region. Turkey, as an ally and good friend of Washington, offers clear advantages to the U.S. . . . Mr. Bush should understand, and urge others around him to act accordingly. Turkey as a safeguard of peace is more precious than Turkey as a war party."[43] A columnist for the daily *Yeni Safak* added, "What the Americans didn't fully understand then [March 2003], and perhaps still don't today, is that Turkey has matured as a democracy. Politicians need to take account of the public if they want to be reelected, and Erdogan is no exception."[44]

As revealed in chapters 2 and 3, Turkish opinions about the United States, its people, and its institutions have become increasingly negative in recent years. A World Public Opinion survey in 2007 found that 64 percent of Turkish respondents rated the United States as the greatest threat to their country. When asked to explain these results, Dr. Emre Erdogan of the Infakto Research Workshop in Istanbul stated, "the Turkish public perceives the U.S. as the worst enemy of Turkey as a result of intensifying terrorist activities of the PKK in the Southeastern region of the country. The collaboration of the U.S. with the PKK is much more than an urban legend and Turkish media continuously present evidence of the collaboration." He went on to say, "Turkish antipathy toward

41. Graham E. Fuller, "Don't Write Off the Turks," *Los Angeles Times*, April 11, 2005.
42. International Strategic Research Organization (ISRO), "ISRO Turkey Terrorism Perception Survey," Ankara, August 3, 2005.
43. Fehmi Koru, "U.S.-Turkish Relations: The Mirror Has Cracked," *New Anatolian*, March 29, 2005.
44. Amberin Zaman, "Turkey Drifts Further from U.S.," *Los Angeles Times*, December 14, 2004.

the U.S. government has been transferred to an emerging antipathy toward Americans and the U.S. life style."[45]

Democratic, secular, and strategically located Turkey is a vital ally. Indeed, by every measure but one—oil—Turkey is more vital to American national interests than Iraq. Yet it is probably not being excessively alarmist to conclude that in its external orientation Turkey is at a "tipping point." Many Turks feel betrayed by the United States because of its Iraq policy and mistreatment of detainees, as well as by French, German, and other European leaders who have repeatedly asserted that Turkey is not welcome in the European Union.[46]

INDONESIA

Indonesia is an archipelagic country consisting of some 17,500 islands, of which about 6,000 are permanently inhabited. It spans about 3,500 miles and controls three of the world's most important waterways. Indonesia's population of more than 230 million ranks behind only China, India, and the United States in size, and it has by far the world's highest number of Muslims. Indeed, its Muslim population—87 percent of all Indonesians—is greater than that of all the Arab countries combined.

Japan occupied Indonesia during World War II. Three days after the Japanese surrender on August 14, 1945, Indonesian nationalists led by Sukarno and Mohammad Hatta, declared the country's independence from the Netherlands. The Yalta Conference had decreed the return of Indonesia to Dutch rule. Although the United States tended to favor the principle of independence, the Cold War placed Washington in something of a dilemma, caught between a generally skeptical view of colonialism and the interests of a friendly Western European country. An especially heavy-handed Dutch police action in Indonesia led the United States to become an outspoken critic, and at one point it even threatened to suspend Marshall Plan aid to the Netherlands. After four years of fighting and negotiations, Indonesia gained independence with Sukarno as president, and it joined the United Nations in 1950.

Although not bound by any formal treaty ties, relations between Indonesia and the United States have ranged from cool to cordial. During the 1950s, Sukarno was among the leaders of the so-called Nonaligned Movement, a

---

45. "Q & A: Emre Erdogan," available at www.worldpublicopinion.org/incl/printable_version.php?pnt=391 (accessed September 5, 2007).
46. Sabrina Tavernise, "Allure of Islam Signals a Shift within Turkey," *New York Times*, November 28, 2006.

group of countries that steered clear of commitments to either of the two Cold War blocs. The groundwork for the NAM was established at a 1955 meeting in Bandung, Indonesia. At least some officials in Washington expressed exasperation with the NAM; for example, Secretary of State John Foster Dulles famously declared, "non-alignment is immoral" because, he asserted, the West-East conflict was one of freedom versus Godless tyranny.

During the following decade Sukarno, who became "president for life" in 1963, ruled in an increasingly dictatorial manner. In foreign affairs he leaned closer to Asian communist countries, emphasizing the theme of a "Jakarta-Phnom Penh-Beijing-Hanoi-Pyongyang axis" to combat neocolonialism and imperialism. In domestic affairs his ties to the Communist Party of Indonesia (PKI) did little to endear him to Washington.

In 1965, however, an uprising, in which it appears that PKI members within the military played a role, led to a bloodbath in which right-wing gangs killed an estimated three hundred thousand communists and their sympathizers. General Suharto led the military against the PKI uprising, and when Sukarno was forced to resign, Suharto was appointed acting president in 1967. Starting in 1968 he was elected for seven five-year terms until forced to resign in 1998. Suharto, whose foreign policies leaned toward the West and maintained close ties to the United States, Western Europe, Australia, and Japan, was generally viewed and lauded in Washington as a staunch anticommunist, which earned him generous military aid. Upon Suharto's departure his vice president, Abdurrahman Wahid, assumed the presidency, but he was impeached for incompetence shortly thereafter, at which point Sukarno's daughter, Megawati Sukarnoputri, became president. She lost the 2004 election to the current president, Susilo Bambang Yudhoyono.

Within the context of generally cordial relations during the Suharto era, human rights issues at times have strained relations between Washington and Jakarta. Communists were brutally suppressed, as were some religious, ethnic, and separatist groups in such areas as East Timor, Aceh, Papua/Irian Jaya, and others. When Indonesia invaded East Timor in 1975, Secretary of State Henry Kissinger told President Suharto that it was acceptable if done "quickly and cleanly."[47] Human rights concerns led the U.S. Congress to cut off military training assistance grants in 1991. The grants were partially restored in 1995, but they were cut off again in 1999 following a bloody rampage killing hundreds in East Timor, where a referendum revealed strong support for independence

---

47. Jane Perlez, "A Book about East Timor Jabs Indonesia's Conscience," *New York Times*, August 17, 2006.

from Indonesia.[48] The programs were again reinstated in 2005, after the massive tsunami that devastated Indonesia at the end of 2004 and certification by the State Department that Indonesia was in compliance with human rights requirements.

The September 11 terrorist attacks on the United States immediately led to statements of support from the Indonesian governments and, notably, from President Megawati, who had embarked on an already-scheduled visit to Washington. Megawati vocally condemned the brutal attacks on the United States and expressed Indonesian sympathy for the loss suffered by America.[49] Official documents published by the Department of Foreign Affairs for the Republic of Indonesia reaffirmed the statements made by Megawati. The Joint Statement between the United States of America and the Republic of Indonesia, published September 19, 2001, following the meetings between Presidents Bush and Megawati, reaffirmed her statement condemning "the barbaric and indiscriminate acts carried out against innocent civilians" and underscoring the notion that "terrorism also increasingly threatens Indonesia's democracy and national security."[50] An additional document, detailing the statement made regarding religious tolerance and terrorism by both Presidents Bush and Megawati, restated Indonesian sympathy and condolences, as President Megawati expressed her "deepest sympathies" on behalf of the "210 million people of Indonesia."[51] Not only did the Indonesian government support the United States directly following the attacks but expressions of sympathy and solidarity with America also emanated from the media and public.

Following the 9/11 attacks, there were also significant fears and discussion in Indonesia about the effects these atrocities would have on a putative "clash of civilizations" between the Muslim and Western worlds. Voices in Indonesia urged restraint, and there was opposition to any conclusion that this sort of clash was indeed inevitable; an editorial that pointed out "there are probably more people building bridges of dialogue between civilizations than there are those fighting between civilizations."[52]

---

48. The State Department 2002 human rights report was a scathing indictment of Indonesia's "poor" record, http://www.state.gov/g/drl/rls/hrrpt/2002/18245.htm.
49. Anthony L. Smith, "Reluctant Partner: Indonesia's Response to U.S. Security Policies," Asia-Pacific Center for Security Studies, March 2003, http://www.apcss.org (accessed June 27, 2005).
50. Department of Foreign Affairs for the Republic of Indonesia, "Joint Statement between the United States of America and the Republic of Indonesia on Terrorism and Religious Tolerance," September 19, 2001, http://www.deplu.go.id/2005/ (accessed June 29, 2005).
51. Ibid.
52. Ulil Abshar-Abdalla, "One World Still," Inside Indonesia, July–September 2001, http://www.insideindonesia.org/edit69/ulil.html (accessed June 28, 2005).

Perhaps the first indication that the Indonesian government would not support the war in Afghanistan also emerged from the statement of solidarity by the two presidents, when Megawati emphasized "the importance of taking into account the views of the Muslim world as the United States leads an appropriate response to the events of September 11th." As leader of the world's most populous Muslim nation, Megawati cited the "importance of differentiating between the religion of Islam and the acts of violent extremists."[53]

The American invasion of Afghanistan received scant support in Indonesia. Political elites expressed numerous concerns, including the fear that the global war on terrorism, spearheaded by the incursion in Afghanistan, was simply a pretext for the United States to "flex its muscles" and assert its supremacy in the Muslim world.[54] Some of them further stated that bin Laden should be granted a fair hearing at an international court and that negotiations with al Qaeda were a more appropriate response than armed intervention. The invasion of Afghanistan was faulted for failing to address the root causes of the attacks. Finally, the most vocal expression of disapproval from the Indonesian government came from Vice President Hamzah Haz, who blamed the September 11 attacks on America's "sins."[55] Despite the vocal post-9/11 expressions of support from the Indonesian government, the war in Afghanistan was neither supported nor viewed as legitimate.

In addition to disapproval by the Indonesian government, the public also articulated its discontent with American policies, initially through large demonstrations in Jakarta, many of which were aimed at the U.S. embassy, in anticipation of a U.S. attack in Afghanistan. One publication discussed the attitude in Indonesia as a manifestation of the "twin towers effect"—the destabilizing and violent reaction that the attacks would have throughout the entire world, including in Indonesia: "If America continues to retaliate against Afghanistan there will no doubt be a negative reaction in Indonesia. . . . [T]he threats that are sure to follow further retaliatory strikes will be directed not only at America, but also the British, the IMF, World Bank, etc."[56]

For most Indonesians, the issue of war in Afghanistan was clear-cut. The same editorial that called for restraint in assuming a clash of civilizations between the Western and Muslim worlds also stated that "of course we should op-

53. Department of Foreign Affairs for the Republic of Indonesia, "Joint Statement between the United States of America and the Republic of Indonesia on Terrorism and Religious Tolerance."
54. Smith, "Reluctant Partner."
55. Ibid.
56. Revrisond Baswir, "The Twin Towers Effect," *Inside Indonesia*, January–March 2002, http://www.inside indonesia.org/edit69/Revrisond.html (accessed June 24, 2005).

pose the American attacks [in Afghanistan]" as "the Afghan people have suffered long enough from war ever since the Soviet invasion in 1979."[57] Further,
some Indonesians even regarded Osama bin Laden as a hero. A student at a
prominent Indonesian university, Gadjah Mada, conducted informal surveys in
the days following the 9/11 attacks to gauge the attitude of university students
toward the al Qaeda leader. Along with pro-Osama propaganda such as stick-
ers, T-shirts, and a book that flooded the market following 9/11, *Osama bin
Laden melawan Amerika* (Osama bin Laden versus America), these informal interviews also provide a glimpse of the popular mind-set of many Indonesians
regarding the war in Afghanistan.[58] They revealed that disapproval of American
policies and support for rogues such as Osama bin Laden could be found not
only among the impoverished but also among university students.

Expressions of opposition to the invasion of Afghanistan were justified
throughout the Indonesia media for numerous reasons and were regarded as
neither blind support for Osama nor unthinking hatred for the United States.
The notion that the United States was using the terrorist attacks to stigmatize
Islam was widespread. According to many Indonesians, "it was as if Islam was
replacing communism as American enemy number one, in spite of repeated
denials by the U.S. government."[59] Moreover for some Indonesians, the "U.S.
military offensive against Afghanistan was not so much an effort to eliminate
Osama bin Laden and al Qaeda, but more a move to safeguard U.S. [oil] resources."[60] Critics of American air strikes against the Taliban, resulting in col-
lateral casualties among innocent civilians, pointed out that the United States
had supported the Taliban against Soviet invaders during the Cold War.

Several important organizations in Indonesia also expressed discontent
with American foreign policy. The American Indonesian Chamber of Com-
merce noted how Indonesia's minister of foreign affairs, Hassan Wirajuda—an
American-educated lawyer with degrees from the Fletcher School of Law and
Diplomacy, Harvard, and the University of Virginia Law School—warned the
United States that if the "U.S. military campaign continued into the Muslim
Ramadan fasting month . . . the impact could be destabilizing on predomi-

57. Abshar-Abdalla, "One World Still."
58. Quoted by Katie Brayne, "Osama bin Cool," *Inside Indonesia,* January–March 2002, http://www.inside
indonesia.org/edit69/osamabincool.org (accessed June 25, 2005).
59. Clyde Prestowitz, "Why Moderate Muslims Are Annoyed with America," *Jakarta Post,* September 10, 2003,
http://www.econstrat.org/RogueNation/cprestowitz_jakartapost_091.html (accessed June 25, 2005).
60. Ibid.

nantly Muslim countries, including Indonesia."[61] The United States–Indonesian Society also outlined the reactions in Indonesia to the "global war on terrorism" as detailed by the International Crisis Group in Jakarta, which voiced the view that U.S. directives must be suspect.[62] Statements of these prominent Indonesian governmental organizations reinforced the widespread disapproval of the war in Afghanistan.

Critical views of the Afghanistan invasion were but a preface to the much more vocal opposition to American policy leading up to, during, and after the American invasion of Iraq. The first statement among many by Indonesian leaders was a declaration by the government welcoming the Iraqi decision to permit the return of the United Nations Security Council Inspection Team, in accordance with Security Council Resolution 1441. The government hoped that "this positive response from Iraq will pave the way to a peaceful solution to the problem in Iraq."[63] A statement made by Foreign Minister Wirajuda to the fifty-seventh session of the UN General Assembly reaffirmed the Indonesian disapproval of any unilateral action against Iraq. Responding to the possibility of a unilateral U.S. invasion, Wirajuda stressed that "nowhere is the necessity for multilateralism more glaring than in our response to the scourge of our time: international terrorism. And nowhere is the role of the United Nations more vital. . . . [A]ny unilateral use of force risks not only undermining the authority of the United Nations, but would also carry the grave potential of destabilizing the immediate region, and indeed beyond, with its attendant humanitarian implications."[64] Indonesia's coordinating minister for security reiterated the desire for a peaceful solution of the Iraq crisis, warning in December 2002 that unilateral American action could instigate a severe reaction throughout the world.[65]

The Indonesian government continued to emphasize the importance of a peaceful and multilateral approach during the months prior to the invasion of

61. "Political Affairs," *American Indonesia Chamber of Commerce* 16, no. 2 (2001), http://www.aiccusa.org/October%202001%20olook/page7.html (accessed June 26, 2005).

62. Sidney Jones, "Indonesia's Reaction to the War on Terrorism," United States–Indonesian Society, October 28, 2003, http://usindo.org/Briefs/2003/Sidney%20Jopnes%2011–28–03.html (accessed June 26, 2005).

63. Department of Foreign Affairs for the Republic of Indonesia, "Indonesia Welcomes Iraq's Decision with Regard to the UN Inspection Team," September 18, 2002, http://www.deplu.go.id/2005.html (accessed July 2, 2005).

64. N. Hassan Wirajuda, "Statement by H.E. Dr. N. Hassan Wirajuda, Minister for Foreign Affairs, Republic of Indonesia, at the 57th Session of the UN General Assembly," Department of Foreign Affairs for the Republic of Indonesia, September 18, 2002, http://www.deplu.go.id/2005/html (accessed July 3, 2005).

65. Susilo Bambang Yudhoyono, quoted in Smith, "Reluctant Partner."

Iraq. A formal statement in February 2003 stressed that the "Government of the Republic of Indonesia remains steadfast in its principled view that the question of Iraq's alleged build-up of weapons of mass destruction must be dealt with through the United Nations Security Council. . . . In this regard, the Government of the Republic of Indonesia fully shares and supports the idea of strengthening the UN Inspection Team in Iraq."[66] In anticipation of the possible outbreak of war in Iraq, the Department of Foreign Affairs issued a formal press release, reaffirming its "principled position of opposing unilateral military action towards Iraq," announcing the temporary closing of the Indonesian embassy in Iraq, and additionally supporting public opposition to the war: the "Indonesia Government understands and shares the sentiment and sympathy of the Indonesian society who oppose the war."[67]

The American invasion of Iraq precipitated additional declarations of strong disapproval from Jakarta. In a formal statement issued March 20, 2003, the government stressed how it "strongly deplores the unilateral action taken by the United States. . . . Indonesia deeply regrets that the multilateral process through the UN Security Council has been sidelined. . . . War will not only fail to resolve the problem, but it will cause humanitarian tragedy."[68] One of the most vocal critics of the war, Foreign Minister Wirajuda, voiced some of the harshest comments regarding the war in Iraq following the fall of Baghdad, describing the situation as a quagmire that the United States could have avoided had it not chosen to act unilaterally. Some months later he stated, "An arbitrary preemptive war has been waged against a sovereign state—arbitrary because it is without sufficient justification in international law." He went on to ask, "Does that mean that any state may now individually and arbitrarily decide to use force preemptively against any other state perceived as a threat?"[69]

In contrast to countries where the Iraq issue led to heightened tensions between the government and the public, or where official declarations of disapproval were carefully worded so as not to upset Washington, in Indonesia statements by political elites were pointedly and vehemently critical of U.S. actions in Iraq.

---

66. Department of Foreign Affairs for the Republic of Indonesia, "Statement on the New Initiative for the Question of Iraq," February 14, 2003, http://www.deplu.go.id/2005/html (accessed July 1, 2005).
67. Department of Foreign Affairs for the Republic of Indonesia, "Press Release: Indonesia Opposes Military Action towards Iraq," March 18, 2003, http://www.deplu.go.id/2005/html (accessed July 2, 2005).
68. Department of Foreign Affairs for the Republic of Indonesia, "Indonesia Strongly Deplores Unilateral Action against Iraq," March 20, 2003, http://deplu.go.id/2005/html (accessed July 3, 2005).
69. Raymond Bonner, "Indonesian Official Rebukes U.S. over Iraq War," New York Times, December 8, 2003.

Discussions of the war in Iraq in the Indonesian media, including consideration of developments such as the ongoing insurgency and the January 2005 elections, exemplify the continuing disapproval. Widespread coverage of developments in the war featured the ongoing violence, including suicide bombings and attacks on U.S. soldiers.[70] The capture of an Indonesian TV reporter was extensively covered in the press, sparking additional discontent among the public and media.[71] Arguments against the war were largely based on principles and humanitarian concerns and rarely contained references to Muslim solidarity or hatred of the United States.

Many articles in the Indonesian media echoed government assertions that the unilateral approach to Iraq was a critical mistake; for example, "Strong adherence to international law and multilateral institutions should be the basic approach to solving international problems, including that of postwar Iraq. Multilateralism must be an essential part of the global security paradigm."[72] While recognizing the critical need for a response to international crises, a key argument was that "security cooperation" is integral to maintaining security and prosperity on an international level by combining the intelligence and efforts of multilateral coalitions.[73]

Top officials in Washington predicted that most Iraqis would be grateful for removal of the oppressive yoke of Saddam's rule, but many editorials in Indonesia doubted, even before the Iraqi insurgency, that American intentions were altruistic. The American invasion was routinely attributed to interests in oil, and while many Indonesians appear to have recognized that this is an overly simplistic response, nonetheless the attitude was that "Iraqis are not wrong to believe that they would have not been 'liberated' by American troops if they grew carrots for a living instead of pumping oil." A further reason for opposing the war was that its most likely long-term outcome "is still a civil war and the partition of the country."[74] While the capture of Saddam was a welcome development, there were

70. "Suicide Bombers Kill 10 in Iraq," *Antara News*, June 14, 2005, http://www.antara.co.id/en/seenws/index.php ?id=4391 (accessed July 6, 2005).

71. "Indonesian TV Reporter Goes Missing in Iraq," *Antara News*, February 18, 2005, http://www.antara.co .id/en/seenws/index.php?=927.html (accessed July 3, 2005).

72. Bantarto Bandora, "Genuine Multilateralism Vital to World Security," *Jakarta Post*, December 18, 2003, http://www.indonesia-house.org/PoliticHR/PHR1203.html (July 3, 2005).

73. Susilo Bambang Yudhoyono, "Part 1 of 2: The Challenge of Security for the World Economy," *Indonesia Focus*, November 23, 2004, http://www.indonesia-house.org/PoliticHR/PHR1203/1215Ind.html (accessed July 3, 2005).

74. Gwynne Dyer, "Saddam's Capture: Will It Make Any Difference?" *Indonesia House*, December 18, 2003, http://www.indonesia-house.org/PoliticHR/PHR1203/121803.html (accessed June 27, 2005).

doubts that it would end Iraqi resistance, lead to a relatively smooth transformation of Iraq into a democratic state, or reduce international terrorism."[75]

The inability of Americans to find any evidence that Iraq had weapons of mass destruction or ties to al Qaeda reinforced the view, widespread in Indonesia, that the invasion of Iraq lacked legitimacy. The Indonesian media reported that because it was very unlikely that Iraq could have destroyed, hidden, or moved WMDs, the resumption of inspections by the United Nations was a more desirable, peaceful, and viable means of containing any dangers in Iraq than war. The realization that the American justifications for invading Iraq were false fueled the opinion that the conquest of Iraq using "democracy as its war cry is a mockery which people all over the world increasingly understand."[76]

The January 2005 elections were not widely regarded as indicative of progress or harbingers of hope for dealing with violence and poverty in Iraq. Discussions of the elections often focused on the tensions that were likely to instigate violence between the competing ethnic groups in Iraq. While the establishment of a true democracy in Iraq would be welcomed by Indonesians, the attitude regarding the elections remained that "even if the general election should proceed smoothly, difficulties can be expected to remain in the way of effective governance. . . . As some Indonesian observers predicted, so long as the United States remains in charge of overseeing the procedures, the establishment of a true and stable democracy in Iraq will not be possible, or difficult to achieve to say the least."[77]

Indonesia was mentioned as a possible candidate for contributing to the foreign presence in Iraq amidst the escalation of violence during the summer of 2005. Although Indonesia has the world's largest Muslim population and has participated in peacekeeping missions since the 1960s, Jakarta routinely rejected any calls for supporting either a peace or reconstruction process in Iraq, concluding that the "U.S.-made crisis" does not justify immediate Indonesian intervention.[78] Continued violence in Iraq has only solidified the opinion that the war was a deplorable American undertaking in which Indonesia should avoid all involvement. Moreover, there were substantial doubts that the Iraq

---

75. Amin Saikil, "Bush May Wish Saddam Had Been Killed," *Indonesia House,* December 16, 2003, http://www.indonesia-house.org/PoliticHR1203/12160.html (accessed June 27, 2005).
76. Tabassum Zakaria, "Think Tank Report: Iraq WMD Not Imminent Threat," *Indonesia House,* January 8, 2005, http://www.indonesia-house.org/PoliticHR/2004/01/010804.html.
77. "Iraq: Is Democracy Viable?" *Jakarta Post,* December 19, 2004, http://www.thejakartapost.com (accessed July 3, 2005).
78. "Staying out of Iraq," *Jakarta Post,* January 30, 2005, http://www.thejakartapost.com (accessed June 26, 2005).

war was an effective response to international terrorism. According to a Congressional Research Service study, "Some Indonesian analysts view the United States as focused on the 'search and destroy' aspect of the war against terror, and feel that the United States has not focused sufficient attention to winning the 'hearts and minds' aspects of the struggle."[79]

The Pew Global Attitudes Project also brought forth evidence of widespread public opposition to the Iraq war.[80] As revealed in table 2.14, in May 2003, 78 percent of Indonesians stated that the government was correct in not supporting the U.S.-led invasion in Iraq. Indonesians were only slightly more equivocal on this matter by June 2005, as 70 percent stated that the government did the right thing in not supporting the U.S. endeavor and another 16 percent did not know whether the policy was right or wrong. Additionally, only 13 percent of those polled in June 2005 believed that the world is a safer place without Saddam, whereas 50 percent actually stated that the world had become more dangerous. Only 13 percent of Indonesians believed that the January 2005 elections would lead to a more stable and democratic Iraq. Seventy-nine percent preferred a world order with another powerful country besides the United States.[81]

Candidates in the October 2004 presidential election in Indonesia—Hamzah Haz, Amien Rais, Megawati Sukarnoputri (the incumbent), General Wiranto, and Susilo Bambang Yudhoyono—did not differ sharply on views of the United States or American foreign policy. They all ran on broad, secular nationalist platforms, and while none could afford to ignore the Islamic vote, pandering to this population did not include either denunciations of the United States or promises to oppose any U.S. efforts.[82] The ultimate winner, Susilo Bambang Yudhoyono, in fact concurred with his predecessor, Megawati Sukarnoputri, echoing her statements regarding maintaining a friendship with the United States while opposing actions deemed to be unjustified, notably the invasions of Afghanistan and Iraq.

When Secretary of Defense Rumsfeld visited Jakarta in June 2006, Indonesian Minister Juwono Sudarsono lectured him about the proper way to deal with terrorism. After offering advice in a private meeting, Sudarsono repeated

79. Quoted in Michael R. Gordon, "Indonesian Scolds U.S. on Terrorism Fight," *New York Times,* June 7, 2006.

80. Pew Research Center, *Views of a Changing World,* June 2003, http://www.pewglobal.org (accessed June 25, 2005).

81. Pew Research Center, *U.S. Image Up Slightly, but Still Negative,* 2005, http://www.pewglobal.org (accessed June 28, 2005).

82. "Indonesian Presidential Poll Nears," *BBC News,* July 2, 2004, http://www.newsvote.bbc.co.uk/mpapps/page tools.bbc.co.uk/2/hi.html (accessed July 8, 2005).

it at a joint session with the press: "As I was telling your secretary just recently, just two minutes ago, that your powerful economy and your powerful military does lend to misperception and a sense of threat to many groups right across the world, not just in Indonesia." He added, "It is important to us because, as the world's largest Muslim country, we are very aware of the perception, or misperception that the United States is overbearing and overpresent and overwhelming in every sector of life in many nations and cultures." The analysis of the meeting suggested that the Jakarta government "is concerned about public opinion regarding efforts to collaborate with the Bush administration."[83]

Indonesia has not always followed Washington's lead on how best to cope with terrorism, but its approach has gained plaudits from one of its regional neighbors whose citizens were victims of the Bali bombings. According to the Australian foreign minister, "If you want an example of a country that's done a good job in dealing with the issue of terrorism and radicalism, then exhibit A is Indonesia. They have not always done as westerners have suggested they do but they have nevertheless done an extraordinary job in getting results."[84]

The tsunami that hit Indonesia with devastating impact on December 26, 2004, is estimated to have claimed between 200,000 and 310,000 victims. Offers of international aid came from many quarters including the United States. In addition to the $857 million from the U.S. government for tsunami relief and reconstruction, private American citizens and companies raised more than $1.4 billion for the devastated areas.

The Indonesian government applauded the response of the world community. In May 2005 President Yudhoyono addressed a conference of USINDO (a U.S. nonprofit organization whose purpose is to increase awareness and understanding of Indonesia in the United States) by stating that "the best badge of honor you [Americans] can proudly wear is our [Indonesia's] great admiration and respect for your tremendous contribution, to the peoples of Indonesia." Yudhoyono went on to stress that "[t]here has been an incredibly deep emotional connection between America and Indonesia since the tsunami. . . . You should all be proud of what America has done to help the tsunami victims."[85] Foreign Minister Wirajuda, although a vocal critic of the Bush administration's foreign policies, also pointedly expressed Indonesian thanks for the U.S. aid to

83. Gordon, "Indonesian Scolds U.S. on Terrorism Fight."
84. John Aglionby, "Indonesia 'Has Best Strategy on Terrorism,'" *Financial Times*, March 6, 2007.
85. Susilo Bambang Yudhoyono, "Address by H.E. Dr. Susilo Bambang Yudhoyono, President of the Republic of Indonesia, at a Dinner Tendered by USINDO, Washington, DC," May 25, 2005.

the reconstruction and relief following the tsunami. Addressing the UN Commission on Human Rights, Wirajuda stated that "Indonesia is very grateful" for the global emergency response led by the United States to the earthquake and tsunami disaster.[86] The Indonesian political elite largely set the tone for the response of the Indonesian media and the public to the United States in the aftermath of the tsunami relief effort.

The American response to the tsunami was widely discussed in the Indonesian media. The *Jakarta Post* praised the increase in aid from $35 million to $350 million, the presence of the aircraft carrier USS *Abraham Lincoln* near Banda Aceh as a center for distribution of relief efforts, and cash donations by U.S.-based oil conglomerate ExxonMobil.[87] Personal interviews of grateful recipients of U.S. aid printed in the Indonesian media exemplified the overwhelming gratitude toward the American relief effort.

The tsunami was often discussed as heralding a new era in the Indonesian-American relationship, as the outpouring of sympathy and aid from America perhaps signaled an opportunity for these two countries to become closer partners in world affairs. The tsunami "created tremendous momentum. Let us ride on the crest of the waves, and look at this terrible event as a turning point in cultivating a new constructive attitude and behavior, paving the way for reconciliation."[88] The goodwill expressed toward the United States did not dissipate in the months following the disaster, as editorials and articles describing the efforts of America in the relief effort continued to be published in the Indonesian media. In contrast to the frequently critical opinions about American actions in Iraq, many in the Indonesian media expressed the view that the American response revealed "no ulterior motives than humanitarian solidarity and empathy. . . . [T]here has never been such an outpouring of empathy and solidarity before towards Indonesia and our sufferings."[89]

There were, however, a few dissenters who felt that the assistance to tsunami victims was not motivated merely by generosity or righteousness but rather that the increase and visibility of U.S. aid could "go a long way towards winning

86. Susilo Bambang Yudhoyono, "Statement by H.E. Dr. N. Hassan Wirajuda, Minister for Foreign Affairs, Republic of Indonesia, at the 61st Session of the UN Commission on Human Rights," March 15, 2005, Department of Foreign Affairs for the Republic of Indonesia, http://www.deplu.go.id/2005/html (accessed July 7, 2005).

87. "World Sends Cash, Food, Medical Teams to Sumatra," *Jakarta Post*, January 3, 2005, http://www.indonesia-house.org/Humanitarian/2005/01/010205.html (accessed July 2, 2005); and "ExxonMobile Ups Tsunami Donation," *Jakarta Post*, January 21, 2005, http://www.thejakartapost.com/misc.html (accessed July 8, 2005).

88. M. T. Zen, "The Soul of Aceh Reconstruction," *Jakarta Post*, March 19, 2005, http://indonesia.house-tsunami.info/index/php?option=com_content.html (accessed July 3, 2005).

89. Jusuf Wanandi, "RI and the International Community in the Tsunami's Aftermath," *Jakarta Post*, January 15, 2005, http://www.thejakartapost.com/asp.html (accessed July 8, 2005).

the 'hearts and minds' of the Muslim 'street' while ameliorating its overly 'muscular' and unilateral foreign image." In fact, some of the Indonesian media cited Secretary of State Colin Powell's own words, when he stated the American relief effort would give "the Muslim world and the rest of the world . . . an opportunity to see American generosity, American values in action." From that perspective, the tsunami disaster was framed as an opportunistic venture, giving the U.S. military the "opportunity to demonstrate to friends and potential foes alike the awesome U.S. capacity to mobilize and deploy large amounts of troops and equipment at short notice to remote parts of the globe."[90]

American tsunami aid had a significant impact on Indonesian opinions of the United States. Of those polled by the 2005 Pew Global Attitudes Project, 79 percent stated that the relief effort contributed to a more favorable view of the United States.[91] Another survey, commissioned by a U.S. nonprofit group, Terror Free Tomorrow, and conducted by an Indonesian polling agency, LSI, came up with similar results. According to LSI, 65 percent of Indonesians stated that they now felt more favorable toward the United States because of the American response to the tsunami, with 71 percent of those under 30 concurring with that statement. Even among those who voiced sympathy for Osama bin Laden, 71 percent still agreed that the U.S. tsunami relief resulted in a more favorable attitude toward America.[92] A later Pew poll revealed a significant drop in confidence in Osama bin Laden and in support for suicide bombings against civilians.[93]

The tsunami crisis is a potent example of the significant impact that American policies can have on the opinion of publics abroad. The Indonesian political elite, the media, and the population overwhelmingly expressed gratitude while continuing to oppose American policies in Afghanistan and Iraq.

The sources and impact of Indonesian public attitudes toward the United States may at first glance appear to be simple and clear-cut. Indonesia is an overwhelmingly Muslim country, as are the targets of the American invasions of Afghanistan and Iraq. Yet the Indonesian response did not appear to hinge solely on religion and ideology. Within the broader context of usually cordial relations and generally favorable views of the United States during the pre-Sep-

90. Mark J. Valencia, "The International Politics of Tsunami Aid," *Jakarta Post,* February 7, 2005, http://www.thejakartapost.com/asp.html (accessed July 8, 2005).
91. Pew Research Center, *U.S. Image Up Slightly, but Still Negative.*
92. Patrick Goodenough, "Tsunami Aid Changed Some Muslims' Attitudes Towards U.S., CNSNews.com International Editor," March 9, 2005, http://www.cnsnews.com/ForeignBureaus/archive/200503/FOR2005.html (accessed June 28, 2005).
93. Pew Research Center, Pew Global Attitudes Project, *Conflicting Views in a Divided World,* May 23, 2006.

tember 11 years, the "war on terrorism," especially as it was used to justify the invasion of Afghanistan and Iraq, was often viewed not only as contrary to Indonesian preferences for multilateral action but also as an exercise to hypocrisy and double standards. According to a 2007 World Public Opinion survey, 73 percent of Indonesians believed that a U.S. goal is "to weaken and divide the Islamic world." Washington was seen as far less concerned with terrorism when the targets were not American.

Owing to the very close concordance of opinions on these issues among leaders, the media, and the general public, it would be hard to argue that the public views of the United States were the driving force behind Indonesian policy. As revealed by the 2004 presidential election, there was a broad consensus for maintaining good relations with Washington, while refusing to pander to Washington or to go along with such undertakings as the wars in Afghanistan and Iraq.

However critical Indonesian opinions may have been during the 2002–4 period, the tsunami aid effort in 2005 also indicates the importance of American policy in influencing Indonesian opinion. After a hesitant start, Washington and the American public acted with wisdom and generosity, and of equal importance, these actions were widely if not universally interpreted as expressions of genuine humanitarian concern. The appearance in Indonesia of three well-known and admired American leaders—former presidents George H. W. Bush and Bill Clinton, as well as Secretary of State Colin Powell—added to the visibility of the aid effort and no doubt also contributed to reversing the precipitous decline in favorable views of the United States.

MEXICO

Many observers describe relations between Mexico and the United States as a "love-hate" relationship. Like many clichés, this term has at least a grain of truth. The two countries share a long and highly porous frontier; a history in which Mexico lost almost half of its territory to its northern neighbor; and increasingly intimate, if unequal, economic ties.

During a period of less than a decade, the United States acquired vast Mexican territories that today constitute parts or all of Arizona, California, Colorado, Kansas, Nevada, New Mexico, Oklahoma, Texas, Utah, and Wyoming. The United States annexed the Republic of Texas in 1845, and the Mexican War of 1846–48, concluded by the Treaty of Guadalupe-Hidalgo, resulted in additional territorial conquests by the United States. The Gadsden Purchase in 1853, which settled a dispute about the southern boundaries of the present states of Arizona and New Mexico, brought an additional 45,534 square miles to the United States and fixed the Mexican-American frontier at its present location.

The 1910 Mexican revolution against the Porfirio Diaz, who had ruled since seizing power in 1876, and the subsequent civil war there led the Woodrow Wilson administration to send American troops into Mexico. Wilson, exasperated by the events in Mexico, including the assassination of President Francisco Madero, asserted, "I am going to teach the South American republics to elect good men."[94] Troops were sent first to occupy and take charge of the customs house in the port city of Vera Cruz in 1914 and, later, in an unsuccessful effort to capture Pancho Villa, who had raided the town of Columbus, New Mexico. Fourteen thousand regulars took part in the search for Villa, and another 140,000 regulars and National Guard troops patrolled the border between the two countries. The last American forces were withdrawn from Mexico in 1917, just before the United States entered World War I.

Mexico played an unwitting role in the American declaration of war against Germany. Just prior to declaring unrestricted submarine warfare, German Foreign Minister Alfred Zimmermann wired his ambassador in Mexico City, stating that if it proved impossible to keep the United States out of the war, "we make Mexico a proposal of alliance on the following basis: Make war together, make peace together, generous financial support and understood on our part that Mexico is to reconquer the lost territory in Texas, New Mexico, and Arizona."[95]

The "Good Neighbor Policy" of the Franklin D. Roosevelt administration was intended to reassure Latin American countries that the many interventions of the preceding decades would be replaced by a policy of hemispheric cooperation. A test of that policy came in March 1938, when the Mexican government expropriated all foreign oil holdings. The United States refused to join an international boycott of Mexican oil, and the issue was settled in 1942 with small Mexican compensation payments. Mexico declared war on Germany the same year. Although it did not take part in military operations during the war, the bracero program brought Mexican workers into the United States to replace some of the thirteen million Americans who served in the armed forces, and some others crossed the border to join the U.S. military.

---

94. *The Cabinet Diaries of Josephus Daniels,* ed. E. David Cronon (Lincoln: University of Nebraska Press, 1965), 6–7.
95. National Archives and Records Administration, Zimmermann Telegram, Record Group 59, General Records of the Department of State, 1756–1979.

Mexico was a charter member of the United Nations, and it joined the Rio Pact in 1947. For the next several decades, however, it conducted a relatively autonomous foreign policy marked on occasion with anti-American rhetoric as a way of fostering and maintaining nationalist sentiments. Some of its policies also revealed a willingness to defy Washington. For example, alone among Rio Pact members, Mexico refused to cut diplomatic ties with the Fidel Castro regime in Cuba. It was also very critical of American interventions in support of the government in El Salvador and of the contra rebels against the Sandinista regime in Nicaragua, and it generally advocated greater cooperation among less-developed countries as a means of reducing dependence on the United States.

By the 1980s, however, Mexico took a number of major steps toward opening up its previously closed economy and making connections to an increasingly globalized economy. It joined the General Agreement on Tariffs and Trade—the predecessor to the present World Trade Organization—in 1982. That process accelerated during the following decade as Mexico joined the Asia-Pacific Economic Cooperation (APEC) in 1993 and the Organization for Economic Cooperation and Development (OECD) in 1994. It also joined Canada and the United States in forming the North American Free Trade Agreement (NAFTA) in 1994. Although Mexico is today the world's fifth-largest oil producer, it did not become a member of the Organization of Petroleum Exporting Countries (OPEC) cartel.

Mexico, a middle-income country with a GDP of over $6,400 per capita, has the world's eleventh-largest population, has the twelfth-largest economy, and ranks only behind Saudi Arabia, Russia, the United States, and Iran with a daily oil production of 3.8 million barrels per day.[96] Remittances from Mexicans living abroad, mostly in the United States, are a major source of foreign exchange, totaling over $13 billion annually, a figure that exceeds even revenues from tourism and is third behind only crude oil exports and foreign investments. Census Bureau figures reveal that the American population includes almost eleven million persons born in Mexico, a figure that is greater than the total of foreign-born from the next nine countries: China, Philippines, Vietnam, India, El Salvador, Korea, Cuba, Canada, and the Dominican Republic. The

---

96. The economic figures are drawn from the Economist, *Pocket World in Figures* (London: Profile Books, 2007). As is true of most Latin American countries, the per capita GDP figures for Mexico hide vast income inequalities.

growth in the Mexican-born population represents an increase of 20.7 percent during the 2000–2005 period.[97]

In 1994–95 Mexico faced a major financial crisis as international investors withdrew vast sums from Mexico, leading to a collapse of the peso. The Clinton administration organized an international rescue effort by which Mexico received an international loan package of $52.3 billion, including $20 billion from the United States. The loan from the United States has been repaid.[98]

The 2000 presidential elections in Mexico and the United States brought to office two leaders with somewhat similar backgrounds—both had had business careers, had been state governors, and shared a probusiness outlook. The election of Vicente Fox to a six-year term was a milestone in Mexican political history because it ended seventy-one years of PRI (Partido Revolucionario Institucional) rule and the voting was free from the illegalities that marked many PRI victories.

The two presidents met at Fox's ranch in Guanajuato only a month after George Bush's inauguration. They faced a formidable agenda of issues, the most important of which were immigration and the status of the millions of undocumented Mexican workers in the United Sates. Others included control of drug trafficking, water rights, pollution, and a number of trade-related concerns. Political prudence suggested that President Fox could hardly be indifferent about relations with the United States, and especially about the immigration issue. When asked to assess the top foreign policy goals for their country, Mexicans placed "protecting the interests of Mexicans in other countries" (88 percent), "promoting the sale of Mexican goods in other countries" (85 percent), and "stopping the flow of illegal drugs into the U.S." (83 percent) at the top of the agenda.[99]

Despite the initial high hopes for NAFTA on both sides of the border, there were palpable signs of discontent in both countries. Self-financed third-party presidential candidate Ross Perot, who received 19 percent of the popular vote in 1992 and about half that amount four years later, had largely based his campaigns on strident opposition to globalization and the outsourcing of jobs to Mexico and other lower-wage countries. Mexican discontent centered on such questions as vast subsidies to American farmers that had allowed them to sell

---

97. Rick Lyman, "New Data Show Immigrants' Growth and Reach," *New York Times*, August 15, 2006. A table listing the foreign-born population for twenty countries appears in the same issue.

98. Jorge I. Dominguez, "Mexico," in *Encyclopedia of U.S. Foreign Relations*, 3:136.

99. Centro de Investigación y Docencia Económicas (CIDE) and Consejo Mexicano de Asuntos Internacionales (COMEX), *Mexico y El Mundo: Global Views 2004; Mexican Public Opinion and Foreign Policy*, September 2004.

corn, pork, and other agricultural products at prices that threatened to ruin many Mexican farmers.[100] While 64 percent of Mexicans approve of NAFTA, 70 percent also believe that the United States benefits more than they do from the agreement, and when asked whether rich countries negotiate trade agreements fairly with poor ones, two-thirds disagreed.[101]

Presidents Bush and Fox established a cordial relationship at the February 2001 meeting, and there were indications that a good start had been made on the issues, including the most contentious one—immigration. Both presidents also had political reasons for wanting improvement of cross-border relations. Latinos, who had become the largest minority group in the United States, traditionally voted for Democratic candidates; thus even moderate inroads in the Latino community might well provide Bush with important payoffs in the 2004 presidential election. Although Fox could not run for a second term in 2006, significant steps toward resolving immigration issues would greatly enhance his stature, as it has been estimated that more than half of Mexicans are related to someone living in the United States.

The discussions resumed at the presidential level when Fox visited Washington at the beginning of September 2001. Although Bush was not willing to grant amnesty to all undocumented Mexicans in this country, if for no other reason than the lack of support for such a move in Congress and especially within his own Republican Party, there were signs of continuing progress.

Only days after President Fox returned to Mexico, the terrorist attacks on New York and Washington stunned the United States and the world. Although the initial reaction of the Mexican government was somewhat lukewarm, surveys undertaken before and immediately after the September 11 attacks revealed that most Mexicans were well disposed toward the United States. As noted in table 2.1, about two-thirds of Mexicans held favorable views of their northern neighbor in surveys undertaken by the State Department in 1999–2000 and by the Pew Research Center in 2002. The results of these polls essentially mirrored those emerging from three other surveys undertaken shortly after the terrorist attacks. On a thermometer scale of 0 (cold) to 100 (warm), Mexican respondents rated the United States at 68 degrees. In a Latinobarometer survey, 63 percent gave the United States a favorable rating, and in a poll by BGC S.C. in Oc-

---

100. Although agricultural products account for only 4 percent of the Mexican GDP, 18 percent of Mexicans are employed in agriculture.
101. CIDE and COMEX, *Mexico y El Mundo*.

tober 2001, 40 percent of Mexicans stated that American policies were having a favorable effect on Mexico, whereas only 25 percent disagreed.[102] Other findings on this score appear in chapter 2. These revealed that in 2002 Mexican respondents were overwhelmingly opposed to having another superpower (table 2.7) and favored the U.S. war on terrorism by a margin of 52 percent to 37 percent but five years later that support fell to 31 percent (table 2.11); moreover, few of those taking part in the 2002 and 2007 surveys felt that Washington paid much attention to Mexico's national interests (table 2.8).

The September 11 attacks immediately pushed relations with Mexico far down on Washington's foreign policy agenda. Most importantly, the immigration question was completely reframed. What had previously been viewed as a humanitarian concern, an effort to ensure American businesses and agriculture had a regular labor supply (supporters of immigration reform), or protection of American jobs and concern for the strict enforcement of the legalities of the immigration process (opponents of immigration reform) now became an issue of homeland security arising from the fear that the porous boundary between the two countries might well serve as an inviting route for terrorist infiltration into the United States. The Mexican hopes expressed during President Fox's visit that there might be important breakthroughs on the issue by the end of the year, perhaps unrealistically optimistic under the best of circumstances because of divisions in Congress and lack of enthusiasm among the general public, were clear victims of the September 11 attacks.

The U.S. invasion of Afghanistan to capture the al Qaeda leader who openly boasted of the group's part in the terrorist attacks, and to overthrow the Taliban regime in Kabul that had provided a base for al Qaeda, received support in Mexico according to some surveys and opposition according to others. Support emerged from a Pew Research Center survey in 2002 in which 52 percent of Mexican respondents supported the war on terrorism. In contrast a Latinobarometer survey found that fully 74 percent of Mexicans opposed the invasion of Afghanistan, a figure topped only by the 80 percent of Argentines who expressed the same view. Differences in question wording and the time of the surveys may account for the disparate responses. The lack of uncertainty about the identity of the September 11 perpetrators apparently weighed significantly in the judgment by some Mexican respondents that the American response con-

---

102. These figures are drawn from Leticia Juarez G., "Mexico, the United States, and the War in Iraq," *International Journal of Public Opinion Research* 16, no. 2 (2004): 331–43; and Marta Lagos, "World Opinion: Terrorism and the Image of the United States in Latin America," *International Journal of Public Opinion Research* 15, no. 1 (2003): 95–101.

stituted a justified use of military force, whereas others, perhaps mindful of the long record of American interventions in Latin America, disagreed.

Evidence of Mexican support for the war in Afghanistan is mixed, but the long run-up to the U.S.-led invasion of Iraq in March 2003 gave rise to a quite different—unambiguously critical—response. Despite a lack of enthusiasm within the Bush administration for taking the Iraq issue to the United Nations Security Council, it did so in the fall of 2002 largely at the insistence of Secretary of State Colin Powell. Mexico sat on the Security Council as one of ten nonpermanent members. In the face of some public opposition at home, Mexico nevertheless joined the other fourteen members in voting for Security Council Resolution 1441, whereby Iraq was ordered to admit UN inspectors to determine whether the Saddam Hussein regime was in violation of the post–Gulf War ban on weapons of mass destruction. Mexico's willingness to follow Washington's lead on this and the lack of progress on immigration issues precipitated the resignation of Foreign Minister Jorge Castaneda in January 2003. Castaneda described the post-9/11 president Bush as "aloof, brusque, and on occasion abrasive," and on the Iraq issue, "I was never asked, 'What is it you need in order to be more cooperative with us? What can we do to help?'"[103]

The next step on the road to war was Security Council Resolution 1442, sponsored by the United States, Great Britain, and Spain, which authorized the use of force against Iraq. Washington was fully aware that either France, Russia, or both would almost certainly exercise their veto power on SC 1442, that Germany would oppose it, and that China would be unlikely to vote in favor. The United States nevertheless lobbied hard for support among the other eight Security Council members, hoping to gain some policy legitimacy for the invasion, while isolating Russia, France, and Germany as naysayers in the effort to overthrow the Saddam Hussein regime and its alleged weapons of mass destruction.

Although the Mexican government was the target of intense pressure from Washington, it faced a dilemma. Mexican public opinion, which according to some polls had supported the American effort to defeat terrorists, was overwhelmingly opposed to an attack on Iraq. Table 4.1 reveals a dramatic turnabout, during the period between the two military undertakings in Afghanistan and Iraq, in views of the United States among relatively affluent Mexicans who

103. Roger Cohen, David E. Sanger, and Steven R. Weisman, "Challenging Rest of the World with a New Order," *New York Times,* October 12, 2004.

might be more inclined to be pro–United States. The October and November 2001 surveys, conducted during the military operations that overthrew the Taliban regime in Afghanistan, revealed very strong favorable opinions about the United States. The surveys in March 2003, undertaken first on the day of the U.S.-led invasion of Iraq and then seven days into the war, found that fewer than one Mexican respondent in three viewed the United States in a favorable light.

While trying to identify the precise source of changes in public opinion can be somewhat hazardous, it seems a reasonable conjecture in this case that many Mexicans made a distinction between the war in Afghanistan as a legitimate response to the terrorist attacks, on the one hand, and, on the other, the invasion of Iraq as a war of choice based on less than compelling evidence about weapons of mass destruction. Further evidence in support of this reasoning emerges from two other survey questions. Sixty-one percent of Mexican respondents asserted that the evidence presented by Americans about Iraqi WMDs was "not true," and when asked about the use of force against Iraq, 65 percent opposed the invasion prior to the war, and fully 95 percent expressed the same view after the war had started.[104]

Mexico initially hedged on its vote on SC 1442. An American official made it quite clear that those who failed to support it would pay a "price for noncompliance."[105] When informal canvassing of the nonpermanent Security Council members revealed that a formal vote on SC 1442 would result in an embarrassing defeat for Washington, the United States withdrew it. President Bush

TABLE 4.1. Mexican Opinions of the United States, 2001–3

"What is your opinion of the United States: Excellent, good, so-so, bad, or very bad?"

	Excellent (%)	Good (%)	So-So (%)	Bad (%)	Very Bad (%)
October 9, 2001	12	44	17	17	5
November 1, 2001	8	57	19	12	1
March 19, 2003	2	29	17	39	17
March 26, 2003	1	24	17	34	20

Source: Leticia Juarez G., "Mexico, the United States, and the War in Iraq," *International Journal of Public Opinion Research* 16, no. 2 (2004): 333.

Note: These surveys sampled the 37 percent of households with telephones, not the entire Mexican population.

---

104. Juarez, "Mexico, the United States, and the War in Iraq."

105. Ed Vulliamy, Peter Beaumont, Nick Paton Walsh, and Paul Webster, "America the Arm-Twister," *Observer*, March 3, 2003, http://www.globalpolicy.org/security/issues/iraq/attack/2003/0302.

announced the decision in a televised speech on March 17, stating that the United States would feel free to act against Iraq without Security Council approval. Shortly thereafter, President Fox followed the Bush announcement with a speech stating that Mexico would have voted against SC 1442. Fox's speech, widely viewed in Mexico as well as in some border towns in the United States, was described as the best in his career. A survey revealed that 78 percent described it as a "good message," and Fox's favorable ratings in Mexico rose to a new high of 68 percent.[106] As noted in the preceding, opposition to the Iraq invasion rose to a near-unanimous 95 percent shortly after the conflict started.

American officials reacted with anger at both the timing and content of President Fox's speech, viewing it as a gratuitous slap at Washington. Shortly thereafter the United States retaliated by canceling the traditional reception in Mexico City celebrating Mexico's military victory over French and traitorous Mexican forces at Pueblo on May 5, 1862.

Events during the years since the ouster of the Saddam Hussein regime in Baghdad have done little to generate support among Mexicans for the Iraq undertaking. The absence of evidence on Iraqi weapons of mass destruction, the abuse of prisoners at the Abu Ghraib prison and the Guantanamo Bay facility, and an insurgency that continues to take a heavy toll among Iraqi civilians have apparently trumped the good news about successful elections in 2005 and the creation of a national unity government in Baghdad the following year. Some Mexicans have drawn parallels between the treatment of Mexicans in American prisons and of Iraqis at Abu Ghraib, and indeed, Mexico has submitted petitions to the United Nations concerning the treatment of its nationals, including the use of capital punishment, by the American law enforcement system.

The immigration issue continues to roil relations between the two countries. When the two presidents met in Monterrey, Mexico, in 2004, Bush proposed a liberalized immigration plan that would permit undocumented workers in the United States to apply for legal temporary worker status. Although 83 percent of Mexicans approved of the proposal, it did not meet all of Mexico's hopes. But just as it is clear that Fox was under great pressure at home to achieve significant immigration reforms, Bush faced pressures from Congress to place border security at the top of the immigration agenda and to oppose amnesty for undocumented Mexicans. Senators John McCain (R-AZ) and Edward Kennedy (D-MA) have worked together on legislation that comes close to Bush's preferences, but such a plan faced very strong headwinds in the House of

---

106. Juarez, "Mexico, the United States, and the War in Iraq."

Representatives. The 2007 immigration reform bill died in the Senate when, despite a strong plea for support from President Bush, only 12 of 49 Republican senators voted in favor. Former Mexican Foreign Minister Jorge Castañeda assessed the broader impact of the Senate vote.

> Very few things could make as much of a difference in Mexico, Ecuador, Peru, Colombia and the Caribbean as a generous, broad-minded and workable reform of immigration. It would show that the United States really wants to mend fences (rather than simply erect them). For many senators, this is an irrelevant factor; they believe that immigration is a domestic matter and that the needs and desires of other countries should not be taken into account. But this is shortsighted. These are not the best of times for the United States in Latin America; allowing relations to deteriorate still further means playing directly into the Venezuelan [Hugo Chávez] president's hands. That, perhaps, is something worth pondering.[107]

Opponents of immigration reform can also count on powerful voices in the media. Former presidential speechwriter for Richard Nixon and presidential candidate Patrick Buchanan has maintained political visibility by raising the specter of American institutions and values drowning in a flood of Hispanic immigrants from below the border, and he is not alone in this respect.[108] CNN television commentator Lou Dobbs rarely loses an opportunity to condemn American leaders for their failure to stem the inflow of immigrants into the United States and the outflow of jobs to low-income countries, and a distinguished Harvard political scientist has expressed fears that America is losing its national identity.[109]

Although Mexicans have strong feelings about immigration issues and they believe that their country should often cooperate with the United States, one possible agreement is off the bargaining table. Any proposal that would present more opportunities for Mexicans to work in the United States in exchange for greater American access to Mexico's oil, gas, and electricity is opposed by an overwhelming margin of 71 percent to 18 percent. A similarly strong majority opposes obtaining more American financing for economic development in return for greater access to Mexican energy resources.[110]

---

107. Jorge G. Castañeda, "Immigration's Lost Voices," *Los Angeles Times*, June 13, 2007.
108. His book *State of Emergency: The Third World Invasion and Conquest of America*, his magazine, *The American Conservative*, and his monthly newsletter, *The American Cause*, are largely devoted to the immigration issue.
109. Samuel P. Huntington, *Who We Are: The Challenge to America's National Identity* (New York: Simon and Schuster, 2004).
110. CIDE and COMEX, *Mexico y El Mundo*.

The September 11 terrorist attacks and subsequent U.S. responses coincided with growing democratization in Mexico, as notably exemplified by the precedent-shattering election of Vicente Fox as president. This development suggests, at least in the abstract, that Mexican leaders should have become more sensitive to public opinion. Given the ubiquitous American impact on many aspects of life across the border, it appears likely that even Mexicans with a very modest knowledge of and interest in politics may pay more attention when the issues revolve around the United States and its policies. If nothing else, the number of Mexican citizens with relatives living in the United States would give many a personal stake in relations between the two countries.

The evidence reviewed here suggests that most Mexicans have maintained at least moderately favorable opinions of the United States. Moreover, a great many Mexicans have expressed their admiration for aspects of American society by crossing the border—"voting with their feet" through the normal immigration channels or otherwise—in the search for better economic opportunities for themselves and their families. Yet the long-standing views of the United States as a bully who is quite insensitive to the interests of others have been magnified by the Iraq war. Repeated American military interventions in Latin America, most recently the invasion of Panama in 1989, sustain the bully image. Although Mexico has few traditional interests in Afghanistan or Iraq, a skeptical view of unilateral, preemptive American military action is perhaps understandable in the light of past history. During the run-up to the invasion of Iraq, a sign warned, "Today Iraq, tomorrow Mexico."

The Centro de Investigación y Docencia Económicas (CIDE) and Chicago Council on Foreign Relations (CCFR) survey, conducted about fourteen months after the dustup arising from Mexico's decision not to support Security Council Resolution 1442 authorizing the use of force against Iraq and shortly after nominal handover of power to a provisional authority in Baghdad, provides a good snapshot of the ambivalent "love-hate" opinions about the United States south of the border. The previously cited score of 68 degrees on a thermometer scale—matched only by judgments about Japan—indicates continuing favorable views of the United States. Moreover, Mexican assessments of major international threats would not evoke much dissent from most Americans: drug trafficking (89 percent), chemical and biological weapons (86 percent), international terrorism (86 percent), and a world economic crisis (81 percent). But these responses do provide only a partial picture of how Mexicans view their powerful neighbor to the north.

Although most (57 percent) Mexicans favor an active international role rather than staying out of world affairs (34 percent), when asked whether Mexico should pursue its own foreign policy or follow the U.S. lead in foreign affairs, the margin in favor of the former option is a formidable 89 percent to 5 percent. Even among opinion leaders, who are generally much more internationalist than the general public, the comparable figures are an almost identical 89 percent and 7 percent. By a margin of almost two to one, respondents to the same mid-2004 survey rejected the proposition that "the U.S. has a generally positive influence in the world." Although not a strong vote of confidence in American foreign policy, that result is better than those that emerged from the three most recent Pew surveys (table 2.3). Most Mexicans welcome an active international role for the United States, but both the general public and opinion leaders overwhelmingly reject the proposition that Washington should act as the "world's policeman."[111]

Finally, the survey also asked respondents to express their feelings about the United States on dimensions of liking, friendship, and trust. The results, summarized in table 4.2, indicate that however much Mexicans admire and hope to replicate the many facets of the American success story, the low level of trust in the United States indicates an imposing hurdle on the path of improving relations between the two countries.

TABLE 4.2. Feelings toward the United States, 2004 and 2006

	Percent Responses		
		2006	
	2004	General Public	Leaders
Admiration	29	34	64
Indifference	46	25	25
Disdain	20	32	7
Fraternity	20	27	—
Indifference	46	25	—
Resentment	26	38	—
Trust	20	26	51
Indifference	33	16	6
Distrust	43	53	41

Source: Centro de Investigación y Docencia Económicas (CIDE) and Consejo Mexicano de Asuntos Internacionales (COMEX), *Mexico y El Mundo, Global Views 2004: Mexican Public Opinion and Foreign Policy,* September 2004; and CIDE and COMEX, *Mexico and the World 2006: Public Opinion and Foreign Policy in Mexico,* 2006.

111. The figures in this and the previous paragraph are drawn from CIDE and COMEX, *Mexico y El Mundo.*

What are the possible policy consequences, if any, of Mexican views of the United States? Because the overall level of education among Mexicans falls far short of that in the United States, it might be assumed that they have only a limited interest in and knowledge of foreign affairs, and thus that their views have little impact. In fact, 87 percent of Mexicans are "very" or "somewhat" interested in "news about the relations of Mexico with other countries," a figure that compares favorably with that of Americans, and they have reasonably good knowledge about such important events as the Mexican position on the U.S.-led invasion of Iraq and the Bush administration's proposals on immigration reform.[112] That said, it would be stretching the evidence to assert that it has proven the power of public opinion in driving foreign policy decisions by the Fox government. But a more modest conclusion seems reasonable: in its search for accommodation with the United States on the crucial immigration issue, and in its decision to distance itself from Washington's undertaking in Iraq, Mexican leaders have acted in ways that were wholly consistent with public sentiments about the United States and its policies, and a failure to do so would have courted serious adverse political consequences at home.

CANADA

Robert Thompson, a British Columbia member of the right-wing populist Social Credit Party, asserted in 1973 that "Americans are our best friends whether we like it or not."[113] That frequently quoted quip provides some insight into relations between the two North American neighbors. History, language, democratic institutions, trade, and many other elements have forged important links between Canada and the United States that are likely to influence most issues. More than five thousand miles of shared frontier ensure physical intimacy but not necessarily perpetually identical definitions of national interests. As indicated in the data presented in chapters 2 and 3, Canadians have generally viewed the United States and the American people favorably, but such issues as the war in Iraq have led to serious questions about many aspects of Washington's policies.

Canadian-American relations since America's independence reveal a record of increasing cooperation despite a good deal of conflict during the years immediately following American independence. During the Revolutionary War

112. CIDE and COMEX, *Mexico y El Mundo.*
113. Quoted by President Bush in an address in Halifax, N.S. David Stout, "Bush Courts Canadians, but without Budging on Iraq," *New York Times,* December 1, 2004.

some forty thousand colonials, the United Empire Loyalists, fled to Canada, and their properties were expropriated without compensation. The War of 1812 brought Canada, still a part of the British Empire, into conflict with the United States. The remainder of the nineteenth century saw the resolution of some border issues by treaties, including the Rush-Bagot Treaty in 1817 and the Webster-Ashburton Treaty in 1842. Canada attained dominion status in 1867, but its foreign relations were still largely conducted through London. Canada and the United States did not exchange ambassadors until 1927.

Canada entered World War I in 1914 and World War II in 1939, in both cases well before the U.S. entry into those conflicts. Even before the Pearl Harbor attack, a number of Americans went to Canada to enlist in the Royal Canadian Air Force. Although enlistment in the armed forces of another country entails loss of American citizenship, special legislation made it possible to do so without penalty in this case. Wartime cooperation between western members of the anti-Nazi alliance far outstripped occasional differences. The persistent tensions that roiled relations between Charles de Gaulle's Free French forces and what he called "the Anglo-Saxons" were notably absent in Canadian-American relations.

With the onset of the Cold War, Canada joined the North Atlantic Treaty Organization (NATO) as a charter member in 1949, and it was also tied to the United States through joint operation of the North American Air Defense Agreement (NORAD), an air defense system established in 1957. When North Korea launched an invasion of South Korea in June 1950, triggering UN Security Council sanctions against the Pyongyang regime, Canada was one of sixteen countries that contributed armed forces to the American-led military effort. It did not take part in the Vietnam War on the grounds that it was a member of the International Control Commission that was to monitor the 1954 Geneva Agreement that brought to an end France's conflict in Indochina. That point aside, there was little public support in Canada for participation in the conflict. Canada also sent a small military contingent to the Security Council–sanctioned and American-led alliance that expelled Iraqi invaders from Kuwait in 1991.

Canada has long prided itself on its participation in various peacekeeping missions. Canadian Lester Pearson proposed that UN peacekeepers be deployed in the Middle East following the Suez crisis of 1956, a plan for which he was awarded the Nobel Peace Prize. Since 1947, Canadian armed forces have participated in 72 peacekeeping missions in Croatia, Bosnia, Somalia, Cambodia, Rwanda, Haiti, Kosovo, East Timor, Eritrea, and Afghanistan. As of May 2007, 2,500 Canadian military personnel were serving in Afghanistan.

Canadian leaders occasionally have found that it is good politics at home to disagree with the United States. Prime Minister Pierre Elliott Trudeau recognized the communist regime on mainland China, drawing the ire of President Nixon, who, it might be noted, followed the same course some time later with his pathbreaking trip to meet Mao Tse-tung and his colleagues. The United States recognized the Beijing regime as the sole authority in China in the resulting "Shanghai Communiqué." Much to the displeasure of Washington and the powerful "Cuba lobby" in the United States, Canada has also maintained diplomatic and trade relations with the Castro regime in Cuba.

A more recent example emerges from the decision on February 24, 2005, by the Liberal Paul Martin government not to take part in the American national missile defense system. Polls in 2004 yielded very mixed responses on the issue. A Pollara survey in February found that seven in ten respondents favored taking part in the NMD system, but an Ipsos-Reid survey the following month indicated that 69 percent opposed doing so, including 48 percent who were strongly opposed. As the decision neared, support for NMD, as revealed in most polls, tended to decline. Although participating in the NMD system would be virtually cost-free for Canada, the Liberal government faced an uphill election in 2006, and the NMD system lacked powerful support, even among the members of the opposition Conservative Party. Based on a postdecision poll, one observer concluded that "Paul Martin would have flown into a public opinion hurricane had he decided to take part in Bush's missile program," although that may have slightly overstated the depth of opposition.[114] To assuage the United States, Martin's decision was paired with a pledge to seek increased defense spending.

The 2006 elections brought a minority Conservative government, led by Stephen Harper, to power in Ottawa. The campaign largely revolved around domestic concerns such as corruption in the previous Liberal Jean Chrétien government, health care, other government services, and taxes, all of which were cited by more than 10 percent of the voters as the most important issues. Canadian-U.S. relations also entered into the debates, as Martin and Harper both accused the other of being more likely to put Canadian forces into harm's way in Iraq, but the latter was more outspoken in asserting the need for improving relations with Washington.[115]

---

114. "Canadians Back PM's Stance on Missiles," *Brockton Recorder and Times,* March 23, 2005.
115. Harold D. Clarke, Allan Kornberg, Thomas Scotto, and Joe Twyman, "Flawless Campaign, Fragile Victory: Voting in Canada's 2006 Federal Election," *PS: Political Science and Politics* 39 (October 2006): 815–19. See also Munroe Eagles, "Canadian-American Relations in a Turbulent Era," *PS: Political Science and Politics* 39 (October 2006): 821–24.

Canada and the United States are increasingly enmeshed in close trade relations. An effort in 1911 by the Liberal Canadian government for a reciprocal trade agreement failed as a result of opposition by Conservatives and the business community. In 1988–89, the Conservative Mulroney government negotiated and passed a free trade agreement with the United States. The 1994 North American Free Trade Agreement, linking Canada, the United States and Mexico, resulted in a doubling of trade between the United States and Canada within a decade. Canadian exports to and imports from the United States constitute 85 percent and 59 percent, respectively, of Canadian trade. Conversely, 17 percent and 24 percent of American imports and exports are linked to Canada. Canada is by far the top American trade partner, far outstripping Japan. The U.S. imports include 1.6 million barrels per day of oil. The United States also imports significant amounts of natural gas and hydroelectric power from Canada.[116]

Although the 1994 trade agreement linking the United States, Canada, and Mexico in a free trade zone has given rise to dramatically increased trade among its members, it has not always been free of controversy. In response to pressures from the lumber industry, in May 2002 Washington imposed 19 percent countervailing duties and 9 percent antidumping duties on all Canadian softwood lumber shipped to the United States on the somewhat dubious grounds that Canada was indirectly subsidizing its lumber industry by not charging sufficient "stumpage fees" for trees felled on government lands. Canada responded by filing appeals with NAFTA and the World Trade Organization. In the face of several decisions in favor of Canada—most recently in August 2006 when the World Trade Organization (WTO) ruled that the tariffs are unfair—the United States has argued that, notwithstanding the adverse WTO and NAFTA rulings, the issue should be settled by direct negotiations between Ottawa and Washington. When faced with the likelihood that the United States would continue to reject NAFTA and WTO rulings, the recently elected Stephen Harper government negotiated an agreement whereby the United States would return $4 billion of the $5.3 billion tariffs collected since 2002.[117]

Although softwood lumber accounts for only 3 percent of Canadian exports to the United States, the issue generated considerable debate. Some critics described the lumber tariffs as an overarching symbol of Canadian discontent with their powerful neighbor. In response to perceived American bullying

---

116. The trade data are drawn from Economist, *Pocket World in Figures.*
117. Ian Austen, "Canada: Lumber Ruling for Canada," *New York Times,* August 16, 2006.

and selective playing by the rules, there were proposals to retaliate by placing tariffs or other restrictions on Florida oranges or California wines. According to one survey, 50 percent and 40 percent, respectively, favored retaliation against oranges and wines. Others, especially in the business community, opposed retaliatory moves as wholly unrealistic and counterproductive, especially if they might involve any reduction of crude oil exports to the United States.

A lesser trade issue concerns Canadian firms filling mail orders for pharmaceuticals, which typically sell for considerably lower prices in Canada, across the border. President Bush did not win many plaudits when he warned that drugs shipped from Canada might not be safe. As one critic, former foreign minister Lloyd Axworthy, put it, "We're a Third World country? I mean, his attitude is extraordinary, and people do resent that."[118]

The attacks on the twin trade towers took almost three thousand lives, including twenty-five Canadians. Rumors that the nineteen hijackers who perpetrated the attacks had entered the country through Canada were quickly dispelled, but American officials criticized Canada for insufficient border security.[119]

The September 11 attacks led members of NATO, including Canada, to invoke Article 5 of the alliance treaty—it stipulates in effect that an attack on one is an attack on all—for the first time. When the Taliban regime in Afghanistan refused to assist in efforts to capture the al Qaeda leaders who had openly boasted of their role in the terrorist attacks, the United States initiated military action in Afghanistan. The call for assistance by the United States brought forth many favorable responses, including landing rights, overflight rights, and intelligence sharing. But Washington effectively stiff-armed NATO on military operations. Deputy Defense Secretary Paul Wolfowitz succinctly summarized Washington's position: "if we need collective action, we'll ask. We don't anticipate that at the moment." That response placed some NATO leaders in an embarrassing position as they had risked their own political capital in supporting the United States, only to be rebuffed.

The U.S. military quickly drove the Taliban government out of Kabul, but there remained the more difficult tasks of pacifying the rest of the country and

---

118. Quoted in Stephen Frank, "Our Take on America: Canadians Don't Like Bush and Are Worried about the U.S. Election." *Time Canada*, November 1, 2004.

119. The border security issue persists. According to U.S. critics, Canada's generous asylum policy and welfare system have made it "a favored destination for terrorists and international criminals." Some Canadians counter that the United States has focused so intently on its borders with Mexico that it has neglected its frontier with Canada. Joshua Kurlantzick, "Terrorist Suspect," *New Republic Online,* June 7, 2006.

capturing or killing the top al Qaeda leaders. Canada contributed two thousand military personnel for those tasks. Although Defense Minister Art Eggleton stated candidly that it would be a long war (his description, "We have said from the beginning that this would be a long campaign," was a prescient and refreshing contrast to the overly optimistic assessments regularly coming from Washington), the Canadian public provided strong support for the military undertaking in Afghanistan.[120] A Leger Marketing survey in mid-October revealed that 81 percent supported it, and two Gallup polls, in October and four months later, yielded very similar results—66 percent and 73 percent, respectively, in favor. Despite a tragic accident in which a U.S. aircraft mistakenly dropped bombs on a Canadian unit, killing four paratroopers in April 2002, support for military participation in Afghanistan has not collapsed. As it has become increasingly clear that the elected Afghan government controls only a small part of the country surrounding Kabul, the "peacekeeping" mission has been transformed into one that involves combat, inevitably resulting in casualties. While there are discordant voices in Canada, some calling for an immediate pull out of all forces and others chastising the government for failing to undertake a massive increase in defense spending, the military undertaking in Afghanistan continues to enjoy at least modest public support.[121] One observer described Canada's involvement in Afghanistan as "the cornerstone of the country's foreign policy," but at least some polls suggest something short of consensus on the issue.[122] By a narrow vote, the House of Commons extended Canada's military deployment by two years, through February 2009.[123] In the light of increasingly heavy Canadian casualties, an Ipsos-Reid survey in July 2007 revealed that support for the Afghanistan mission has declined to 50 percent.[124]

The United States and Great Britain fought as allies in World War I, World War II, the Korean War, and the Gulf War, and in each case they were joined by Canada. When American and British forces launched the invasion of Iraq on March 20, 2003, it was the first time that they went to war together without

---

120. "Art Eggleton Says US-Led War in Afghanistan Could Last Years," *Hill Times*, November 5, 2001.

121. For example, an op-ed essay by sociologist John Conway denounces Canadian participation in an effort that he describes as an imperial American undertaking. "Bring Troops Home and Sack Hillier," *Record*, March 25, 2006.

122. Mike Blanchfield, "52% of Canadians Support Operation: Kandahar Deployment," *National Post*, March 4, 2006, but a *Toronto Globe and Mail* poll during the same month revealed lower support.

123. Clifford Krauss, "Canada Leader Wins on Extending Afghan Tour," *New York Times*, May 18, 2006. Prime Minister Harper has also stopped flying the flag at half-mast for Canadian troops killed in Afghanistan and has limited media coverage of bodies returning from Afghanistan.

124. Reuters report, *New York Times*, July 25, 2007.

Canadian participation. Unlike widespread support for the invasion of Afghanistan just weeks after the terrorist attacks on New York and Washington, the NATO alliance was deeply divided on the issue of Iraq, as was the UN Security Council. Owing to the absence of compelling evidence about the two bases on which proponents of the invasion built their case—alleged Iraqi possession of weapons of mass destruction and Baghdad's close ties to al Qaeda—Canada as well as many other traditional American allies questioned the need for and timing of military operations against Iraq.

When the Bush administration launched its public relations effort to gain congressional and international support for military action against the Saddam Hussein regime in September 2002, polls in Canada revealed considerable ambivalence about the issue. While there were prominent voices in Canada asserting that human rights violations by the sadistic Saddam Hussein regime in Baghdad and the realistic need to remain on good terms with the powerful neighbor to the south required Ottawa to join the United States in the Iraq undertaking, public opinion surveys revealed far less enthusiasm for doing so.[125] According to an Ipsos-Reid survey, 56 percent of Canadians described Iraq as an international threat, but at about the same time only 22 percent in a Leger study agreed that an invasion of Iraq would be justified. Several other surveys undertaken during the final months of 2002 revealed growing but not overwhelming Canadian unease about military action in Iraq, but when viewed in their totality, there was a striking absence of a powerful consensus on the question. For example, a Strategic Counsel study found that 51 percent believed that there was "no good reason" for attacking Iraq, whereas 41 percent believed that Saddam Hussein should be overthrown, even in the absence of evidence about Iraqi weapons of mass destruction.[126]

A perhaps more revealing picture of Canadian attitudes emerged from surveys in which respondents were asked about their country's participation alongside the United States in any military action against Iraq. These questions

---

125. Proponents of Canadian participation included Michael Ignatieff, then a historian at Harvard University and now a Liberal member of Parliament. Although the early favorite, he lost the 2006 election for leadership of the Liberal Party. John Granatstein is a historian who has written extensively on relations between the United States and Canada. Both Ignatieff and Granatstein have argued strenuously that if Canada is to be taken seriously in international affairs, it must undertake massive increases in defense spending, and moreover, it cannot afford to alienate Washington on such issues as Iraq. Michael Ignatieff, "Canada in the Age of Terror—Multilateralism Meets a Moment of Truth," *Policy Options* 24 (February 2003): 14–18; and J. L. Granatstein, *A Friendly Agreement in Advance: Canada-US Defence Relations Past, Present, and Future* (Ottawa: C. D. Howe Institute, 2002). The latter has called anti-Americanism "Canada's national religion." Quoted in Clifford Krauss, "Canada May Be a Close Neighbor, but It Proudly Keeps Its Distance," *New York Times*, March 23, 2005.
126. Mike Blanchfield, "Canadians Back Iraq Attack," *Edmonton Journal*, September 9, 2002.

revealed that the role of the United Nations Security Council was a crucial variable. Just weeks before the invasion of Iraq, a JMCK survey found that 60 percent of those taking part replied that UN backing should precede Canadian support for military action. Similarly, an early 2003 SES Canada Research group survey posed this question:

> Some people think that Canada should support the United States if it decides to unilaterally invade Iraq to topple Saddam Hussein because the U.S. is our ally. Others think that we should not support our U.S. ally without the approval of the United Nations. Which of these best reflects your views?

While 26 percent would support U.S. unilateral action, more than twice as many (66 percent) would withhold that support in the absence of United Nations approval.[127]

Frequent polling during and immediately after the U.S.-led military action against Iraq revealed a continuing lack of Canadian public enthusiasm for the Iraq war, though the short and successful military campaign did change some minds. For example, a March 2003 Leger Marketing survey found that only one-third of Canadians felt that the war was justified, but that number jumped to almost one-half (46 percent) after the fall of Baghdad. A month later, an Ipsos-Reid survey for CTV and the *Globe and Mail* found respondents evenly split at 48 percent to 48 percent on the invasion.[128]

The Canadian decision not to join the "coalition of the willing" did not go unnoticed in Washington. The U.S. ambassador to Ottawa, Paul Cellucci, asserted that he was "upset and disappointed" and that Canada's failure to join the United States would have "consequences." President Bush canceled a visit to Ottawa in the wake of the Canadian action.[129]

Nor did that refusal to join the United States in the invasion win unanimous plaudits in Canada. The Vancouver Board of Trade sent a letter to Ambassador Cellucci stating that it was "shocked and embarrassed" by the Canadian failure to participate in the Iraq war, and the Conservative Party leader in Parliament, Stephen Harper, also attacked Prime Minister Chrétien for failing to join the United States in the invasion of Iraq.[130] Some other business leaders

---

127. Bill Rodgers, "No War without U.N.," *Edmonton Sun,* February 20, 2003.
128. "Canadians Split over U.S.-Led War: Poll," *Agence France Press-English,* April 7, 2003.
129. Paul Cellucci, *Unquiet Diplomacy* (Toronto: Key Porter Books, 2005).
130. David Hogben and David Reevely, "We Support War in Iraq, Board of Trade Tells U.S.," *Vancouver Sun,* March 28, 2003; and Tom Cohen, "U.S. Criticism Intensifies Debate over Canada's Refusal to Join Iraq War," Associated Press, March 25, 2003.

were equally critical and expressed fears that the close trade ties between the United States and Canada might be damaged.[131]

Events since the fall of Baghdad have included such successes as the capture of Saddam Hussein and three elections in 2005 leading to a new Iraqi constitution and government. These have been offset by an increasingly violent insurgency that, according even to some top American military leaders, could escalate into a full-fledged civil war. In the light of these developments, it is hardly surprising that few Canadians regret Ottawa's decision to abstain from participation. The overwhelming support that Canadians expressed in 2002 for the U.S.-led effort to fight terrorism had fallen sharply since then—to 37 percent in 2007—probably because the Iraq invasion was perceived as a distraction from rather than a contribution to dealing with terrorism (table 2.11). Moreover, whereas in May 2003 Canadians supported their government's decision not to join in the invasion of Iraq by a two-to-one margin, two years later that support had risen to a margin of 80 percent to 17 percent (table 2.14).

Liberal Party Prime Minister Chrétien stepped down in December 2003 and was replaced by Paul Martin, who, in turn, lost office to a minority Conservative government as a result of a general election in 2006. Prime Minister Harper was eager to improve relations with Washington and took a number of steps in that direction. The joint U.S.-Canadian NORAD air defense system was renewed in May 2006, and Harper suggested that the decision to pull out of the national missile defense system might be revisited. He has also increased the size of the Canadian military contingent in Afghanistan and added $1.26 billion to the budget for border security.[132] But he would surely face a firestorm of protest should he even contemplate sending Canadian armed forces to Iraq, replacing those from Italy, Spain, or other countries whose military units have been withdrawn. According to a July 2005 Gallup poll, four-fifths of Canadians doubted that peace and security would be restored within a year, and fully 71 percent thought that Iraq was unlikely to experience peace and security in less than five years. Events on the ground during the subsequent months indicate that those rather pessimistic diagnoses are also quite realistic. They suggest that no Canadian government, even one committed to placating Washington, is likely to send its armed forces into such a quagmire. More generally, the head of a minority government cannot afford to be seen as "Bush's poodle."

---

131. Bernard Simon, "Canada Feels Repercussions for Staying out of Iraq War," *International Herald Tribune*, April 2, 2003.
132. Eagles, "Canadian-American Relations in a Turbulent Era."

The survey evidence summarized in chapters 2 and 3 reveals that Canadians generally have favorable views of the United States (table 2.1), its people (table 3.1), many of its institutions, and its science and technology (table 3.7).[133] Despite frequently asserted fears that Canada's cultural identity is being swamped by American movies, television, music, and print media, three Pew polls indicated that more than three Canadians in four approve of American entertainment products (table 3.8), although many fewer were enthusiastic about the spread of U.S. customs in their country (table 3.10). More generally, most Canadians agreed with the proposition that the United States is "a beacon of hope" (table 3.2). In summary, when the questions ask Canadians to express their views about "what America is," the responses are generally quite favorable, although in some cases more critical views have increased in the past few years.

When Canadians were asked to judge "what America does," especially in the international arena, the picture becomes far bleaker. To be sure, few Canadians believe that the world would be safer if there were another military superpower to compete with the United States (table 2.7), and most of them agree that there are circumstances in which the preemptive use of force is legitimate (table 2.9). On the other hand, few Canadians believe that Washington pays much attention to the vital interests of other countries, including Canada (table 2.8), or that the United States plays a mainly positive influence in the world (table 2.3). And few Canadians approve of the American way of doing business (table 3.9). In a 2005 *National Post* survey, 37 percent of Canadian respondents identified "terrorism" as the major threat to national security. An equal number of respondents stated that "American foreign policy" was the most important threat. It is not very difficult to identify some sources of disquiet. Shortly after the September 11 attacks, the American "war on terrorism" received support from more than two-thirds of Canadians, but that support eroded sharply when Washington included the invasion of Iraq as a central part of the antiterrorist effort (table 2.11). Ottawa's decision not to join the "coalition of the willing" in Iraq was widely hailed by the Canadian public (table 2.14); and most Canadians doubted that post-Saddam U.S. policies in Iraq were meeting the needs of the Iraqi people (table 2.18), although a plurality stated that they were contributing to regional stability in the Middle East (table 2.20). Finally, when asked directly whether tensions between the two countries could be traced primarily to dif-

---

133. In addition to the figures in table 3.1, an Angus Reid poll in December 2004 found that 80 percent of Canadians had favorable opinions of Americans.

ferences in values or policies, by a margin of more than three to two Canadians pointed to policy differences (table 3.13).

Although most Canadians feel close to the United States on many values and business practices, they are also prepared to follow an independent path on foreign affairs. When a 2005 survey of Canadians and Americans asked for responses to the proposition "Canada should follow its own interests, even if this leads to conflict with other nations," 61 percent agreed. Respondents in the Atlantic provinces (75 percent) and British Columbia (81 percent) expressed the strongest agreement, in contrast to those in Quebec (38 percent), and men (70 percent) outstripped women (54 percent) in their support.[134]

Despite sharp differences on Iraq and some trade issues, Canada and the United States seem destined to remain "best friends" for the foreseeable future. There will no doubt continue to be those who are determined to alienate the other country by means of verbal bombshells. Carolyn Parrish, a member of Canada's House of Commons asserted, "Damn Americans. I hate those bastards," an observation that Prime Minister Chrétien called "unacceptable." He did not, however, discipline her. A Republican attack television commercial in 2006 asserted, "Canada can take care of North Korea. They're not busy." Given Canada's recent decision to increase its military contingent in Afghanistan, it is hardly surprising that Canada's ambassador in Washington expressed his displeasure to a White House official.[135] But it will probably take more than such childish rhetoric to inflict a fatal blow to the natural and historic bonds between the two countries.

AUSTRALIA

Australia, the sixth-largest country by land area, has long maintained strong ties to the United States. Although one is a superpower and the other is not even the dominant power in its region, the two countries share a number of core values and experiences. Both were British colonies whose settlers rapidly supplanted the native peoples in their vast countries, who established successful democratic governments and capitalist economies, and who are predominantly Caucasian, Christian, and English speaking. The two countries have fought to-

---

134. *The Niagara Report*, SES and University of Buffalo, 2006, http://www.niagarareport.buffalo .edu/index/shtml.
135. Cellucci, *Unquiet Diplomacy*, 133; and Ian Austen, "Republican Attack Ad Offends Canada," *New York Times*, October 27, 2006.

gether in every war since World War I. In addition to World War II, the Korean War, the Vietnam War, and the Gulf War of 1991, Australia joined the "coalition of the willing" that, under U.S. leadership, ousted the Saddam Hussein regime in 2003.

During the heyday of the British Empire, Australia looked primarily to London for its security, and it contributed military units to the British campaigns against Germany during both World Wars. Australian combat divisions totaling 330,000 troops suffered horrendous casualties during World War I, including 60,000 killed.[136] Canberra also contributed military units to the allied effort against Nazi Germany during World War II, but by 1942 the threat of a Japanese invasion forced Australia to withdraw its troops from the North African campaign against Germany and to rely increasingly on the United States for its survival. After a series of early defeats beginning with the Pearl Harbor attack, American victories at the naval battles of Midway and the Coral Sea began to turn the tide against Japan. Subsequent victories in New Guinea and other nearby Pacific islands thwarted the threat of a Japanese invasion.

The onset of the Cold War during the late 1940s, the victory of the Communists in China in 1949, and the invasion of South Korea by North Korea in 1950 provided ample incentives for security cooperation between Washington and Canberra. The Japanese Peace Treaty, signed in San Francisco in 1951, formally brought an end to the Pacific War. As an additional incentive for Australia and New Zealand to sign the treaty, the United States joined these two countries in the tripartite ANZUS (Australia–New Zealand–U.S.) pact. That alliance persists, although in a somewhat truncated form. When the Auckland government banned nuclear-armed and nuclear-powered ships from visiting its ports in 1987, Washington broke its alliance ties to New Zealand rather than signal which of its ships might be carrying nuclear weapons. ANZUS thus lives on with Australia-U.S. and Australia-New Zealand security ties.

When the Liberal-National Party (L-NP) coalition came to power in 1976, it issued a Defense White Paper, focusing on "self-reliance, development of the Australian Defence Force (ADF) and the rejection of the use of 'threats' in the defence planning process." Twenty years later, when the L-NP took power under John Howard, it undertook another review of the national defense strategy, stressing the close defense relationship with the United States, expanding of the

---

136. Robert G. Sutter, "Australia," in *Encyclopedia of U.S. Foreign Relations,* 1:116.

combat capabilities of the ADF, and supporting a more global foreign policy role for Australia.[137]

Australia and the United States have also maintained strong economic relations. The United States accounts for about 8 percent of Australian exports and slightly over 14 percent of its imports.[138] The Australia–United States Free Trade Agreement (AUSFTA) took effect on January 1, 2005, opening new trade opportunities. Australia and the United States also stood together as the only developed countries to oppose the Kyoto Protocol on global warming.

But economic relations are not without some discordant notes. U.S. agricultural subsidies have been a special and continuing source of resentment in Australia because they give American farmers incentives to produce large surpluses and a significant advantage in selling wheat and other farm products on world markets, thus depressing prices for all sellers. Whereas agriculture accounts for 2 percent of American employment, the comparable figure for Australia is twice as large, and thus the loss of international markets is felt much more deeply. In the aftermath of the September 11 terrorist attacks, the United States and many other wealthy countries pledged to reduce or eliminate farm subsidies, but the collapse of the "Doha Round" trade negotiations in 2006 put an end, at least for the foreseeable future, to serious efforts to implement such expressions of good intentions.

A quick review of the survey data presented in chapters 2 and 3 reveals that Australians have generally maintained quite positive views of the United States (table 2.1) and, especially, of the American people (table 3.1). On the latter question, only respondents in Canada and Great Britain were slightly more favorably inclined toward Americans. In 2003, majorities agreed that the United States is "a beacon of hope and opportunity" and "a force for good" in the world (table 3.2). Moreover American ideas of democracy (table 3.5), science and technology (tables 3.7 and 3.11), and entertainment products (table 3.8) received strong approval, as did the effort to deal with global terrorism (table 2.11). As noted, Australia sent armed forces to Afghanistan, and it joined the "coalition of the willing" in Iraq, policies that, according to a 2003 Pew survey, had strong public support (table 2.14).

In a few respects, however, Australians were less enthusiastic. Only France and Turkey gave the United States lower ratings on its business practices (table

137. Thomas-Durell Young, "The Australian-United States Security Alliance," in *Australia's Security in the 21st Century*, ed. J. Mohan Malik (St. Leonards: Allen and Unwin, 1999).
138. The trade and other economic figures in this paragraph are drawn from Economist, *Pocket World in Figures*.

3.9); Washington's agricultural subsidies no doubt contributed to this negative judgment. A Roy Morgan Research poll for the BBC in 2003 revealed that fully 82 percent of the respondents stated that Australia should *not* copy the way that the American economy is run.[139] As was true of most publics abroad, increasing Americanization of their country was not warmly applauded by Australians (table 3.10). Concerns about American arrogance (table 3.4), its influence in the world (table 2.3), and the degree to which Washington paid attention to Australian vital interests (table 2.8) also reflected some disquiet about a generally very cordial alliance relationship.

Finally, an overwhelming majority (93 percent) of Australians believe that their country is a better place to live than the United States, and 82 percent stated that they would not want to live in the United States. But these figures seem less an indictment of American society than a sense of satisfaction with the quality of life in Australia. There is at least some basis for those feelings as, according to the "Human Development Index," Australia ranks third in the world, only slightly behind two Scandinavian countries and just a shade above the United States.[140]

As is clear in many of the previously cited tables, the Pew Global Attitudes Project and other polling organizations undertook somewhat fewer surveys in Australia than in NATO and several other countries, and there is a relative dearth of data after 2003. That limitation is offset at least in part, however, by public opinion surveys conducted by Australian organizations. These will be cited where relevant to supplement those summarized in chapters 2 and 3.

The September 11 terrorist attacks on New York and Washington brought forth immediate expressions of support and sympathy from most Australians. The victims of the attacks included twenty-three Australian citizens who had been working at the World Trade Center towers. Australian prime minister John Howard was visiting Washington when the third of the hijacked airliners slammed into the Pentagon. A poll by Colmar Brunton Research only two days later revealed that 63 percent believed that the United States would go to war against the perpetrators, and 66 percent expressed the opinion that Australia should participate. Only one in ten respondents thought that "it's not our problem," while a slightly larger minority feared that taking part would have negative consequences for Australia's multicultural domestic environment. Interest-

---

139. Roy Morgan Research, *What Australia Thinks of America,* finding no. 3641, June 19, 2003, http://www.roymorgan.com/news/polls/2003/3641/index.cfm?printversion=yes.

140. The HDI data are from Economist, *Pocket World in Figures.*

ingly, 43 percent of those advocating Australian participation cited the importance of showing support for Washington, whereas only 23 percent felt that it was most important to punish the perpetrators.[141]

Another poll later that week confirmed strong support for the United States. When asked, "would you personally be in favour or against America retaliating with force against those it believes responsible for the terrorist attacks," 69 percent asserted that they were in favor, with fully half "strongly in favour." The follow-up question about "involvement by Australian armed forces" yielded very similar results, with seven in ten respondents favoring their country's participation.[142]

Armed with clear public support, the Howard government in Canberra agreed to invoke Article 4 of the ANZUS treaty, and it committed 1,550 troops to military operations in Afghanistan, a decision that received continued public support. After the deployment in November 2001, those approving Australian participation rose to 71 percent, with only one-quarter that many expressing disapproval.[143] Supporters felt that by acting in support of the United States, Australia was honoring its ANZUS treaty obligations. The military contingent in Afghanistan was later scaled back, but after the London bombings in July 2005, an additional 150 special forces troops were deployed there.

There were two striking features of Australia's involvement in Afghanistan. First was the fear—remarkably prescient as it turned out—that the United States lacked a serious commitment to rebuilding Afghanistan and that it would abandon the country before completing the task. Second, there was extensive bipartisan support for Australian involvement there, in striking contrast to the deep partisan divisions on participation in the Iraq war. An opposition Australian Labor Party (ALP) spokesman asserted in mid-2005 that "Australia needs to ensure that the task we began in Afghanistan is completed."[144]

Although there was a close correspondence between public opinion and the policies of the Howard government, in the light of subsequent events, especially the war against Iraq, it seems unlikely that Australian actions were merely a response to a groundswell of support for deployment of armed forces to Afghanistan. Even in the absence of widespread public approval, the Howard

---

141. "NSW: Australians Stunned by US Terrorist Attacks," AAP NEWSFEED, September 13, 2001, Academic, LEXIS-NEXIS (accessed October 14, 2006).

142. Newspoll, survey undertaken September 14–16, 2001.

143. IPSOS Reid survey, conducted between November 19 and December 17, 2001.

144. Guy Rundle, "To Hell in a Handcart," *Australian*, October 9, 2002; "Labor Opposes More Troops to Iraq, Backs Afghan Force," *Age*, July 12, 2005; "Terror Threat from Afghanistan: ALP," *Age*, July 12, 2005; and "Australia Must Finish the Job in Afghanistan," *Age*, July 13, 2005.

government would likely have pursed the same policies. That is, perceived alliance obligations and a strong belief that Australia should align its policies with Washington would likely have trumped public opinion, even had it been opposed.[145]

Australia contributed to the coalition assembled by President George H. W. Bush to expel the Iraqi armies that had invaded Kuwait in the summer of 1990. It also joined the United States in the limited "Desert Fox" operation against Iraq in 1998. These actions gained strong approval from the Australian public.[146] By early 2003, as it became increasingly clear that American armed forces would invade Iraq, Australia was the third country—behind the United States and Great Britain—to join "the coalition of the willing" with the deployment of two thousand troops.

That decision did not meet with universal approval. As in many countries, the issue of support from the UN Security Council loomed large in the minds of many Australians. Three surveys during the weeks prior to the invasion asked whether respondents were "in favour or against Australian troops being involved in military action if the U.N. supported such action." The polls found that 57 percent, 56 percent, and 61 percent favored such action. When asked to express their views if the UN did not support military action, support fell precipitously to 18 percent, 22 percent, and 25 percent.[147]

On February 16, 2003, about five hundred thousand Australians had joined in peace rallies to protest the prospect of war in Iraq, and polls indicated something short of a groundswell of support for Australian participation. Nevertheless, surveys during the run-up to the invasion of Iraq revealed a trend of slightly rising support for sending troops to Iraq. Four Roy Morgan polls found that support for sending troops ranged between 40 percent (September 2002) and 51 percent (March 2003), while opposition declined from 54 percent to 46 percent during the same period. At the same time a majority stated that the United Nations should have supported military action against the Saddam Hussein regime.[148] Thus, even when the issue had been rendered moot by the

145. Henry Albinski, "Australia's American Alliance in the Aftermath of September 11th, *Australian Review of Public Affairs,* October 11, 2001.
146. U.S. Department of Defense, *Operation Desert Fox,* http://www.defenselink.mil/specials/desert_fox/; and Roy Morgan Research, *Majority of Australians Approve Sending Troops to Gulf If America Launches Military Action against Iraq,* finding no. 3057, February 24, 1998.
147. NewsPoll, February 2, March 2, and March 16, 2003.
148. Roy Morgan Research, *Australians Approve Action against Iraq: Believe UN Should Have Supported Military Action,* finding no. 3616, special poll published March 27, 2003.

invasion, many Australians still yearned for legitimation of the invasion from the UN.

Public enthusiasm for the Australian military presence in Iraq declined somewhat during the year following the capture of Baghdad as a growing insurgency gave lie to optimistic U.S. expectations that relative calm and security would prevail in the post-Saddam era. As early as July 2003, two-thirds of those taking part in a NewsPoll survey asserted that the U.S. government "misled the Australian public about whether Iraq had weapons of mass destruction," and a majority of those believed that it did so "knowingly."[149] Shortly after the initial phase of the Iraq war, ending with the fall of Baghdad, Australia withdrew most of its combat forces. Surveys in February, May, and December 2004 showed a steady decline (46 percent, 40 percent, and 32 percent) in respondents who agreed that "it was worth going to war in Iraq." Moreover, the December 2004 survey revealed the wide partisan differences in responses. Whereas half of the governing L-NP members judged that the war was worth it, only 21 percent of the opposition Australian Labor Party members gave the same response.[150]

Other surveys corroborated a sense of dissatisfaction with U.S. policy in Iraq. When asked, "If the new Iraqi Government asked us to stay in Iraq, should we continue to have a military presence in Iraq or not," respondents agreed to the Australian presence in Iraq by a margin of 63 to 28 percent. When the question was if "the UN asked us to stay in Iraq," support rose to 84 percent, but when asked if "the US asked us to stay in Iraq," support for an Australian presence in Iraq fell to only 30 percent.[151] It is also worth noting that the question about the UN brought forth strong support from members of all political parties, whereas that on the United States gave rise to strong partisan divisions.

The October 2004 election provided at least a partial test of support for the Howard government's Iraq policy. Despite growing misgivings about events in Iraq and Australian participation in that conflict, John Howard led the L-NP to its fourth consecutive electoral victory. A Roy Morgan study prior to the election provided a fairly clear answer to this seeming anomaly. When given a list of eleven issues and asked to state the three most important issues in their electoral decision, "defense and national security" (21 percent) ranked in seventh place, well behind health services and hospitals (63 percent), education (34 percent), crime/law and order (33 percent), and reducing taxes (30 percent). Simi-

---

149. NewsPoll, July 18–20, 2003.
150. NewsPoll, February 8, May 2, and December 19, 2004.
151. Roy Morgan Research, *Our Troops Should Stay in Iraq until Job Done but Not at USA Request,* finding no. 3726, April 2, 2004.

lar priorities emerged from a postelection survey undertaken by NewsPoll.[152] In addition, some voters may have feared electing a leader who might alienate Washington by his opposition to U.S. policies. ALP leader Mark Latham had made it clear that if his party won the election, he would bring home the Australian troops by Christmas. Half of those taking part in a preelection survey expressed the fear that if the ALP won the election, it would damage relations with the United States. In the light of its electoral triumph, the Howard government felt free to reverse a campaign promise, increasing the size of the Australian contingent in Iraq by 450 combat troops shortly after the election. Howard did not mention the United States, stating that the additional troops were being sent at the request of Japan and Great Britain.[153]

Although Australian casualties in Iraq have been almost miraculously low through 2006—one pilot who flew with the British Royal Air Force and two media personnel covering the war—public support has continued to decline. Three Roy Morgan polls undertaken in April 2004, 2005, and 2006 are revealing. When Australians were asked whether they favor a military presence in Iraq, or bringing the troops home, the former option was favored in 2004 by a margin of 50 percent to 46 percent. Those preferring to keep troops in Iraq fell to 44 percent and 32 percent in the 2005 and 2006 surveys, whereas the "bring them home" option rose to 53 percent in 2005 and to 63 percent in 2006.[154] According to Newspoll, in October 2006 only 22 percent of Australians felt that it was worth going to war in Iraq, down from 46 percent two-and-half years earlier. A Lowy survey the same month found strong doubts about two of America's goals in Iraq: 67 percent doubted that the war would spread democracy, and 84 percent felt that it would not reduce the threat of terrorism.[155]

By any standards, Australia has been a staunch ally of the United States during the turbulent years since the September 11 terrorist attacks. Its deployment of military forces to Afghanistan received—and continues to receive—strong public support, largely because that campaign is perceived as a direct contribution against terrorist organizations. Although Australia has not suffered a direct terrorist attack, the 2002 bombing in nearby Bali, Indonesia, in which eighty-

152. Roy Morgan Research, *Health and Education Still Top Issues*, April 14, 2004; and NewsPoll, February 2005.
153. Raymond Bonner, "Australia Will Send More Troops to Iraq," *New York Times*, February 23, 2005. For a summary of foreign personnel and financial contributions in postwar Iraq, see Jeremy M. Sharp and Christopher M. Blanchard, *Post-War Iraq: Foreign Contributions to Training, Peacekeeping, and Reconstruction*, Congressional Research Service Report, RL32105, Washington, DC, July 7, 2006.
154. http://www.world.publicopinion.org/incl/printable_version.php?pnt196.
155. "Fewer Australians Believe Iraq War Is Worthy, Opinion Poll," Xinhua General News Service, October 31, 2006; and Malcolm Farr, "Most of Us Think War's Futile: Poll," *Daily Telegraph*, October 3, 2006.

eight Australians perished, and the July 2005 bombings in London have under-scored the international nature of threats from al Qaeda and similar organizations.

Many Australians have drawn a sharp distinction between the invasions of Afghanistan and Iraq. The latter undertaking has divided Australians, in part because a majority had asserted that any action against Iraq should be contingent upon approval of the UN Security Council. The Pew Research Center included Australia in its major "Global Attitudes" survey in the weeks following the capture of Baghdad in April 2003. In many respects that was the high point of the Iraq campaign, as the hated Saddam Hussein regime had been driven from power and casualties suffered by the U.S.-led coalition forces were much lower than many had feared. Indeed, Australian forces escaped without any battle deaths. At that point, 59 percent of Australians agreed that their government had made "the right decision" in taking part (table 2.14), two-thirds supported the U.S. war on terrorists (table 2.11), and 61 percent felt that the coalition forces had done enough to avoid civilian casualties during the conflict (table 2.16). Yet even at the moment of seeming victory, there was some disquiet about whether the interests of the Iraqi people were being adequately taken into account (table 2.18) and whether the volatile Middle East region had been rendered more stable as a consequence of the war (table 2.20).

Almost two years later the Lowy Institute undertook a major survey on Australian foreign policy that included a number of issues concerning the United States.[156] The good news is that more than seven in ten respondents supported the ANZUS alliance, but in other respects the results revealed that public support for the United States and its policies had eroded sharply since mid-2003. Even the executive director of Lowy, Allan Gyngell said, "I have to say that the results of the survey have jolted some of my assumptions."[157] The John Howard L-NP government had closely tied its policies to the United States, and he was once derisively described as "Washington's deputy sheriff in the region." The L-NP had been reelected only months earlier, but the Lowy survey suggested that it was despite rather than because of its foreign policies. The survey asked Australians if they had positive or negative feelings about fifteen countries and regions in the world, and the United States (58 percent positive) ranked eleventh, far behind the United Kingdom (86 percent), Europe (85 percent), Japan (84 percent), China (69 percent), France (66 percent), and the

156. Ivan Cook, *Australians Speak 2005: Public Opinion and Foreign Policy* (Sydney: Lowy Institute for International Policy, 2005).
157. Raymond Bonner, "U.S. Image Sags in Australian Poll," *New York Times*, March 29, 2005.

United Nations (65 percent), and ahead of only Indonesia, the Middle East, Iran, and Iraq.

More specific questions yielded at least partial explanations for these results. When asked, "Thinking of how much notice Australia takes of the views of the United States in our foreign policy, on the whole do you think we take too much, too little, or the right amount of notice," 68 of the respondents chose too much, 2 percent too little, and 29 percent the right amount. When Australians were asked a similar question about the United Nations, the results were strikingly different: 14 percent chose too much, 33 percent too little, and 48 percent the right amount. It is worth recalling, in this respect, that even in mid-2003, at the moment of military triumph in Iraq, only 8 percent of Australians believed that Washington pays much attention to their country's vital interests (table 2.8).

Still another Lowy question asked respondents to state how worried they are about several "potential threats from the outside world." That nuclear proliferation, global warming, international terrorism, and international epidemics led the list is hardly surprising, but these perceived threats were followed by "Islamic fundamentalism" and "U.S. foreign policies"; the latter two were each cited by 57 percent of respondents as causing them to be "very worried" or "fairly worried." The looming superpower of the region—China—was similarly cited by only 35 percent of those taking part in the survey.

Finally, the Lowy study asked for judgments about the Australia–United States Free Trade Agreement that had gone into effect at the beginning of 2005, as well as about preliminary negotiations on a similar agreement with China. The AUSFTA divided the public into three almost equal parts: good for Australia (34 percent), bad (32 percent), and no difference/unsure (34 percent). Responses on a proposed trade agreement with China were somewhat more favorable: good (51 percent), bad (20 percent), and no difference/unsure (29 percent). One reason for the lukewarm response to AUSFTA may have been its unequal terms. It opens Australian markets to 99 percent of American exports, but it continues to protect U.S. markets in several categories, by retaining bans of Australian fast ferries; limits on sugar, dairy, and beef products; and exclusion of most textiles.[158]

The Australian government has called for elections in December in 2007. Prime Minister Howard and opposition leader Kevin Rudd have taken diametrically opposing views on Iraq. If victorious, the latter pledged to withdraw all

---

158. Tim Colebatch, "Why Latham Should Reject the FTA," *Age,* July 20, 2004.

Australian forces from Iraq, reflecting the views of 70 percent who told a Newspoll survey in late 2006 that the war was not worth fighting. In contrast, Howard has reiterated his strong support for the United States, asserting, "If America is defeated in Iraq, it is hard to see how the longer-term fight against terrorism can be won. We were right to go into Iraq, and we would be wrong to get out of it." Although Australia increased its forces in Afghanistan, Howard insisted that he would not increase its commitment of 1,400 troops in Iraq, nor would he redeploy them to Baghdad.[159] When asked in a February 2007 survey, "Do you think we should continue to fight in Iraq or bring our forces back to Australia," a margin of 64 percent to 29 percent preferred the latter option.[160] President Bush, in Australia for the Asia Pacific Economic Cooperation meeting in September 2007, met with Howard and Rudd, who publicly and privately reiterated their positions on the future of Australian troops in Iraq. Howard and his party suffered a major defeat in the election; Howard even lost his own seat. But Rudd's victory was not solely the result of his position on Iraq. Such domestic issues as pensions were important in the views of many voters.

As noted at the outset, the United States and Australia have a long history of close ties and cooperation, especially on crucial issues of war and peace. Though the Australian population of some twenty-two million is dwarfed by those of its major regional neighbors—notably China, India, Japan, and Indonesia—there are compelling reasons why the United States should pay careful attention to the state of its relations with Canberra. The Iraq war, now widely acknowledged to be a disaster even by some of its erstwhile cheerleaders in Washington, has clearly taken a severe toll on how many in Australia view the United States and its policies. Continued support for the ANZUS pact should reassure the United States, and Prime Minister Howard has made it clear that his government stands firmly with Washington because of "the need to maintain the common fight against people who are enemies, not just of Australia and Britain and the United States, but they are the enemies of all civilizations."[161] Moreover, most Australians would no doubt agree with the view expressed shortly after the invasion of Iraq: "Who would I rather stand with in a

---

159. Paul Starick, "Surge into Iraq Could Spell Trouble for Libs," *Advertiser* (Australia), January 10, 2007; Ben Ruse, "Words Not Backed by Action," *West Australian*, January 12, 2007; and Raphael Minder, "Australia May Double Troops in Afghanistan," *Financial Times*, February 22, 2007.
160. Roy Morgan International survey, February 14–15, 2007, http://www.roymorgan.com/news/polls/2007/4140.
161. Jason Koutsoukis, "Common Fight to Dominate PM Talks with Allies, *New Age*, July 11, 2005.

time of crisis—Asia or the U.S.? Definitely the U.S."[162] And yet, in other respects the declining level of Australian public approval for this country is a cause for concern that Washington would be well advised not to ignore. When fast-growing but highly authoritarian China is viewed more favorably than the United States, there is surely no place for complacency.

MOROCCO

America's relations with Morocco extend back to the earliest days of the republic. Morocco was the first country to recognize the independence of the thirteen breakaway American colonies, doing so within a year of the signing of the Declaration of Independence in 1776. In 1787 the two countries entered into a Treaty of Peace and Friendship that, though renegotiated in 1836, continues in force today, and it constitutes the longest unbroken treaty relationship in U.S. history. The 1906 Algeciras international conference reaffirmed Morocco's independence, but six years later the Treaty of Fez brought Morocco under French control. During World War II Franklin D. Roosevelt urged France to grant Morocco independence. When it failed to do so, the Istiqlal independence movement initiated open warfare. After imposing a ruler who was widely deemed illegitimate, in 1955 France allowed the respected Sultan Muhammed V to return from exile, and on March 2, 1956, the "Celle-Saint Cloud" agreement granted independence to the Kingdom of Morocco. Five weeks later, Morocco signed an agreement with Spain, ending that country's protectorate over Moroccan northern provinces. On April 22, 1956, Morocco joined the United Nations. Although the run-up to its independence was not free of conflict, Morocco achieved it without having to suffer the tragic experience of its neighbor Algeria—a long, brutal, and ultimately failed French effort to maintain control.

The population of some thirty-three million in Morocco is overwhelmingly—over 98 percent—Muslim. When asked whether they consider themselves national citizens or Muslim first, respondents chose the latter response by a wide margin of 70 percent to 7 percent.[163] Nevertheless, Morocco has been relatively free of religious tensions that have characterized some of its neighbors in North Africa and the Middle East. The tiny Jewish community has not suffered as a result of overwhelming public opposition to Israel's policies, and some Jews—including senior economic policymaker Andre Azoulay—have ac-

162. Reader response to "Is Australia's Relationship with the United States a Help or Hindrance?" *New Age*, April 4, 2003.
163. Pew Research Center, *U.S. Image Up Slightly, but Still Negative.*

tually served as advisers to the king. That said, few Moroccans hold favorable views of either Christians (38 percent) or Jews (8 percent).[164]

The Kingdom of Morocco is a constitutional monarchy that enjoys some of the trappings of a democracy. Under the most recent (1996) constitution, a bicameral parliament is popularly elected with multiple parties vying for seats. The 2002 election to Chamber of Representatives was the "first free, fair and transparent election ever held in Morocco."[165] The state monopoly on the media ended in 2003 and the press enjoys some freedom,[166] but the king can dismiss the prime minister, dissolve parliament and call for new elections, or rule by decree. He is also head of the armed forces and is the "Commander of the Faithful," the country's religious leader. Thus, there is little doubt that he is "the decider."

Despite some policy differences—over serious human rights violations, the Palestinian issue, the Iraq war, and the continuing and unresolved Moroccan claims of control over Western Sahara, a former Spanish colony—relations between Washington and Rabat have generally been quite cordial. The Peace Corps has operated in Morocco since 1963, and currently there are almost two hundred PC volunteers working there. A 1982 accord granted the United States the right to establish air bases in Morocco in crises. After Iraq's invasion of Kuwait in 1990, King Hassan II joined the UN-sanctioned and U.S.-led Gulf War coalition against Iraq. Despite widespread public support for Iraq, including a huge demonstration in support of Saddam Hussein, he nevertheless dispatched Moroccan troops to help defend Saudi Arabia.

King Hassan sent Moroccan troops to the Sinai front in the 1973 Arab-Israeli War, but following the "Declaration of Principles" between Israel and the Palestine Liberation Organization, he invited Israeli prime minister Yitzhak Rabin to visit Morocco in September 1993.

Hassan II died in 1999 and was succeeded by his son and present ruler, King Muhammed VI, who has used his extensive powers to enact a number of major domestic reforms on such questions as family law and the rights of women. Women constitute about one-third of judges, teachers, and doctors.[167] He has also been somewhat willing to confront in a limited way the many human rights abuses during his father's reign, although the perpetrators have not been

---

164. Ibid.
165. Carol Migdalovitz, "Morocco: Current Issues," Congressional Research Service, May 4, 2006, 1.
166. But not without significant limits, as journalists who published an article, "How Moroccans Laugh at Religion, Sex and Politics," have discovered. "Morocco: 2 Journalists on Trial for Others' Jokes," *New York Times*, January 9, 2007; and Laila Lalami, "Censorship's New Clothes," *New York Times*, February 3, 2007.
167. C. R. Pennel, *Morocco: From Empire to Independence* (Oxford: One World Press, 2003), 176.

brought to justice.[168] In 1999 and 2003 he freed about 17,000 prisoners and re-duced the sentences of some 68,000 others, and 8,862 were pardoned in 2007 to celebrate the birth of his second child.[169]

While maintaining a pro-Western foreign policy, some significant policy differences have roiled relations between Rabat and Washington in recent years. U.S. support for Security Council Resolution 1495 on the future of Western Sahara, developed by former secretary of state James Baker, was widely viewed in Morocco as favoring the Algerian position on the issue. The *Economist* newspaper expressed a typical view: "The public opinion is disappointed. U.S. popularity is at its lowest level. . . . Washington is ungrateful today; it turns a blind eye to 40 years of commitment with the Western bloc at the time of the cold war and the first Gulf war."[170] A proposed UN referendum has repeatedly been postponed. King Muhammed VI has proposed a reasonable plan whereby Western Sahara would enjoy autonomous status under Moroccan sovereignty, but it faces an uphill battle in gaining widespread international support.[171]

Morocco also opposed the U.S.-led invasion of Afghanistan, and Muhammed VI refused to join the "coalition of the willing" for the invasion of Iraq in March 2003. Widespread demonstrations, including one hundred thousand who took part in an antiwar protest in Rabat a month before the invasion, as well as some polling data indicated overwhelming public opposition to the war against Iraq, but the extent, if any, to which the king's decision reflected the need to align his policies to public opinion is far from clear.

In the light of its generally Western-leaning foreign policies and moderate domestic policies, it is not surprising that radical Islamic terrorist groups have been active in Morocco.[172] On May 16, 2003, shortly after the fall of Baghdad, Casablanca was wracked by bombings that killed forty-five, including thirteen suicide bombers, by an Islamic movement, the Ansar al-Mahdi group. The government arrested thousands of Islamists and claimed to have uncovered some terrorist cells linked to al Qaeda. Three months earlier Osama bin Laden de-

---

168. "Morocco Confronts Rights Abuses in Its Past, but Not the Abusers," *New York Times*, December 26, 2004; and Neil MacFarquhar, "In Morocco, a Rights Movement, at the King's Pace," *New York Times*, October 1, 2005.
169. Library of Congress, "Morocco," May 4, 2006, 6; and "Morocco Pardons Nearly 9,000 Prisoners," *New York Times*, March 2, 2007.
170. "Moroccan Paper Criticizes U.S., Spain Positions in Security Council over Sahara," *Morocco-USA, Politics*, August 6, 2003, http://www.arabicnews.com. For a fuller discussion, see Carol Migdalovitz, "Western Sahara: Status of Settlement Efforts," Congressional Research Service, September 29, 2006.
171. Frederick Vreeland, "Will Freedom Bloom in the Desert?" *New York Times*, March 3, 2007.
172. Thomas Omestad, "The Casbah Connection," *U.S. News and World Report*, May 9, 2005.

scribed Morocco as having an "oppressive, unjust, apostate ruling government," and thus was "most eligible for liberation."[173] Following the Madrid bombings in March 2004, Spanish authorities arrested sixty suspects, including forty Moroccan immigrants. The government has continued to play an active role in dealing with terrorism, including the arrest in September 2006 of fifty-six al Qaeda suspects.[174]

Data presented in chapters 2 and 3 provide an overview of how Moroccans have viewed the United States during the past few years.[175] After an overwhelming (77 percent) favorable judgment at the turn of the century, subsequent surveys reveal a precipitous decline coinciding with the Iraq war (table 2.1) and, interestingly, something of a revival in support in 2005, when almost half of those surveyed expressed a positive view of the United States, but that support fell to an abysmal 15 percent in 2007. Few Moroccans believe that Washington pays much attention to their country's vital interests (table 2.8), but following the terrorist bombing in May 2003, strong opposition to the U.S. war on terrorism has declined somewhat in 2004, only to fall precipitously three years later (table 2.11). The invasion of Iraq was judged to hurt rather than help in that effort (table 2.21). Morocco's decision not to join the "coalition of the willing" against Iraq received overwhelming public support (table 2.14). As a result of the Iraq war, most Moroccans taking part in Pew surveys asserted that the needs of the Iraqi people have been neglected during the postwar era (table 2.18), the United States is less trustworthy and less sincere in promoting democracy (table 2.19), and the Middle East region is less stable (table 2.20).

When asked about America's motives for invading Iraq, Moroccans chose responses that were rather different from those announced by Washington (Saddam Hussein's alleged weapons of mass destruction and ties to the al Qaeda perpetrators of the September 11 terrorist attacks). In the eyes of many Moroccans, the United States acted to control Mideast oil (63 percent), to dominate the world (60 percent), to protect Israel (54 percent), and to target unfriendly Muslim governments (46 percent). Interestingly, these judgments about American policy were almost identical to those in another Muslim coun-

---

173. "Moroccans Say Al Qaeda Masterminded and Financed Casablanca Suicide Bombings," *New York Times,* May 23, 2003, quoted in Migdalovitz, "Morocco," 2.

174. Associated Press, "17 in Terror Ring Arrested, Morocco Says," *New York Times,* November 21, 2005; and Craig S. Smith, "Moroccan Terror Plot Foiled with 56 Arrests, Officials Say, *New York Times,* September 7, 2006.

175. The Pew surveys in Morocco were conducted in urban areas only.

try with which the United States has also generally maintained good relations—Turkey.[176]

The events of 2003–4, notably the Iraq war, clearly coincided with increasingly critical views of the United States and its foreign policies, but many of those taking part in these surveys also expressed favorable opinions about important aspects of American life and society. They were initially far less critical of "Americans" than of the United States (table 3.1) but by 2007 Moroccans were less supportive. The same pattern appeared on American ideas of democracy (table 3.5). Their admiration of science and technology persisted (table 3.7), and, on balance, they also liked the American ways of doing business (table 3.9). Unlike publics in some predominantly Muslim countries, Moroccans on balance favored such American entertainment products as movies, television, and music in 2003, but since then their opinions have changed for the worse (table 3.8). Although they were decidedly unenthusiastic about Americanization of Morocco (table 3.10), many of them agreed that those who emigrated to America enjoyed a better quality of life (table 3.12).

Surveys other than those summarized in chapters 2 and 3 confirm that Moroccans held the United States in low esteem during the period surrounding the Iraq war. Zogby surveys revealed that favorable attitudes about America in 2002 (38 percent) declined by more than two-thirds to 11 percent two years later.[177] A survey conducted by Shibley Telhami in the weeks prior to the invasion of Iraq unearthed very similar findings. Only 6 percent of Moroccans viewed the United States favorably, and they predicted that a war with Iraq would increase terrorism (87 percent), while contributing little to peace (1 percent) or democracy (2 percent) in the Middle East.[178]

The sources of anti-American attitudes emerge very clearly from the 2004 Zogby survey (table 4.3). Moroccans taking part in the study expressed consistently favorable views about the American people, science and technology, freedom and democracy, movies and television, products, and education. The results also provide a comparison of Moroccan opinions with those of its neighbors in the Middle East–North African region. In most respects Moroccans' views of American values, institutions, and products are more favorable, especially when compared to those of publics in Saudi Arabia and Lebanon. But when respondents were asked about American policies toward Arabs and

---

176. Pew Research Center, *A Year after Iraq War.*
177. Zogby International, *Impressions of America, 2004,* tables 1, 3a, 3b, 3c, 4a, and 4b.
178. Shibley Telhami, "Arab Public Opinion on the United States and Iraq," *Brookings Review* 21 (summer 2003): 24–27.

Palestinians and the issues of terrorism and Iraq, the similarities across the five countries far outweigh the minor differences between them. In a word, very few respondents in any of the countries polled by Zogby had a favorable judgment about any aspect of American policy on some of the major issues in the region.[179] In the case of Morocco, neither age nor gender differences were significant. For example, only 1 percent of men and a like number of women supported American policy in Iraq. In a March 2007 World Public Opinion survey, 78 percent of Moroccans stated that Washington seeks to divide and weaken the Islamic world. These assessments provide scant support for the thesis, propounded by a number of analysts who have pondered the declining support abroad for this country, that most countries of the world oppose America because it is the premier and most successful exemplar of modernity and they would do so irrespective of Washington's foreign policy actions.

Although the survey data provide ample evidence that Moroccans are critical of the United States in many respects, there were also some interesting indications of some improvement in 2005 (table 2.1), a period that witnessed few U.S. successes in Iraq and Afghanistan and little progress in dealing with the Palestinian issue, before another sharp decline two years later. Why, then, were

TABLE 4.3. Arab Attitudes toward U.S. Values, Products, and Policies, 2004

	Percent Favorable				
	Morocco	Saudi Arabia	Jordan	Lebanon	UAE[a]
Science/technology	90	48	83	52	84
Freedom/democracy	53	39	57	41	39
American people	59	28	52	39	46
Movies/television	60	35	56	30	54
Products	73	37	61	39	63
Education	61	12	59	38	63
Policy toward					
Arabs	4	4	8	5	7
Palestinians	3	3	7	4	5
Terrorism	13	2	21	10	9
Iraq	1	1	2	4	4

Source: Zogby International, *Impressions of America*, 2004, 3.

Note: Although Egypt was also included in this six-nation study, responses to this item are not included. On most other items, Egyptian responses were more critical of the United States than those of the other five countries.

[a]United Arab Emirates.

---

179. Zogby International, *Impressions of America*, 2004, tables 1, 3a, 3b, 3c, 4a, and 4b.

there a few signs of at least a temporary ebbing of anti-American sentiments in Morocco?

Several possible explanations come to mind. King Muhammed VI, whose role in Moroccan politics is crucial, has enacted moderate domestic reforms that are more in line with Western and U.S. values than those espoused by Islamic fundamentalists, especially with respect to women's rights. Such features of Moroccan society as bars, unveiled women, mixed-gender beaches, and reforms in family law dealing with divorce, child custody, the minimum age of marriage for women, and polygamy are anathema to some Muslims. Indeed, they precipitated a protest rally of some five hundred thousand in March 2000. According to one hypothesis, the "true clash of civilizations" revolves around competing conceptions of the proper role of women.[180] To the extent that this is a valid diagnosis of international cleavages, the king's policies would appear to place Morocco on the Western side. This is not to say, however, that there are no challenges to such reforms. The Islamic Party for Justice and Development (PJD), the only legal Islamist party, tripled its representation by capturing forty-two seats in the 2002 parliamentary elections. Because the Ministry of Interior discouraged it from running in all electoral districts, these results probably understate the PJD's strength.[181] In the 2007 elections, marred by a record low turnout of 37 percent, the PJD won 46 seats, finishing just behind the Istiqlal part of the ruling coalition. According to its parliamentary leader, Mustapha Ramid, "part of society is coming back to Islamic values, some in moderation, some with extremism."[182]

A second possible explanation centers on the threat of terrorism. Although there has been no repeat of the Casablanca bombings, Moroccans have been implicated in several other bombings, including the 2004 attack on trains in Madrid that killed 191 and injured 1,400. Whereas a 2004 Pew survey found that only 38 percent of Moroccans asserted that violence against civilian targets in defense of Islam is "never" justified, that figure rose sharply to 79 percent only a year later. Support for the proposition that suicide attacks in Iraq are often or sometimes justified fell to a still disturbing high of 56 percent. Confidence in Osama bin Laden "to do the right thing in world affairs" also declined sharply, from 49 percent in 2003 to 26 percent in 2005.[183]

Moreover, when asked about threats to their country, 60 percent of respon-

180. Ronald Inglehart and Pippa Norris, "The True Clash of Civilizations," *Foreign Policy* (March/April 2003): 62–70.
181. Migdalovitz, "Morocco," 1.
182. Omestad, "The Casbah Connection."
183. Pew Research Center, *Image Up Slightly, but Still Negative.* The survey was completed before the London bombings in July 2005.

dents replied that "Islamic extremism" is a "very great" threat, and another 13 percent characterized it as a "fairly great" threat. To put these figures into context, responses in other Muslim countries provide some basis for comparison: the "very great" threat option was selected far less frequently in Pakistan (28 percent), Turkey (22 percent), Indonesia (15 percent), Lebanon (9 percent), and Jordan (2 percent). A follow-up question asked about the sources of Islamic extremism. Moroccan respondents looked inward, identifying poverty and lack of jobs (39 percent) and lack of education (18 percent), whereas publics in some other countries, notably Jordan and Lebanon, cited U.S. policies and influence as the roots of extremism. Thus, while severe doubts persist about the effectiveness of what Washington calls its "global war on terror," many Moroccans apparently have had second thoughts about violence, suicide bombings, and the role of Islamic extremists.

U.S. policy would also appear to deserve some credit for at least a temporary softening of several aspects of anti-American sentiments. Part of it lies in what Washington did *not* do. Even when Morocco declined to join the invasion of Iraq, officials in Washington refrained from the kinds of sophomoric jibes that had been directed at Germany, France, Belgium, Turkey, and other allies who had expressed doubts about American intentions during the run-up to the invasion, and who ultimately chose not to follow the United States into Baghdad. Nor did they indulge in such actions as canceling the Cinco de Mayo reception in Mexico to express displeasure at Mexico's failure in the UN Security Council to support military action against Iraq. Apparently at least some administration officials understood that undermining a moderate Islamic leader in a politically sensitive region over differences about Iraq would serve the national interests of neither country.

In addition, the United States undertook several initiatives that were intended to send a clear signal that, despite policy differences on Iraq, Washington recognized and appreciated the history of generally cooperative relations between the two countries.

On the eve of its invasion of Iraq, the Bush administration proposed a bilateral free trade agreement (FTA) with Morocco, the first such pact with an African country. Negotiations ended about a year later. The U.S. Congress approved the agreement, which covers about 95 percent of industrial and consumer goods, in 2004, and the Moroccan parliament followed suit in January 2005.[184] The overall level of trade between the two countries is relatively mod-

---

184. For a fuller discussion, see Raymond J. Ahearn, "Morocco-U.S. Free Trade Agreement," *Congressional Research Service*, May 26, 2005.

est—about $500 million of U.S. imports and an equal volume of exports—and it is only a small fraction of Morocco's trade with France and Spain. Thus, for the immediate future the symbolic importance of the agreement outstrips its economic significance, except in one important respect. The FTA, which went into effect in 2006, opens Moroccan markets to highly subsidized American agricultural products. Although agriculture constitutes about 15 percent of Morocco's GDP, it accounts for 44 percent of the labor force. About one hundred thousand Moroccans engaged in an unauthorized protest against the FTA. The Rabat government was able to gain at least a temporary exemption for wheat, but other agricultural sectors may fare less well. One danger is that if the FTA undermines local agriculture, it would accelerate migration to cities and to Europe.[185]

In addition to the FTA, in 2004 President Bush designated Morocco as a "major non-NATO ally," a category that includes Australia, Israel, and several other countries. In addition to its symbolic value, countries with that status are able to purchase and stockpile American arms more easily.[186] The United States also gained access to Moroccan military ports and bases in exchange for foreign military aid.

Finally, although Morocco has received rather modest amounts of foreign aid, especially when compared to Egypt, the figure in 2005 ($28.5 million) represented a substantial increase from the previous year. Moreover, Morocco was designated as a beneficiary of the U.S. Millennium Account Program in recognition of its political, economic, and educational reforms.[187]

Critics might dismiss these American actions as largely symbolic, but that misses the point that symbolic actions can be an important tool in the diplomatic repertoire. In the light of Morocco's refusal to join the "coalition of the willing" in Iraq, they represent a useful exception to President Bush's dictum "you are with us or you are with the terrorists."

America's reputation among Moroccans has clearly taken a big hit since the days that the State Department survey found approval from 77 percent of respondents. U.S. policies on Morocco's claim to Western Sahara, the Palestinian issue, and the war in Iraq have contributed to the sharp decline in public support. Yet the situation seems less ominous than that in another moderate Is-

185. Khatoun Hadar, "Moroccans Unsettled by Free Trade Deal with U.S.," *Daily Star* (Beirut), March 18, 2004, http://www.bilaterals.org (posted April 24, 2004); and Gregory W. White, "Trade as a Strategic Instrument in the War on Terror? The 2004 US-Moroccan Free Trade Agreement," *Middle East Journal* 59 (autumn 2005): 597–616.
186. Economist, *Pocket World in Figures;* "U.S. Rewards Morocco for Terror Aid," BBC News, June 4, 2004, http://news.bbc.co.uk/2/hi/africa/3776413.stm; and "Major Non-NATO Ally (MNNA) Status," Center for International Policy, http://ciponline.org/facts/mnna.htm.
187. Library of Congress, Federal Research Division, "Country Profile: Morocco," May 2006, 13.

lamic country—Turkey. Unlike Turkey, Morocco has the luxury of geographic separation from Iraq, and it does not have a separatist group such as the Kurds whose future may hinge at least in part on the ultimate outcome of American efforts to cope with the deepening civil war in Iraq. But American policy has also contributed at least in part to the differences in how Moroccans and Turks view the United States. In its dealings with Rabat, Washington has avoided the ham-handed blunders that have contributed so deeply to Turkish disenchantment with the United States.

SOUTH KOREA

The early history of Korean-American relations provides a good deal of ammunition for Korean nationalists who harbor deep doubts about reliance on Washington to support and sustain their vital national interests.[188] Following the example of Commodore Matthew Perry's "opening" of Japan to foreign penetration and the Treaty of Kanagawa in 1854, an initial effort to open Korea was a debacle that resulted in sinking of the U.S. ship *General Sherman*. The two countries eventually entered into diplomatic relations in 1882, during a period when Russia, Japan, and China vied for influence and trade access to what had been called "the Hermit Kingdom." Japan's victories in wars with China (1894–95) and Russia (1904–5) established that country as the dominant power in East Asia. The U.S.-brokered Treaty of Portsmouth in 1905 ending the Russo-Japanese War dashed the hopes of Koreans demanding independence, in part owing to President Theodore Roosevelt's contempt for Korea. The Taft-Katsura Agreement in 1905 essentially acknowledged the primacy of Japanese interests in Korea in exchange for recognition of American primacy in the Philippines. Korea was annexed five years later by Japan, which ruled it with exceptional brutality until Japan's defeat in 1945.

President Woodrow Wilson's "Fourteen Points" for a postwar settlement included not only a proposal for establishing a general international organization but also for self-determination for Poland and for peoples living in the German and Ottoman empires. He failed to mention restoration of Korea's independence, and the Versailles settlement left Korea under Japan's control, in part because Japan had joined the war on the side of the victorious Allies.

---

188. Among many other sources, I have relied on good brief summaries in Edward A. Olson, "Korea," in *Encyclopedia of U.S. Foreign Relations*, 3:23–28; and Eric V. Larson, Norman D. Levin, Seonhae Baik, and Bogdan Savych, *Ambivalent Allies: A Study of South Korean Attitudes toward the U.S.* (Santa Monica, CA: RAND Corporation, 2004), chap. 2.

The Cairo Conference of allied leaders during World War II addressed the future of the German, Italian, and Japanese empires. Korea was mentioned with a vague promise of independence "in due course." The Yalta Conference, the last wartime meeting of Roosevelt, Churchill, and Stalin, made no reference to the future of Korea.

World War II ended with Japan's surrender in August 1945. Temporary Russian and American zones of occupation were established as an administrative convenience for processing the surrender of Japanese troops in Korea. The Cold War that emerged not long after the guns of World War II had cooled left Korea divided along the 38th parallel. The Soviets controlled the northern—and at that time the more industrialized and prosperous—sector where they established the Democratic People's Republic of Korea (DPRK) in 1948 under control of a communist leader, Kim Il Sung. The southern sector was initially deemed to be of little strategic interest by military advisers to the Truman administration. UN-administered elections in 1948 in what became the Republic of Korea (ROK) brought to power the American-educated and authoritarian Syngman Rhee. Kim and Rhee both aspired to unify the countries under their control, and there were occasional skirmishes along the border, as well as clashes among various groups within the ROK. Most of the U.S. occupation forces left in 1949.

On June 25, 1950, North Korea mounted a full-scale invasion of its southern neighbor, an action that dramatically changed the nature of Korean-American relations. Although his military advisers had earlier told President Truman that "the U.S. has little strategic interest in maintaining the present troops and bases in Korea,"[189] Truman framed the issue more broadly: failure to respond to the North Korean aggression would doom the nascent United Nations, just as the world's failure to take action after the Japanese invasion of Manchuria in 1931 revealed the impotence of the League of Nations. Thus, Truman sent American air and ground forces to South Korea. Owing to a Soviet boycott of the UN, the Security Council was able to condemn the invasion and invited members to assist South Korea. During the opening weeks of the war, the North Koreans overran all but the Pusan sector on the southern tip of the peninsula. A dramatic military landing at Inchon turned the military tide in favor of the allies. Following a dubious U.S. decision to reunify the country by overrunning the DPRK, based in part on assurances by General Douglas MacArthur that China would never dare to respond militarily, China made good on its threats to in-

---

189. Quoted in Olson, "Korea," 25.

tervene. Allied forces were driven back across the 38th parallel before a successful counterattack stabilized the front near where the war had started.

More than two additional years of bitter fighting followed. The bloody war that cost the United States 142,000 casualties, of whom 54,000 were killed, ended with an armistice on July 27, 1953, leaving the dividing line between the two Koreas not far from the 38th parallel.[190] President Rhee refused to sign the armistice, and to date there has been no treaty formally ending the war.

The postwar years witnessed a number of important developments that have affected the ways in which the South Korean public has viewed the United States. A mutual defense treaty in 1954 that formally committed the United States to protect South Korea has been backed up with deployment of some thirty-seven thousand U.S. troops. Even with the subsequent redeployment of the Second Infantry Division to Iraq, substantial numbers of American troops remain in South Korea. The authoritarian Syngman Rhee was driven from power by protestors in 1960, but his successors included two military "friendly tyrants"—Park Chung Hee and Chun Doo Hwan—who were widely perceived to have American support.

Just as the North Korean invasion of June 1950 was a major turning point in U.S.-ROK relations, so suppression of the Kwangju demonstrations represented another such critical event. Park Chung Hee was assassinated by the head of the Korean CIA in 1979. General Chun Doo Hwan overthrew the interim Choi Kyu Hah government in May 1980, an action that triggered widespread opposition. Street demonstrations by protesters in Kwangju were put down over ten days by the military, with extensive loss of life. Many believed that the United States was complicit in the suppression because U.S. general John Wickham permitted twenty thousand South Korean troops under his command to take part. The validity of those charges remains controversial, although they appear to be supported by at least some documentary evidence. General Wickham asserted that the United States would support Chun if he emerged as president, and shortly thereafter President Jimmy Carter stated, "We would like to have a complete democracy in South Korea with full and open debate, free press and elected leaders. The Koreans are not ready for that, according to their own judgment, and I don't know how to explain it any bet-

---

190. These figures are from Olson, "Korea." Larson et al., *Ambivalent Allies,* cite much lower numbers of casualties (137,000) and deaths (30,000) on p. 11. Most other sources found on the Internet seem to agree that the United States suffered about 103,000 wounded and 33,000 combat deaths, plus an unknown number of noncombat deaths.

ter."[191] Such observations added credence to the view that Washington preferred to overlook its professed democratic ideals in favor of support for Chun Doo Hwan, known to be a staunch anticommunist who had served in the American war in Vietnam. That support continued under the Reagan administration. According to one observer, "The shift in emphasis [among prodemocracy South Koreans] from a struggle against a dictatorship to a struggle against the U.S. is one of the most significant developments of the 1980s and could have a far-reaching impact on U.S. interests in Northeast Asia."[192]

In 1987, demonstrators protested Chun Doo Hwan's plan to pass power to retired general Roh Tae Woo. The widespread popularity of opposition reform movements led to important democratization steps acceptable to all reformers. Thus the election of Roh Tae Woo initiated an era of democratically elected governments in Seoul.

In recent decades Korea has also undergone a dramatic economic transformation from a poor agricultural country into a major industrial power. While the DPRK has suffered economic disaster after disaster, including famines, under the repressive dynasty of Kim Il Sung and his wayward son, Kim Jong Il, the ROK enjoyed significant economic growth. During the decade starting in 1994 its annual real growth rate of 8.5 percent ranked third in the world, behind only China and Thailand; during the next decade its growth rate fell to 4.9 percent, but that was still higher than that of the United States or any member of the European Union except Estonia. Korea has become the world's eleventh-largest economy, ranking tenth in industrial output and ninth in manufacturing, and as the world's twelfth-largest exporter it is a major factor in such international markets as electronics and automobiles. As measured by the "Human Development Index," South Korea ranks twenty-eighth in the world, well ahead of Argentina, Russia, and Brazil and only slightly behind Italy, New Zealand, and Germany.[193]

Other indicators of Korea's growing international importance include hosting the 1988 Olympic Games, cohosting the 2002 World Cup with Japan, and

---

191. Quoted in Tim Shorrock, "The Struggle for Democracy in South Korea in the 1980s and the Rise of Anti-Americanism," *Third World Quarterly* 9 (October 1986), 1204.
192. Shorrock, "The Struggle for Democracy in South Korea," 1208. For similar assessments of the Kwangju prodemocracy protests and their brutal suppression, see Gweon Yong-lib, "The Changing Perception of America in South Korea: Transition or Transformation?" *Korea Journal* (spring 2004): 152–77, which argues that the events destroyed the emotional belief that the United States is a beneficial ally and the only reliable guardian of South Korea; and Hwang Jong-yon, "Rethinking Korean Views on America: Beyond the Dichotomy of Pro- and Anti-Americanism," *Korea Journal* (spring 2004): 103–8.
193. The economic figures are drawn from Economist, *Pocket World in Figures*.

the election in 2006 of Ban Ki-moon as secretary-general of the United Nations.

Some of these developments provide the context for the ways in which the Korean public has viewed the United States. The data presented in chapters 2 and 3 reveal a complex mixture of favorable and unfavorable opinions. A predominantly favorable view of the United States at the turn of the century had eroded somewhat—from 58 percent to 46 percent—by the time that Iraq became a crucial issue, but it rose back to its prewar level in 2007 (table 2.1). Questions about the American role in the world yielded a very mixed set of responses. On the one hand, the United States was judged to contribute to peace and stability in the East Asian region (table 2.5), and there was little enthusiasm for the emergence of another superpower (table 2.7). At the same time, a majority of Korean respondents came to express doubts that the United States is a positive influence in the world (table 2.3), that American military superiority contributes to a safer world (table 2.6), and that the preemptive use of force is "often" or "sometimes" justified (table 2.9). As was the case in most countries, very few Koreans believed that Washington pays a great deal of attention to the vital interests of their country (table 2.8). The U.S. effort against global terrorism was strongly opposed in three Pew surveys (table 2.11). Although Seoul decided in late 2003 to send three thousand troops into Iraq, it did so with little public support; a poll earlier that year revealed overwhelming approval for staying out of Iraq (table 2.14). Strong majorities felt that the United States and its allies did not try hard enough to avoid civilian casualties in Iraq (table 2.16), criticized by a margin of more than eight to one the lack of attention to the needs and interests of Iraqis during the postwar reconstruction period (table 2.18), and concluded narrowly that the Iraq war had left the Middle East region less rather than more stable (table 2.20).

When questions turned from foreign policy to American values and institutions, Koreans found a good deal more to their liking. Their views of the American people have consistently been very favorable and actually increased after the invasion of Iraq (table 3.1). Although Koreans were less sure that America is "a beacon of hope and opportunity," or "a force for good in the world" (table 3.2), various questions about American society and its institutions revealed that although an overwhelming majority of Koreans described America as "arrogant" rather than "humble," there were many qualities to admire (table 3.4), including ideas about democracy (table 3.5), science and technology (table 3.7), entertainment products (table 3.8), and ways of doing business (table 3.9). There was a split verdict on whether Americans are sufficiently religious (tables 3.4 and 3.6). The prospect of American ideas and customs spreading to Korea (table 3.10) elicited tepid enthusiasm, in part for reasons summarized in table 3.11. Finally, when asked to identify the sources of differences between their country and the United States, a majority of Koreans pointed to policies rather than values (table 3.13).

By any standards the transformation of South Korea from a despised and brutalized Japanese colony into an electoral democracy and major industrial power ranks as one of the great success stories of the late twentieth century. Those achievements, compared to the appalling economic and human rights situation in North Korea, confirm the wisdom of the decision of the United States and its fifteen allies to repel the North Korean invasion in June 1950.

That success has also transformed the U.S.-South Korean relationship to the point that the South Korean public and policymakers in Seoul have become more assertive in identifying and pursuing some interests in ways that do not always conform to preferences in Washington. This is not the place to undertake a detailed discussion of relations between the two countries during the past two decades, but it may be useful to identify a few issues—relations with North Korea, South Korean self-identification and status, trade, and the Iraq war—that may have contributed to public opinion about the United States and the possible policy consequences of those views.

The disintegration of the Soviet Union, Pyongyang's patron, transformed the balance of power between the two Koreas. To greatly oversimplify a complex situation, for many South Koreans the perceived threat from their northern neighbor has greatly diminished, even to the point that it was possible for some to think about an eventual peaceful reunification of the two countries. However, North Korea's actions have regularly thrown cold water on such hopes and have seemed directed at driving wedges between Seoul and Washington. It undertook several tests of its missile program in 1993, 1998, and 2006, and North Korea's bellicose rhetoric—for example, the threat to turn South Korea into a "sea of fire"—did little to encourage those who favored diplomatic engagement with Pyongyang. It participated in various sets of unproductive talks on its nuclear program, it withdrew from the Nuclear Nonproliferation Treaty, and, in 2006, it tested a small nuclear bomb, an action that led the UN Security Council to impose sanctions that may—or may not—cause Pyongyang to rethink its nuclear weapons program. In order to gain Russian and Chinese support, the Security Council resolution explicitly excluded the threat of military force.[194]

---

194. Warren Hoge, "Security Council Supports Sanctions on North Korea," *New York Times*, October 15, 2006.

These actions notwithstanding, support for a "sunshine policy" of reaching out to North Korea has gained considerable support in South Korea. Following a summit meeting in Pyongyang between leaders of the two countries, South Korean president Kim Dae Jung stated:

> The Pyongyang people are the same as us, the same nation sharing the same blood. Regardless of what they have been saying and [how they have been] acting outwardly, they have deep love and a longing for their compatriots in the South. If you talk with them, you notice that right away. . . . We must consider North Koreans as our brothers and sisters. We must believe that they have the same thought. . . . Most importantly there is no longer going to be any war. The North will no longer attempt unification by force and at the same time we will not do any harm to the North.[195]

Whether or not such assertions reflect a realistic understanding of North Korea and its foreign policy goals, survey evidence indicates a growing sense of nationalism and at least some long-term aspirations for national unity. This must be weighed against the remarkable ability of the Kim Jong Il regime to behave in ways that confirm the worst suspicions of its critics.

The nuclear test in 2006 confronted leaders in Seoul with competing domestic political pressures. The United States and the conservative opposition party favored sanctions against Pyongyang, including termination of two joint ventures—the Mount Kumgang tourism project and an industrial plant in Kaesong. Members of President Roh Moo-Hyun's own party preferred to maintain the policy of reaching out to the DPRK despite its intransigence on the nuclear issue. The architect of that policy, former president Kim Dae Jung, reiterated his long-standing views. "It's clear that the sunshine policy has succeeded between the two Koreas, and it could have been more successful were it not for the bad relations between North Korea and the United States."[196] Although not stated directly, that seemed to place the onus for the problem on Washington. Whatever the merits of that diagnosis, it was in line with a survey undertaken just days before the Security Council vote on North Korea's nuclear program. Four in ten respondents blamed the United States for the nuclear

---

195. Quoted in Larson et al., *Ambivalent Allies*, 30.

196. Choe Sang-Hun, "South Korea Grapples with Competing Pressures as It Weighs Its Responses to North Korea," *New York Times*, October 13, 2006. Also, "Discipline and Dialogue: Seoul Walks Tight Rope between Washington and Beijing," *Korea Times*, October 15, 2006; Thom Shanker and Martin Fackler, "South Korea Tells Rice It Won't Abandon Industrial and Tourist Ventures with North," *New York Times*, October 20, 2006; and Norimitsu Onishi, "South Korea Won't Intercept Cargo Ships from the North," *New York Times*, November 14, 2006.

tests, followed by North Korea (37.2 percent), South Korea (13.9 percent), China (2.4 percent), and Japan (1 percent).[197]

South Korea's political and economic successes have also given rise to what might be called "sovereignty" and "status" issues. Opinions of the United States reached a low point in 1995 during negotiations on the first North Korean nuclear crisis. An "Agreed Framework" negotiated between Washington and Pyongyang in October 1994 froze North Korea's nuclear program, allowed international inspection of its nuclear facilities, and promised North Korea heavy water reactors and oil. According to one analyst, the talks between the United States and North Korea "remind[ed] South Korean officials of their own sense of helplessness at being sidelined from an issue that directly impinged on South Korean national interests but was beyond the control of the leadership in Seoul."[198]

A controversy arising at the 2002 Winter Olympics in Salt Lake City also aroused status concerns for many South Koreans. A South Korean speed skater, World Cup Champion Kim Dong-sung, crossed the finish line first and was the apparent winner in the 1500-meter event. However, an Olympic judge disqualified the South Korean skater, ruling that he had interfered with American skater Apolo Ohno, who was then awarded the gold medal. Although the judge was Australian, the brunt of South Korean anger was directed at the United States. Korean newspapers featured what they called a "robbery" in their headlines, and sixteen thousand e-mails, mostly from South Korea, crashed the U.S. Olympic Committee Internet server.[199] Polls at about that time revealed a sharp decline in favorable views of the United States. It should also be noted, however, that the Olympic controversy took place at about the same time that President Bush identified North Korea as part of the "axis of evil," a description that ran against South Korean hopes for the sunshine policy of reaching out to its northern neighbor. That may well have primed many South Koreans to find fault with the United States in the Olympic episode.

The "Status of Forces" agreement (SOFA) between the United States and South Korea has also occasionally been a source of friction even though it was revised in 1991 and 2001 and is now the same as agreements with NATO coun-

---

197. Park Chung-a, "U.S. Most Responsible for Nuclear Test: Poll," *Korea Times*, October 15, 2006.
198. Scott Snyder, *Negotiating on the Edge* (Washington, DC: U.S. Institute for Peace, 1999), quoted in Larson et al., *Ambivalent Allies*, 16.
199. CNNSports Illustrated, "Skating Union Rejects Protest of South Korean's Disqualification," http://www.cnnsi.com (accessed February 21, 2002). The importance of the Olympic episode is also emphasized in Seung Hwan Kim, "Anti-Americanism in Korea," *Washington Quarterly* 26 (winter 2002/2003): 109–22.

tries and Japan. In 2002 an American military truck went out of control and killed two young South Korean girls. In accordance with the SOFA agreement, the soldiers were tried in an American court. Their acquittal in November 2002 resulted in widespread protests and nightly candlelight vigils just prior to the presidential elections. As noted in chapter 1, presidential candidate Roh Moo-Hyun was elected after a campaign in which he was at least moderately critical of the United States. It seems likely that the acquittal of the American soldiers contributed to his vote total, especially among younger voters.

The broader question arising from these episodes is the extent to which South Koreans believe that Washington pays attention to their vital interests. As shown in table 2.8, only 5 percent of South Korean respondents to three Pew surveys across five years (2002–7) selected the "a great deal" option. An analysis of the earlier Pew survey revealed an exceptionally strong correlation between opinions about the United States and judgments about American sensitivity to South Korean interests. Only 5 percent responded "a great deal" to the latter item; among them, 65 percent of them also had a favorable opinion about the United States. In contrast, of those who responded that Washington was "not at all" interested in Korean vital interests, 67 percent also had an unfavorable view of the United States.[200]

South Korea's economic successes have also given rise to some trade issues. Rather than being perceived as a poor country dependent on U.S. aid, South Korea is increasingly viewed in Washington as a competitor. In March 2002 the Bush administration imposed tariffs ranging from 8 to 30 percent on steel imports and targeted a number of major producers, including South Korea. Despite protests and a 2003 World Trade Organization ruling that the tariffs were illegal, they were not lifted until later that year when Japan and other countries threatened to retaliate against some American products.

South Korean and American trade officials concluded a free trade agreement (FTA) in June 2007, barely beating a deadline imposed by the midyear expiration of "fast track authority" wherein Congress must vote "up or down" on trade agreements but may not amend them. Bilateral trade between the two countries exceeds $70 billion annually. Thousands of Koreans engaged in protest against an FTA with the United States, fearing that such an agreement would seriously threaten their heavily protected farmers. Although labeled as an FTA, South Korea and the United States actually agreed to discriminate in favor of exporters or investors based in each other's territory. Farm and auto-

200. Larson et al., *Ambivalent Allies*, 106.

mobile interests can be expected to make their voices heard in the ratification process in Seoul and Washington.[201]

The American invasions of Afghanistan and Iraq have also given rise to modest discord between Washington and Seoul. At the behest of the United States, over a twelve-year period the Park Chung Hee government deployed over three hundred thousand troops in support of the American military effort in Vietnam, where ROK forces suffered sixteen thousand casualties, including five thousand killed. At that time there was little doubt among most South Koreans that the large contingent of American forces in their country was the major deterrent against another invasion from the north, and thus the deployment to Vietnam might be viewed as a quid pro quo for the presence of Americans in South Korea.

A small South Korean contingent joined the multinational forces in Afghanistan after the fall of Kabul. Washington made several private requests in 2002 for a deployment of some twelve thousand South Korean troops to join the "coalition of the willing" that would shortly invade Iraq. Presidential candidate Roh Moo-Hyun could not have failed to note the overwhelming public opposition to such a deployment. Indeed, most South Koreans objected to the inclusion of North Korea, along with Iraq and Iran, as part of the "axis of evil." Had he acceded to Washington's request, he would almost certainly have doomed his electoral campaign. A Pew survey conducted shortly after the fall of Baghdad in 2003 found overwhelming public support for the decision to stay out of Iraq (table 2.14), although in fact seven hundred engineering and medical troops had been in Iraq since May.

Several months later the Roh Moo-Hyun government agreed to a scaled-back deployment of three thousand combat personnel to Arvil in northern Iraq. According to one source, almost 65 percent of those taking part in an October 2003 *Hankook Ilbo* poll supported the deployment.[202] A UN Security Council resolution in support of multinational contributions to aid in the reconstruction of Iraq, just one week before the Roh government's decision, no doubt helped to gain support for it. The National Assembly in Seoul stipulated that South Korean forces were to conduct their reconstruction operations in-

---

201. Martin Wolf, "A Korean-American Strand Enters Trade's Spaghetti Bowl," *Financial Times*, April 3, 2007; David Hale, "It Is a Big Mistake to Kill Bush's Trade Deal with Seoul," *Financial Times*, July 18, 2007.

202. Kyudok Hong, "The Impact of NGOs on South Korea's Decision to Dispatch Troops to Iraq," *Journal of International and Area Studies* 12, no. 2 (2005): 31–46. The author is highly critical of South Korea for failing to meet the American request more quickly, with a larger contingent of forces, and for not placing restrictions on South Koreans' opinions. Harvard-based researcher Sung-Yoon Lee is even more critical of President Roh, accusing him of seeking to destroy the U.S.-ROK alliance by wresting operational control of the two countries' armed forces. "Korea-US: Swan Song for Alliance," *Asia Times*. September 16, 2006, http://www.atimes.com/atimes/Korea/HI16Dg02.html. See also Woosang Kim and Tae-Hyo Kim, "A Candle in the Wind: Korean Perceptions of ROK-U.S. Security Relations," *Korean Journal of Defense Analysis* 16 (spring 2004): 99–118.

dependently rather than under the United States. As the situation in Iraq continues to slide toward a civil war, South Korea has joined Spain, Italy, Poland, and several other countries in reducing its forces there. They are slated to decline to only nine hundred during 2007.

At the 2004 Republican National Convention that nominated him for a second term, President Bush thanked eight countries and their leaders for their courage in assisting the U.S. undertaking in Iraq. He failed to mention either South Korea or President Roh. During a free-wheeling press conference the omission might have been an inadvertent oversight, but in the highly scripted Republican convention, where the president's speech must have been vetted by many members of his staff, it could hardly have been accidental.

Views of the United States held by the South Korea public reflect changes in both the international system and democratization of the political system. The end of the Cold War has reduced but did not eliminate the threat from North Korea, and the sunshine policy of reaching out to North Korea has yet to yield many tangible benefits. Optimistic predictions about Pyongyang's nuclear program suffered a severe setback with the successful test of a small nuclear weapon in October 2006, and the Kim Jong Il regime has not demonstrated a significant commitment toward improving the lives of its citizens.

The six-power negotiations involving both Koreas, China, Russia, Japan, and the United States in February 2007 resulted in a promising step toward curtailing North Korea's nuclear program in exchange for major assistance on energy, but history suggests that even a signed agreement with Pyongyang does not ensure fully satisfactory implementation. For many South Koreans it is a vindication of the sunshine policy, and China appears to have an important stake in a successful outcome, but some staunch Republican conservatives, including former UN ambassador John R. Bolton, have attacked the agreement for "caving in" and abandoning their goal of a regime change in Pyongyang. Moreover, Japan has threatened to withhold aid until North Korea resolves the issue of kidnapped Japanese citizens.

That said, it seems unlikely that many South Koreans will espouse the uncritical views of the United States that were widespread in the aftermath of the Korean War. Indeed, careful analyses of two sets of polling data suggest that the future may be fraught with difficulties for the United States.[203] Both found impressive evidence that Koreans' opinions of the United States are sharply di-

---

203. Larson et al., *Ambivalent Allies,* chap. 4; and Derek J. Mitchell, ed., *Strategy and Sentiment: South Korean Views of the United States and the U.S.-ROK Alliance* (Washington, DC: Center for Strategic and International Studies, 2004). Also, Norimitsu Onishi, "At 50, the Korean Truce Defines a Generation Gap," *New York Times,* July 26, 2003.

TABLE 4.4. South Korean Opinions of the United States, China, Japan, and North Korea, March 2005

"What is your opinion of (country)? Is it favorable or unfavorable?"

| | Percent Favorable Minus Percent Unfavorable | | | |
Group	United States	China	Japan	North Korea
Overall	−4.0	−4.4	−55.6	2.5
Men	−7.0	−7.8	−57.5	4.9
Women	−1.0	−1.1	−53.7	−3.9
Age				
29 and under	−4.2	−6.3	−40.6	5.1
30–39	−15.6	−2.6	−53.4	3.5
40–49	−6.7	−2.9	−57.5	3.5
50–59	7.3	−3.4	−66.0	−3.9
60 and over	12.1	−18.2	−72.8	−28.8
Middle school or less education	−1.9	−15.9	−67.7	−10.5
High school graduate	−3.4	−3.0	−59.1	0.2
College or higher	−6.0	−0.9	−45.9	5.4

Source: Maureen and Mike Mansfield Foundation, *Dong-A Ilbo Korean Attitudes toward Japan and Other Nations,* Asian Opinion Poll Data, March 2005.

Note: Large numbers of respondents (54.2 percent on the United States; 55.6 percent on China; 28.8 percent on Japan; and 46.9 percent on North Korea) answered "neither" or "don't know."

vided by age and education. The American role in defending the ROK during the Korean War and providing security forces since the end of that conflict remains a most salient fact for older Koreans who experienced the war and its immediate aftermath. They have significantly more favorable judgments than those, for example, of the "386 generation," Koreans who came to maturity during the rule in Seoul of authoritarian generals during most of the 1960s, 1970s, and 1980s.[204] Cleavages of similar proportions may be found when respondents to these surveys are classified by education. Better-educated South Koreans were strikingly more inclined to be critical of the United States.

Results of a 2005 *Dong-A Ilbo* survey provide further evidence that age and education are important sources of South Korean opinions about world affairs. As shown in table 4.4, those aged fifty and older expressed favorable opinions of the United States, whereas their younger compatriots were on balance critical. Older respondents were also likely to hold more negative views of China

---

204. The "386 generation" refers to liberals who are in their 30s, attended college in the 1980s, and were born in the 1960s. Hong, "The Impact of NGOs on South Korea's Decision to Dispatch Troops to Iraq," 31–46 n 5.

(which intervened in the Korean War in November 1950), Japan (which has been far less than frank in acknowledging its treatment of Koreans during World War II), and North Korea. Those with a higher level of education were also most critical of the United States, somewhat less negative about China and Japan, and most favorable toward North Korea.

Demography is not necessarily destiny, but such findings suggest that the next generation of South Korean leaders may be less willing to follow Washington's lead on foreign affairs without pondering serious questions about how their national interests are engaged. Thus, in South Korea, as is true in an increasing number of countries, publics are more likely to respond favorably to enlightened foreign policies than to simple rhetoric about axes of evil or assertions that "you are with us or you are with the terrorists."[205] Even were that not the case, it would still behoove Washington to show maturity and thoughtfulness in its foreign relations.

---

205. According to one analysis, South Korean views of the United States have nothing to do with American foreign policy because they are responsive only to domestic structural features. Thomas Kern, "Anti-Americanism in South Korea: From Structural Cleavages to Protest," *Korea Journal* (spring 2005): 237–88.

CHAPTER 5

Explanations for Anti-American Opinions

Almost as soon as Europeans began colonizing the vast area that ultimately became the United States, some foreign visitors who came to these shores shared their observations and evaluations of the American peoples, customs, values, and institutions. Unlike those who emigrated with a view to settling permanently and starting a new and better life here, notable observers such as Alexis de Tocqueville, Charles Dickens, and many others were temporary visitors who were driven by motives ranging from genuine curiosity to a determination to ridicule if not condemn most if not all aspects of life in the "new world." These writings have spawned an even more voluminous literature by Americans depicting how and why foreigners have understood—or misunderstood—the United States. The September 11 terrorist attacks and subsequent responses by the United States have given rise to a flood of speeches, editorials, op-ed articles, and books that analyze the nature and sources of foreign views of the United States.[1]

The evidence reviewed in chapters 2 and 3 indicates that recent years have witnessed widespread erosion of America's image among publics abroad, albeit the changes are far from uniform. Publics in some countries continue to view the United States in a very favorable light, and some aspects of American soci-

---

1. Book-length studies include Stephen Brooks, *As Others See Us: The Causes and Consequences of Foreign Perceptions of America* (Peterborough, Ontario: Broadview Press, 2006); Andrew Kohut and Bruce Stokes, *America against the World: How We Are Different and Why We Are Disliked* (New York: Times Books, 2006); and Peter Katzenstein and Robert O. Keohane, eds., *Anti-Americanisms in World Politics* (Ithaca: Cornell University Press, 2006). The Brooks and Kohut and Stokes books rely heavily on some data from the excellent Pew Global Attitudes Project, of which Kohut is the director.

ety—notably, science and technology—evoke almost universal admiration even in countries that are highly critical in most other respects.

What can account for the often-dramatic changes in the ways in which this country is appraised abroad? What explanations have been offered for the growth of anti-American sentiments? The September 11 terrorist attacks have generated a widespread debate to which vast numbers of politicians and pundits, foreign policy analysts, and area experts have contributed their thoughts. This chapter describes seven of the more popular and quite varied theories about foreign disenchantment with this country—the end of the Cold War, globalization, America's virtues and values, irrationality, strategic scapegoating, ignorance, and U.S. policies—along with brief sketches of the foreign policy implications of each.

THE END OF THE COLD WAR

One plausible explanation for declining support of the United States is the end of the Cold War. In the face of the Soviet threat, cohesion within alliances led by the United States—notably NATO—was widely perceived as a necessary if not sufficient condition for an effective policy of containment. In the eyes of some, the disintegration of the USSR at the end of 1991 reduced the imperatives of alliance cohesion as a top national interest and, with it, the indispensable leadership role of the United States. Indeed, a number of "realist" intellectuals forecast that the end of the Cold War would result in the demise of NATO. In the words of Kenneth Waltz, "NATO's days are not numbered, but its years are."[2] Although the number of "years" was not specified, at this point that appears to have been a less than prescient prediction.

But even with the survival of NATO, the demise of the Soviet Union allowed national interests other than containment of Moscow, at times divergent ones, to come to the forefront. Thus, it might be reasonable to assume that in the absence of Cold War threats, publics and leaders in Western Europe and elsewhere might feel less dependent on the United States, less reluctant to criticize Washington, and freer to pursue a more independent course in world affairs. Examples of issues that might have received less attention when East-West relations and fears of a possible nuclear war dominated world politics include efforts to deal with such environmental issues as global warming (the Kyoto Protocol); coping with such "failed states" as Yugoslavia, Rwanda, Soma-

---

2. Kenneth Waltz, "The Emerging Structure of International Politics," *International Security* 18 (fall 1993): 76.

lia, and Sudan; agricultural subsidies in rich countries that have severely damaged the ability of poor countries to compete in international markets for cotton and other commodities; threats of global pandemics; and a host of immigration issues.

In another important respect the disintegration of the USSR and end of the
Cold War could have affected the ways in which the United States is perceived
abroad. According to balance-of-power theories, when a single country
emerges as the dominant power, fear may impel others to join forces in a coun-
teralliance in order to restore a balance of power. European politics of the seventeenth through twentieth centuries offer a number of examples, but others
could be cited as well. Thucydides attributed the Peloponnesian Wars to the
growth of Athenian power and the fears that it aroused among its neighbors,
including Sparta. They formed the Peloponnesian League to deter and ultimately to defeat Athens.

Despite critical descriptions of the United States as a "hyperpower" by some
French leaders, the post–Cold War era has not witnessed overt balancing
against the United States, probably in part because of its reputation for avoiding imperial territorial expansion outside the Western hemisphere. As noted in
chapter 1, however, even traditional allies are now somewhat less willing to line
up behind Washington on all issues. One observer has described this process as
"soft balancing."[3] But balance-of-power reasoning has not necessarily gone into
permanent eclipse, and thus the possibilities that it might energize a coalition
of lesser powers to join forces in opposition to the United States cannot be
ruled out. It is unlikely that the reservoir of good will generated during World
War II and the Cold War and earlier is inexhaustible. The nature of American
policy is likely to be the key to how others react to its hegemonic position.
Chapter 6 explores aspects of American policy and their impact abroad more
fully.

While explanations that identify the end of the Cold War as the source of
declining support for the United States among publics abroad no doubt have
some validity, if only because it probably permitted latent anti-American sentiments to surface, they are at best incomplete. They might provide some insight
into changing opinions about the United States during the decade between the
collapse of the USSR and the September 11 terrorist attacks, but they would
seem less valuable for providing much insight into the evidence of dramatically

---

3. Robert A. Pape, "The World Pushes Back," *Boston Globe*, March 23, 2003; and T. V. Paul, "Soft Balancing in the
Age of U.S. Primacy," *International Security* 30 (summer 2005): 46–71.

changing assessments of the United States during the years since the assaults on New York and Washington. Indeed, if external threats are seen as a source of internal alliance cohesion, as during the Cold War, the terrorist attacks and subsequent events also should have given rise to sustained support and sympathy for the United States, not necessarily among publics in Muslim countries but certainly in European countries that have also experienced terrorist violence. As revealed by the evidence presented in the previous chapters, favorable views of the United States have declined since 2001 rather than increased in many parts of the world. The somewhat related argument that the United States is hated by enemies and friends because that is the inevitable fate of hegemonic powers is equally unpersuasive.[4] The disintegration of the USSR in 1991 left the United States as the sole superpower, and yet chapters 2 and 3 provide ample evidence that publics abroad generally viewed this country more or less favorably for at least the following decade. That being the case, it is useful to consider other explanations for the growth of anti-American sentiments.

GLOBALIZATION

The past several decades have witnessed a significant increase of globalization—the reduction of barriers to the flow of goods, services, capital, information, people, entertainment products, ideas, and the like. The World Bank, International Monetary Fund, World Trade Organization, and World Economic Forum (in Davos, Switzerland) play important roles in promoting economic globalization, and technologies such as faster transportation, telecommunications infrastructures, and the Internet have accelerated its pace. They have also added to threats of worldwide terrorist networks such as al Qaeda and of global pandemics.

Globalization has produced winners and losers, both within and between countries. As is often the case, when regulations and restrictions are liberalized, the stronger and those with the most financial leverage are more likely to be among the winners. As the world's most powerful economy, the United States and American corporations have on balance benefited from globalization, but it has not given rise to increasing prosperity in all regions. Whereas China, India, and such "Asian tigers" as Thailand, South Korea, Malaysia, and Singapore have benefited, on balance, from globalization, many African countries have been left far behind economically. The protests against the World Trade Orga-

---

4. Niall Ferguson, "Why Our Enemies—and Friends—Hate Us," *Los Angeles Times*, February 26, 2007.

nization meeting in Seattle—"the so-called battle of Seattle"—in 1999 have spawned the World Social Forum, an annual antiglobalization event. Others that often oppose globalization include the Group of Seventy-seven (Third World countries that now number more than the original seventy-seven), Greenpeace, and domestic lobbies in many countries.

Because reducing trade barriers has not benefited all groups equally, antiglobalization groups have also emerged even in countries that have generally gained from increased international trade. Within the United States, workers in the automobile and textile industries, for example, have seen many of their jobs lost to countries with lower labor costs or, less frequently, to immigrants, especially from Mexico. Consequently, anti-immigration and antiglobalization movements have gained considerable traction. Columnist, author, and former presidential candidate Patrick Buchanan has founded *American Conservative* magazine to represent this viewpoint, and viewers of the CNN television channel get almost nightly doses of antiglobalization editorials from Lou Dobbs. Perennial French candidate Jean-Marie Le Pen espouses strong antiglobalization views, and spokespersons for such sentiments may be found in many other countries.

Paul Hollander, who has generally expressed little sympathy for criticisms of America, finds some merit in the thesis that American-led globalization of culture has given rise to anti-American opinions.

> Some of the discontents and criticisms stimulated by American cultural influences abroad, or by traits of American culture at home, are well founded. In particular to the extent that anti-American sentiments have been a response to modernization they reflect legitimate apprehensions. Modernity and modernization (the latter often justifiably called "Americanization") have been a mixed blessing and the United States has been in the forefront of spreading these disruptive processes, hence it is understandably identified with them.[5]

The thesis that anti-American views among publics abroad can be explained primarily as a reaction to globalization is less than compelling however. One admittedly imperfect test of the thesis is to correlate the degree of globalization with opinions about the United States. A. T. Kearney has developed a sophisticated "Globalization Index" (GI) based on twelve measures of economic integration, technological connectivity, political engagement, and personal contact. The most recent GI ranks sixty-two countries, ranging from the most

---

5. Paul Hollander, *Anti-Americanism: Rational and Irrational,* revised edition (New Brunswick, NJ: Transaction Books, 1995), xii.

globalized (Singapore) to the least (Iran).[6] If globalization is a prime source of anti-American sentiments, then the countries with the highest GI ranking should also be among the most critical of the United States. Table 2.1 summarizes opinions of the United States in twenty-seven countries. If we compare the most recent assessments of the United States with the GI rankings, there is little if any systematic relationship. Countries where a majority of publics expressed favorable views of the United States include five with GI scores in the top thirty (Canada, Australia, Great Britain, Italy, and Japan), but also four with low GI rankings (Mexico, Poland, Nigeria, and India). Conversely, publics in some countries with high GI scores also expressed critical opinions about America (Netherlands, Germany, France, and Spain), whereas those in eight countries that had low GI rankings were also critical of the United States (Turkey, Brazil, Russia, Indonesia, Pakistan, Egypt, Morocco, and China).

The globalization thesis also fares poorly by another very imperfect test. The 2003 Pew survey undertaken shortly after the fall of Baghdad and a similar study in 2007 not only asked those taking part for their opinions of the United States but also asked for their views of "the American way of doing business." Responses to the latter question, which would seem to assess at least one facet of globalization, reveal that respondents with the most consistently favorable views of American business practices were South Koreans, Indians, Israelis, Lebanese, Nigerians, Kuwaitis, and Jordanians; majorities in each country stated their approval (table 3.9). But, with the exception of Kuwait and Lebanon, publics in none of these countries expressed negative views of the United States in the 2007 Pew surveys (table 2.1). Although these results are far too skimpy to constitute a definitive test, they offer little support for the thesis that negative views of the United States are rooted primarily in the kinds of economic activities that are the core of globalization.

Nor did the globalization explanation receive support from a State Department study of European attitudes toward the United States. It identified several sources of anti-American opinions, but it dismissed as "fiction" the thesis that globalization is a major factor. "Europeans are not generally negative toward globalization, nor do they primarily associate it with the spread of U.S. influence. Even so-called antiglobalization activists see some aspects of globalization in a positive light."[7]

---

6. "The Globalization Index," *Foreign Policy* (November/December 2006): 74–81. Also at http://www.ForeignPolicy.com, and http://www.ATKearney.com.
7. U.S. Department of State, Office of Research, *Europeans and Anti-Americanism: Fact vs. Fiction; A Study of Public Attitudes toward the U.S.*, September 2002, 1.

A final and perhaps most persuasive finding against globalization as an explanation for critical opinions of the United States emerges from a Eurobarometer survey conducted in October 2003—only a few months after the invasion of Iraq, which had generated strong opposition from most European Union members. The survey found that those with favorable views of globalization outnumbered those who opposed it by a margin of 63 percent to 29 percent. Respondents in Germany (71 percent) and France (63 percent) favored globalization, shortly after they had expressed decidedly critical views of the United States (table 2.1).[8]

This is not to deny the importance of globalization, its widely perceived links to Americanization, or its ability to arouse strong negative feelings. But the globalization thesis would appear better able to explain anti-American views among specific sectors of publics abroad rather than entire populations. Farmers in many countries oppose globalization and seek tariffs, quotas, or both to protect them from competition. Some American farmers welcome "free trade agreements" that open markets abroad, but others support policies that restrict imports, for example, of sugar and even Brazilian ethanol, an effective substitute for gasoline. The United States also provides other illustrations of varied responses to globalization. On balance, most Americans have benefited from the lower trade barriers that have made available low-cost textiles, televisions, and cell phones and a wide range of other goods produced abroad. In contrast, those whose jobs have been outsourced to low-wage areas are highly critical and, as noted earlier, they have found vocal advocates of their views in Patrick Buchanan, Lou Dobbs, and many union leaders. India provides a final example. It has benefited immensely from jobs outsourced by many American corporations, but the prospect of Wal-Mart entering India's $300 billion retail sector has aroused strong protests. The livelihood of an estimated forty million Indians depends on retailing, and few of them are likely to take a kind view of the United States or American business practices if the world's largest and most aggressive retailer enters their market.[9] Because the pattern in India is likely to be found in many other countries, it suggests the value of also considering other explanations for declining support for the United States among publics abroad.

---

8. European Commission Eurobarometer 151b, *Globalization*, November 2003, 15–17.
9. "Wal-Mart's Welcome to India Includes Demonstrations," *New York Times*, February 22, 2007.

AMERICA'S VIRTUES AND VALUES

Upon learning of the September 11 terrorist attacks, the evangelical Protestant minister Jerry Falwell pointed to America's sinfulness: "the pagans, and the abortionists and the feminists, and the gays and the lesbians who are actively trying to make that an alternative lifestyle, the ACLU and People for the American Way—all of them who tried to secularize America—I point the finger in their face and say, 'you helped this to happen.'"[10] His colleague Pat Robertson agreed with him.

Although Falwell's is not a diagnosis that most Americans rushed to espouse, it has gained some traction among conservative critics of contemporary society. For example, Dinesh D'Souza pins the blame for the 9/11 terrorist attacks squarely on the shoulders of "the cultural left," which, he alleges, promotes and defends decadent values that are anathema not only to most Americans but also to Osama bin Laden. Thus, he argues, the terrorist attacks were motivated not by opposition to American policies in the Middle East or the Israel-Palestine issue but rather by a liberal American culture that ran counter to bin Laden's traditional Muslim sensibilities. More broadly, D'Souza locates the sources of anti-American sentiments abroad in the decadence of the left.[11]

Many others hold a more positive opinion of American values. Nine days after hijacked airliners smashed into the World Trade Center and the Pentagon, President Bush addressed a joint session of Congress and the American people about the attacks and how the United States would respond. In the course of his speech, which was frequently interrupted by enthusiastic applause, the president asked, "Why do they hate us?" He answered his own question: "They hate what we see right here in this chamber—a democratically elected government. Their leaders are self-appointed. They hate our freedoms—our freedom of religion, our freedom of speech, our freedom to vote and assemble and disagree with each other."[12]

The president's diagnosis has received favorable responses from many of his supporters, and it has been expanded to include not only terrorists but also all of those who might hold critical views of the United States. For example, the

10. John F. Harris, "God Gave U.S. 'What We Deserve,' Falwell Says," *Washington Post.* September 14, 2001.
11. Dinesh D'Souza, *The Enemy at Home: The Cultural Left and Its Responsibility for 9/11* (New York: Doubleday, 2007).
12. George W. Bush, "Address to a Joint Session of Congress and the American People," Washington, DC, September 20, 2001. Available at http://www.whitehouse.gov/news/releases/2001/09/print/20010920-8.html.

syndicated columnist George Will wrote that the terrorist targets were "symbols of not just American power but of its virtues. . . . They hate America because it is the purest expression of modernity—individuality, pluralism, freedom, secularism." In the same vein, columnist Jonah Greenberg wrote, "the haters need no reason to hate us. It is enough that we are who we are—a free and powerful people. . . . They can't bear our happiness, our prosperity, our power, and most of all the realization that others want to model themselves on us and build their own free societies."[13] One additional example illustrates this line of reasoning. According to Ilya Shapiro, anti-American sentiments are rooted in "resentment, not of the American way of life per se, but rather of the openness, ease of manner, optimism, and entrepreneurial spirit that have defined 'Americanness' since de Tocqueville and continue even in this multicultural age."[14]

Many others locate the sources of anti-American actions and sentiments in a quality that virtually all Americans hold dear, notably freedom. The policy implications of these diagnoses are fairly straightforward. Because the United States is criticized for its virtues and values that are almost universally accepted, then those who oppose America must be unvirtuous. According to many of its proponents, if this country's freedom and related values lie at the root of anti-Americanism, then it is quite appropriate to frame differences in moral terms—the virtuous versus the opponents of those virtues—in a conflict that permits no middle ground or disengaged bystanders. As President Bush has stated many times since the September 11 terrorist attacks, "Either you are with us, or you are with the terrorists."[15]

A closely related thesis locates anti-American opinions in certain American values such as religiosity, individualism, optimism, personal responsibility, American exceptionalism, and the like. A number of cross-national surveys, notably those conducted by the Pew Research Center Global Attitudes Project, have revealed that the degree of attachment to some of these values does indeed distinguish this country from many others.[16] It is also possible, however, to overestimate the extent of the differences. For example, as revealed in table 3.4,

---

13. http://grecoreport.com/why_America_is_hated.htm.

14. Ilya Shapiro, "Why Do They Hate Us?" March 23, 2004, Web site of the Institute of Communication Studies, University of Leeds, UK, http://ics.leeds.ac.uk/papers/vp01.cfm?outfit=pmt&requesttimeout=500&folder=1259&paper=1456.

15. For example, the president's previously cited speech to Congress on September 20, 2001. See also his joint press conference with French president Jacques Chirac on November 6, 2001, and a speech the following day on steps to disrupt terrorist financial networks.

16. See, for example, Kohut and Stokes, *America against the World*.

publics in six countries (Canada, Great Britain, Australian, South Korea, Russia, and France) judged the United States to be "religious," whereas those in Israel, Brazil, and Jordan disagreed. When respondents were asked whether the United States was "too religious" (table 3.6), only in France did a majority agree, whereas 50 percent or more in twelve countries stated that America is "not religious enough." Majorities among publics in all eight Muslim countries selected the latter option, but that was also the majority opinion in Italy, Brazil, South Korea, and Nigeria. In addition, pluralities of more than 40 percent in Germany, Italy, Russia, and Israel selected the "not religious enough" option. Thus, outside France, a country with a long anticlerical tradition, the criticism that publics abroad view Americans as excessively religious, or that this belief may lie at the heart of declining support for the United States, is not borne out by the data.

There is a more serious problem with the thesis that value differences are the primary source of contemporary anti-American opinions. Societal values are almost by definition more or less stable, more likely to change over decades than over months. Southern racial views illustrate the point. Integration of the armed forces by President Truman in 1948, the 1954 *Brown vs. Topeka School Board* decision on school integration, and the Civil Rights Act of 1965 represented major milestones on the road to a more-integrated society, but their impact on public attitudes in the South—and elsewhere—was far from instantaneous.

For similar reasons, if we wish to understand how public attitudes toward the United States changed during the few years since the September 11 attacks, American values are unlikely to provide more than a partial explanation at best. To the extent that optimism, individualism, a sense of national exceptionalism, and the like characterize important elements of societal values, they did so in 1999 as well as in 2007. For example, Kohut and Stokes point out that, by a small margin, Americans were likely to regard religion as less important in 2004 than they did four decades earlier, and weekly attendance at religious services has not changed significantly in a decade.[17] Stated differently, if we wish to understand sharp *changes* in public attitudes abroad over a relatively short period of time, a full answer is unlikely to be found in the relatively *stable* features of American society.

---

17. Ibid., 101, 103–4.

IRRATIONALITY

A fourth and closely related cluster of explanations for anti-American sentiments emphasizes the irrationality of leaders and publics abroad. The essence of the irrationality thesis is that appraisals of the United States are rooted more in the traits of those making the judgments and less in American values, institutions, and policies. In one of several articles on the theme, the widely read syndicated columnist Charles Krauthammer argued that anti-American views, especially among Europeans and Arabs, are deeply rooted in envy of American power and success.

> It is pure fiction that this [post 9/11] pro-American sentiment was either squandered after September 11 or lost under the Bush administration. It never existed. Envy for America, resentment of our power, hatred of our success has been a staple for decades, but most particularly since victory in the cold war left us the only superpower. . . .
> The fact is the world hates us for our wealth, our success, our power.
> They hate us into incoherence. . . .
> The search for logic in anti-Americanism is fruitless. It is in the air the world breathes. Its roots are envy and self-loathing by peoples who, yearning for modernity but having failed at it, find their one satisfaction in despising modernity's great exemplar. On Sept. 11, they gave it a rest for a day. Big deal.[18]

Krauthammer has returned to this theme repeatedly, especially when discussing the policies of Western Europe NATO allies. For example, in a column strongly advocating a U.S. military attack on Iran's nuclear facilities, he acknowledged that such action might entail diplomatic costs.

> [Arab] governments will express solidarity with a fellow Muslim state, but this will be entirely hypocritical. The Arabs are terrified about the rise of a nuclear Iran and would privately rejoice in its defanging.
> The Europeans will be less hypocritical because their visceral anti-Americanism trumps rational calculation. We will have done them an enormous favor by sparing them the threat of Iranian nukes, but they will vilify us nonetheless.

The Iranian leadership, which has rarely missed the opportunity to condemn the United States as the protector of the "illegitimate Zionist entity" (Israel), is also deemed by Krauthammer to be incapable of the type of rational calculation that might deter it from using any nuclear weapons it might acquire:

---

18. Charles Krauthammer, "To Hell with Sympathy: The Goodwill America Earned on 9/11 Was Illusory. Get Over It," *Time*, November 17, 2003, 156.

"Against millenarian fanaticism glorying a cult of death, deterrence is a mere wish."[19]

The essence of this perspective, of which Krauthammer is not the only proponent, is that U.S. actions in the global arena are fundamentally irrelevant because many publics and leaders abroad hate and envy America for what it *is*—rich, powerful, modern, and successful—rather than for what it *does*. Indeed, he argues that anti-Americanism is so deeply rooted in many countries that it has overshadowed the normal calculations of self-interest that are the traditional sources of foreign policy decisions. That being the case, there is no room for normal diplomatic give-and-take to deal with policy differences.

The policy implications for the United States are clear: efforts to compromise, cooperate, and coordinate policies with others are not only doomed but, to use Krauthammer's term, "pathetic." Anti-American views are so deeply embedded among leaders and publics abroad that it would be wholly useless to make any policy adjustments with a view toward ameliorating, if not eliminating, such opinions. Indeed, attempting to do so would be an especially dangerous form of appeasement, merely reinforcing images of the United States as not only an enemy but also a "paper tiger" that may be attacked with impunity. In short, Washington should stand firm in its pursuit of self-defined national interests while resisting temptations to accommodate adversaries, occasionally recalcitrant allies, or, worst of all, international institutions. Whether publics and leaders abroad support or oppose those policies is—and should be—totally irrelevant.

Krauthammer is not the only proponent of the irrationality thesis to explain anti-Americanism abroad. According to Fouad Ajami, findings from recent international polls, including some of those that are analyzed in the previous chapters, "are neither surprising nor profound." Indeed, he accuses pollsters of having a political agenda when reporting their results. "Pollsters report rising anti-Americanism worldwide. The United States, they imply, squandered global sympathy after the September 11 terrorist attacks through its arrogant unilateralism. In truth, there was never any sympathy to squander. Anti-Americanism was already entrenched in the world's psyche—a backlash against a nation that comes bearing modernism to those who want it but who also fear and despise it." Ajami also warns that it would be fatuous for the United States to consider the critical views of publics abroad in shaping its poli-

19. Charles Krauthammer, "Iran Is in the Crosshairs of a U.S. Decision," *Raleigh News and Observer*, September 17, 2006.

cies because they are essentially rooted in nonrational sentiments—perhaps, "psychopathologies" is not too strong a description—that are not amenable to change. Ajami's dismissal of German appraisals of the United States illustrates his understanding of public opinion in much of the world. "The United States need not worry about hearts and minds in foreign lands. If Germans wish to use anti-Americanism to absolve themselves and their parents of the great crimes of World War II, they will do so regardless of what the United States says and does."[20] It might be noted that Ajami, a distinguished student of Middle Eastern cultures, has no special expertise about Germany or World War II.

A similar thesis emerged from a discussion in January 2003 of why France was unlikely to join the United States in an invasion of Iraq. According to Hillel Fradkin, President Jacques Chirac's warning that the Bush administration's views on Iraq are simpleminded, utopian, and arrogant is "close to being beneath contempt."

> It would be preferable if we could count on the support of France and other European and democratic states. It would also be just since only wounded vanity and envy seem properly to explain the posture of the French and others. But envy may prevail and we will have to live with this as well as Middle Eastern distrust if we are to perform the duty our power imposes on us.[21]

British historian Paul Johnson provided yet another version of the envy thesis. "Anti-Americanism is racist envy," a point that he supported by the assertion that "France is not a democracy."[22] These explanations would seem to confirm the observation attributed to the novelist Henry James that "[i]t is, I think, an indisputable fact that Americans are, as Americans, the most self-conscious people in the world, and the most addicted to the belief that other nations of the earth are in a conspiracy to under value them."

The evidence reviewed here has not, on balance, been kind to the thesis that publics abroad are more or less permanently stuck in a "hate America" frame of mind arising from envy, self-loathing, or other nonrational impulses. Publics abroad may often be ill informed about the United States—just as many Americans have a fragile foundation of knowledge about most parts of the world—

---

20. Fouad Ajami, "The Falseness of Anti-Americanism," *Foreign Policy* (September/October 2003): 52–61. The quotations are from pp. 52 and 61. Ajami is reported to have advised Vice President Richard Cheney during the months prior to the invasion of Iraq. Spencer Ackerman and Franklin Foer, "The Radical," *New Republic* 229 (December 1 and 8, 2003): 21. In the same vein, see Russell A. Berman and Arno Tausch. "Yet Another Reason They Dislike Us: Europe Is Rich, but the United States Is Richer," *Hoover Digest* (winter 2005): 69–73.
21. Hillel Fradkin, *National Review Online*, http://www.nationalreview.com.
22. Paul Johnson, "Anti-Americanism Is Racist Envy," July 21, 2003, http://www.Forbes.com.

and they may rely on stereotypes that are poorly grounded in reality. Despite these and other weaknesses they nevertheless seem able and willing to make significant distinctions in their judgments. For example, respondents in many countries expressed critical views about American political institutions but at the same time offered favorable judgments about the quality of life, popular culture, and, especially, science and technology in this country.

Many publics abroad also appear quite able to make significant distinctions in their appraisals of American foreign policy. Reactions to the American-led invasions of Afghanistan and Iraq illustrate the point. Aside from negative public reactions in some predominantly Muslim countries, the intervention in Afghanistan to rout the Taliban regime and to capture al Qaeda leaders received widespread support from publics abroad as a justified response to the September 11 terrorist attacks on New York and Washington, and their governments' policies reflected those opinions. France and Germany have been major contributors in Afghanistan, by far the most important venue for fighting terrorists. The French deployment included combat aircraft, and a Congressional Research Service report found that "[t]he German response to the 9/11 terrorist attacks against the United States was immediate and unprecedented in scope for that country."[23]

With some exceptions, those favorable judgments only rarely carried over to the invasion of Iraq. Washington's failure to come up with any evidence about alleged Iraqi weapons of mass destruction or ties to al Qaeda did little to change minds among those who doubted the wisdom and legitimacy of the intervention. For example, French opposition to the Iraq invasion was not simply a matter of throwing monkey wrenches into Washington's plans in a fit of pique. Many in France, including President Jacques Chirac, looked back to their own disastrous experience in their bloody and failed effort to maintain control over Algeria after World War II. Indeed, Chirac served as a young officer in Algeria during the 1950s, and he drew the conclusion that an occupation of Iraq would encounter many of the same difficulties.[24] Reactions to American tsunami assistance in Indonesia and elsewhere further buttress the point that most publics are quite often able to reassess their judgments of the United States and its actions in the light of new information. In short, American actions seem to matter.

---

23. Francis T. Miko and Christian Froelich, "Germany's Role in Fighting Terrorism: Implications for U.S. Policy," Congressional Research Service, December 27, 2004, 1 (Order Code RL32710).
24. Paul Starobin, "The French Were Right," *National Journal,* November 7, 2003.

STRATEGIC SCAPEGOATING

Yet another and quite different explanation for anti-Americanism locates its source not in irrational impulses but, rather, in carefully calculated strategies by political leaders, especially in Arab and Muslim countries, to distract their publics from gross mismanagement at home by pointing to the United States as the source of their problems.[25] In doing so, they thus absolve themselves of any need to confront directly their own failures.

Exaggerating real or imaginary threats from abroad in order to serve domestic political purposes has been in the playbook of countless leaders since antiquity. Thucydides may have been the first to suggest that leaders may use foreign adventures to buttress their political fortunes at home, but he is certainly not alone in doing so. The French philosopher Jean Bodin wrote, "the best way of preserving a state, and guaranteeing it against sedition, rebellion, and civil war is to . . . find a common enemy against whom [the subjects] can make common cause."[26] American history also yields an example. In the face of secession by southern states, on April 1, 1861, Secretary of State William Seward suggested to recently inaugurated President Abraham Lincoln that he should instigate a war against Britain, France, or Spain as a way of reuniting the country. Fortunately, Lincoln had the foresight to understand that a war against Britain would not succeed in bringing the southern states back into the Union; that being on the brink of a civil war, his government hardly needed to add one of the world's most powerful countries to its list of enemies; and, finally, that among the most serious problems he would face was to deter London, whose textile mills were heavily dependent on southern cotton, from recognizing the Confederate States, thereby adding to the legitimacy of their rebellion.

American history is replete with other examples of strategic scapegoating falling short of war: the depiction of foreigners, especially Catholics, by the "Know Nothing" movement of the mid-1850s; the obligatory "twisting of the [British] lion's tail" on the presidential hustings throughout the nineteenth century; and some of the more lurid depictions by Senator Joseph McCarthy and others of a vast international communist conspiracy, abetted by spies and traitors in the State Department, during the Cold War.

---

25. See, for example, Barry Rubin, "The Real Roots of Anti-Americanism," *Foreign Affairs* 81 (November/December 2002): 73–85. An alternative view is presented in Marc Lynch, "Taking Arabs Seriously," *Foreign Affairs* 82 (September/October 2003): 81–94. See also Paul Hollander, ed., *Understanding Anti-Americanism: Its Origins and Impact at Home and Abroad* (Chicago: Ivan R. Dee, 2004).

26. Quoted in Jack S. Levy, "The Diversionary Theory of War: A Critique," in *Handbook of War Studies*, ed. Manus Midlarsky (London: Allen and Unwin, 1989).

There is little doubt that some contemporary leaders have engaged in strategic scapegoating, using the United States as a foil. Current examples of leaders who have depicted the United States, its institutions, and its policies in venomous terms in order to buttress support at home include Presidents Hugo Chávez of Venezuela and Mahmoud Ahmadinejad of Iran. Their speeches at the opening of the 2006 United Nations General Assembly described the United States and the current administration in lurid terms that fell rather short of the loosest standards of diplomatic decorum.

Less dramatically, French, Russian, German, Canadian, and many other leaders abroad have at times found it expedient to distance themselves publicly from Washington because doing so has been good domestic politics; Gerhard Schroeder's 2002 reelection campaign is a good case in point.[27] That said, to attribute criticism of the United States largely or wholly to scapegoating may seem like an appealing explanation for the same reason as the American virtue and "irrational hatred" theses are appealing: it lays the blame for anti-Americanism wholly on others, and thus it rules out the need for a cold-eyed assessment of one's own policies and their consequences. That is also its weakness, for it constitutes another form of scapegoating.

IGNORANCE

A sixth school of thought locates anti-American views among publics abroad in their ignorance of America and its policies. A benign version argues that public diplomacy efforts have faltered largely for lack of sufficient resources. The U.S. Advisory Group on Public Diplomacy for the Arab and Muslim World, appointed by President Bush in the wake of the September 11 attacks and chaired by retired diplomat Edward Djerejian, compared the present situation with the "golden age" of public diplomacy when Edward R. Murrow headed the United States Information Agency. In a Republican-led reorganization, the USIA, which included the Voice of America and Radio Free Europe, was folded into the State Department in 1999, and its staff was reduced by 40 percent. The Djerejian committee came up with the "startling figure" that the State Department includes only five persons who can speak Arabic sufficiently well to appear on Al-Jazeera, Al-Arabiya, or other television networks and engage fluently in Arabic at a professional level. The committee's reports went on

---

27. For thoughtful appraisals of the role that domestic political calculations can play in sustaining anti-American views, see Sergio Fabbrini, "The Domestic Sources of European Anti-Americanism," *Government and Opposition* (July 2002): 5; and Sophie Meunier, "The French Exception," *Foreign Affairs* 79 (2000): 104–16.

to identify the further need for personnel who are fluent in Farsi, Urdu, Bahasa, Indonesian, Pashto, and other key languages of the area.[28]

Former House Speaker Newt Gingrich has presented a more malign version of the ignorance thesis, asserting that the problem is rooted in a State Department that is unable or unwilling to defend the president's policies.[29] A benign interpretation is that State Department personnel lack sufficient resources or are simply incompetent, but Gingrich also suggested not very subtly that disloyalty is the real source of the problem. Were these just casual comments by a politician who was too young to recall the havoc caused by Senator Joseph McCarthy's charges in February 1950 that the State Department was riddled with disloyal employees and communists? That seems unlikely because Gingrich holds a Ph.D. in history and, further, because he repeated in print charges that he had previously made in a public address: "The State Department was engaging in a deliberate and systematic effort to undermine Bush's foreign policy." As a remedy, he suggested recruiting a "business advisory group from internationally sophisticated corporations" to help sell American policies to publics abroad.

The Bush administration appears to be taking seriously the charge that American public diplomacy has in recent years been ineffective. The president persuaded his trusted adviser of many years, Karen Hughes, to return to Washington following the resignation of two previous ineffective undersecretaries for public diplomacy. Aside from her demonstrated political skills, she has the advantage of excellent access to the president. Whether that will ensure the success of her efforts is less clear. Her recent trip to generate support for the United States in the Middle East has generally been described as a disaster.[30] In commenting on her appointment, an unnamed senior State Department official echoed the conclusions of the Djerejian report: no amount of marketing will change minds in the Muslim world about the war in Iraq or American support of Israel.[31] Based on the evidence analyzed here, there is also little reason to think that publics *outside* the Muslim world can be persuaded to change their generally negative appraisals of the Iraq war. Indeed, recent revelations about

---

28. Edward P. Djerejian, "Briefing on the Report on Public Diplomacy for the Arab and Muslim World," Washington Foreign Press Center, October 3, 2003.

29. Newt Gingrich, "Rogue State Department," *Foreign Policy* (July/August 2003): 42–48.

30. Ilana Ozernoy, "Ears Wide Shut," *Atlantic Monthly* (November 2006): 30–33.

31. Elizabeth Bumiller, "Bush Picks Adviser to Repair Tarnished U.S. Image Abroad," *New York Times*, March 12, 2005.

decision making in Washington before, during, and after the war are likely to buttress critical judgments.[32]

The premise that publics abroad have insufficient information about the United States and its policies is no doubt valid, but it does not necessarily follow that more information will always give rise to more favorable opinions or greater support for American policies. The more basic problem is that critical views of the United States may be rooted in divergent assessments of global threats and opportunities, calculations of vital national interests, and strategies for pursuing those interests.

U.S. POLICIES

The virtues, irrationality, and ignorance theses about the sources of surveys such as those summarized in the preceeding chapter hold that the United States need not—indeed, should not—rethink any major aspects of its foreign policy. Those who believe that publics abroad assess the United States on the basis of what it *is* are likely to dismiss any theses that look primarily to what America *does*, notably in its foreign policy actions, as sources of growing public disaffection abroad. Yet even in the "tough cases"—Arab and Muslim countries—some careful analyses reject the Ajami thesis that their publics and leaders are merely caught up in irrational envy and hatred of the United States. For example, one such study concluded, "we have presented inductive evidence that Arab publics evaluate non-Arab object countries on the basis of those countries' specific foreign policy behaviors throughout the Middle East."[33] A similar conclusion emerges from a statistical study of global public opinion by scholars in Singapore and Japan. "Our results suggest that one potential obstacle to international support for U.S. policy is, paradoxically, U.S. policy itself. . . . If foreign opinion matters, U.S. leaders would be wise to pay more attention to the effects of their actions at that level. They ought to consider how shared security interests can be pursued without alienating publics abroad, and whether the future public-opinion costs of conflict or covert action are worth the security benefits they

---

32. For example, Thomas E. Ricks, *Fiasco* (New York: Penguin Press, 2006); and Robert Woodward, *State of Denial* (New York: Simon and Schuster, 2006).

33. Peter A. Furia and Russell E. Lucas, "Determinants of Arab Public Opinion on Foreign Relations," *International Studies Quarterly* 50 (September 2006): 585–605. See also Marc Lynch, "Beyond the Arab Street: Iraq and the Arab Public Sphere," *Politics and Society* 31 (March 2003): 55–91, for a discussion of the Iraq issue, written prior to the 2003 invasion.

provide."[34] More broadly, pollster Andrew Kohut told a subcommittee of the House of Representatives in 2005, "Over time, our surveys have found that anti-Americanism around the world is driven first and foremost by opposition to U.S. foreign policy."[35]

That judgment reinforces the findings of the previously cited Djerejian report that the sources of anti-American views abroad are primarily to be located in policies and only secondarily in poor public relations efforts to present those policies. According to Djerejian, "let's say policy forms 80 percent of people's perceptions about us. There is that other 20 percent, which is the message."[36] Among those interviewed by the Djerejian committee was Yenni Zannuba Wahid, daughter of Indonesia's former president who had just returned from a year of graduate study at Harvard. Her comments at a videoconference with the group were telling: "There is no point in saying this is a problem of communication, blah, blah, blah. The perception in the Muslim world is that the problem is the policy toward the Israeli-Palestinian conflict and Iraq."[37]

The thesis that problems of support abroad arise from U.S. policies rather than the deficiencies of those who try to sell them also emerges from a brilliant analysis by Clyde Prestowitz, a conservative Republican and former Reagan administration trade representative.[38] Other analysts have gone further, suggesting that only a thorough revision of American policies, especially in the Middle East, will suffice to repair this country's reputation and effectiveness in foreign affairs. For example, a former CIA officer who was once in charge of tracking Osama bin Laden asserts that bin Laden hates the United States not because of our values but because of our policies. For that reason, he counsels that nothing short of an end to American aid to Israel, withdrawal from Afghanistan and Iraq, termination of support for such repressive regimes as Saudi Arabia, and an end to American pressure to keep oil prices low will suffice to undercut the appeals and effectiveness of al Qaeda and other terrorist organizations.[39] Whatever merits such recommendations may have in the abstract, recognition of current political realities in Washington is probably not among them.

34. Benjamin E. Goldsmith, Yusaku Horiuchi, and Takashi Inogushi, "American Foreign Policy and Global Public Opinion: Who Supported the War in Afghanistan?" unpublished manuscript, June 30, 2003.

35. Andrew Kohut, testimony to the U.S. House International Relations Committee, Subcommittee on Oversight and Investigations, November 10, 2005, http://www.au.af.mil/au/awc/awcgate/congress/koh111005.pdf.

36. Steven R. Weisman. "Bush-Appointed Panel Finds U.S. Image Abroad Is in Peril," New York Times (October 1, 2003); and Djerejian, "Briefing on the Report on Public Diplomacy."

37. Jane Perlez, "U.S. Asks Muslims Why It Is Unloved. Indonesians Reply," New York Times, September 27, 2003.

38. Clyde Prestowitz, Rogue Nation: American Unilateralism and the Failure of Good Intentions (New York: Basic Books, 2003).

39. Michael Scheuer, Imperial Hubris: Why the West Is Losing War on Terror (London: Brassey's, 2004).

The concluding chapter will consider to the extent to which certain American foreign policies may have contributed to growing anti-Americanism abroad. The discussion must necessarily fall short of a full-scale analysis of Washington's actions during the past few years. After a brief overview of how U.S. policies during the Cold War may have affected public opinion in some allied countries, the analysis turns to policies that were stimulated by and have been linked, wisely or unwisely, to the September 11 terrorist attacks.

The Impact of American Policies

The previously cited Djerejian committee report that pointed to American policy as the primary determinant of how the United States is viewed abroad was based largely on evidence from Arab and Muslim countries of the Middle East and South Asia. The data presented in previous chapters include but are not limited to publics in some important predominantly Muslim countries. The question to be explored here is the impact of American foreign policies of the past half dozen years on how publics in a wider sample of countries have come to view the United States.

Before turning to more recent policy decisions, it may be useful to examine some results of surveys from earlier decades. The U.S. Information Agency and the Eurobarometer surveys provide some pre–September 11 evidence on how publics in several NATO countries assessed the United States during the years prior to those covered in table 2.1. The results for major allies Great Britain, France, West Germany, and Italy for the years 1954–87 are presented in table 6.1.

Several conclusions emerge from these surveys. They uncovered relatively steady, if not overwhelmingly favorable, appraisals of the United States among publics in Great Britain, West Germany, and Italy. The figures from West Germany reveal consistently strong approval through most of the 1960s. This was a period in which Soviet challenges to the status of West Berlin created a number of major Cold War crises in 1948–49, 1958–59, and 1961. At his 1961 summit meeting in Vienna with newly inaugurated President John F. Kennedy, Nikita Khrushchev raised the specter of another major confrontation over the status of West Berlin. In response Kennedy mobilized some reserve units to reinforce

TABLE 6.1. Opinions about the United States among Major NATO Allies, 1954–87

	Percent Favorable															
	1954	1955	1956	1957	1958	1959	1960	1961	1962	1963	1965	1969	1982	1984	1985	1987
Great Britain	49	60	57	51	61	63	59	65	59	54	65	53	63	53	64	64
France	20	35	26	26	37	39	43	49	45	46	41	46	68	49	54	51
West Germany	61	60	63	64	68	67	68	73	71	76	76	66	71	66	48	50
Italy	59	65	72	70	67	73	64	59	64	71	65	57	71	54	64	61

Source: 1954–69—U.S. Information Agency; 1982–87—Eurobarometer.

the point that the Western powers would not relinquish their positions in that divided city. In August 1961 the Soviets built the notorious Berlin Wall to stanch the flow of refugees from East Germany to West Germany. Kennedy visited Berlin and famously announced at the wall, "Ich bin ein Berliner" (I am a Berliner). In his speech announcing the discovery of Soviet missiles in Cuba on October 22, 1962, Kennedy explicitly warned the Soviets not to use the occasion to challenge the Western position in Berlin. "Any hostile move anywhere in the world against the safety and freedom of the people to whom we are committed—including in particular the brave people of West Berlin—will be met by whatever action is needed." These actions in support of West Berlin no doubt contributed to the strongly favorable appraisals of the United States expressed by German respondents to the USIA surveys.

Later issues such as the deployment of Pershing missiles in Germany in response to Soviet SS-20 intermediate-range missiles gave rise to divisions of opinion about U.S. policy. By the mid- to late 1980s, at least some Germans viewed U.S. actions less as an effective deterrent against the threat from the east and more as an obstacle to hopes for reunification of the country. The 1985 Eurobarometer survey revealed for the first time that fewer than half of German respondents expressed favorable views of the United States. By the turn of the century, a decade after the hated Berlin Wall came down, starting a process that led to peaceful reunification of the divided country, more than three Germans in four offered a favorable assessment of the United States (table 2.1).

Responses in France were both more measured and more volatile in their assessments. The roots of somewhat rocky relations between the French, on the one side, and the United States and Great Britain can be traced at least as far back as World War II. Winston Churchill once stated that "[t]he cross of Lorraine [the symbol of Free French Forces led by Charles de Gaulle] was the heaviest cross I have had to bear." During the postwar era, at least three issues arising from remnants of the French Empire strained relations between Paris and Washington. The first revolved around the collapse of the French effort in Indochina. The United States had provided substantial aid to France during the conflict in Indochina, but by the spring of 1954 it seemed evident that in the absence of a major intervention by the United States and/or Great Britain, the French military campaign would fail. Although the Dwight Eisenhower administration was deeply divided on the issue—as was French society—it ultimately chose not to intervene militarily, at least in part because the British government declined to join in the undertaking.

Two years later, after Egypt had nationalized the Suez Canal, France joined with Great Britain and Israel in an invasion to retake control of the canal and, perhaps, to effect a regime change in Cairo. On learning of the invasion, the United States took the issue to the United Nations Security Council and ultimately voted against its NATO allies on a resolution demanding withdrawal of the invasion forces. Secretary of State John Foster Dulles stated that Suez provided a good occasion for the United States to make a final break with European colonialism, and the United States threatened to use its formidable international economic power in ways that left Paris and London no option but to withdraw.

Algeria, considered by France to be a part of metropolitan France—and thus of a different status than, for example, Indochina—was a third issue on which many of those in France who opposed independence felt that the United States was an insufficiently supportive ally. Although the Eisenhower administration did not officially urge the French to withdraw from Algeria, periodic public statements by Americans such as then-senator John F. Kennedy opposing France in its war against separatists were hardly welcomed by those in France who favored maintaining control in Algeria. The issue was finally resolved in favor of Algerian independence after World War II resistance leader Charles de Gaulle assumed the French presidency.

French assessments of the United States, like those in Britain and Germany, tended to reflect the course of these and other events during the Cold War period. In 1954, when the Viet Minh siege of the doomed French garrison at Dien Bien Phu reached its climax, only one French respondent in five expressed a favorable view of the United States. That figure almost doubled in the following year, only to plummet once again in 1956–57 with the events surrounding the Suez invasion. By the 1960s, French assessments of the United States improved, and favorable opinions reached a peak in 1982. They remained favorable until Iraq became an issue in 2003. By the turn of the century, the United States was viewed in a very favorable light throughout most of Europe, including in countries that had once been a part of the Soviet-led Warsaw Pact. Spain, where the public was evenly divided on the question, and Russia were the only exceptions (table 2.1).

Events can also explain other variations of opinions revealed in table 6.1. The disastrous Suez invasion, which ended Prime Minister Anthony Eden's long and illustrious political career, found Washington using strong economic threats, including sinking the pound on international currency markets, against Britain to force its withdrawal from Suez. While the invasion deeply divided British society, the decline in favorable judgments about the United

States seem clearly linked to that episode. The Kennedy administration's decision a few years later to cancel the Skybolt missile, which the British had counted on to be a mainstay in their strategic deterrent, coincided with declining British sentiments about their ally.[1]

Finally, Italy did not experience such episodes as the Suez invasion or the Skybolt cancellation, but apparently the Pershing missile controversy did affect how Italians viewed the United States, as the generally favorable views dropped sharply between 1982 and 1984.

To summarize, the evidence in table 6.1 suggests that publics in none of these European countries were stuck in a permanent pro-American or anti-American mode of thinking. There were, to be sure, a number of sharp changes in how the United States was appraised during the 1954–87 period, and these changes generally seem to have been explicable reactions to American foreign policy decisions.

SEPTEMBER 11 AND THE INVASION OF AFGHANISTAN

It would be impossible to review all aspects of American foreign policy during the past few years with a view to discerning the extent to which the Djerejian committee report may have been correct in citing those policies as the primary source of anti-American sentiments abroad. Because the survey evidence reviewed in previous chapters suggests that events surrounding the September 11 terrorist attacks and subsequent events in Afghanistan and Iraq—what the Bush administration has called the "global war on terror"—have played a significant role in this respect, the following analysis will focus on them, with less attention to other important international issues.

Any analysis of recent American foreign policies should avoid at least two traps. First, it is important not to lose track of political realities. As noted at the end of chapter 5, a suggestion that Washington should cut off all aid to Israel flies in the face of political realities, as all administrations, both Democratic and Republican, have supported the right of Israel to exist. Equally unrealistic is any suggestion to stop importing oil from the Middle East. Whatever the merits of

---

1. The Suez and Skybolt episodes are analyzed in Richard Neustadt, *Alliance Politics* (New York: Columbia University Press, 1970). That book grew out of a report commissioned by President Kennedy, who was concerned about how and why two such historically close allies could so badly misinterpret each others' interests and actions. Neustadt was scheduled to present the report to Kennedy upon his return from his November 22, 1963, trip to Dallas.

such a proposal, the United States will be depending on oil from that region for the foreseeable future—and probably well beyond that.

Second, there is nothing to be gained by criticizing actions purely on the basis of hindsight and information that was not available at the time. Perhaps someday evidence will emerge to demonstrate that the Bush administration should have been able to pinpoint and avert the September 11 terrorist attacks, but at this point that seems highly unlikely. In contrast, although post–September 11 decisions concerning Afghanistan and Iraq are quite recent and the full archives will not be available for years, there is a good deal of evidence about what leaders in Washington knew and when they knew it.[2]

The September 11 terrorist attacks were front-page news throughout the world, and they immediately brought forth widespread expressions of sympathy, even from such unlikely sources as Libya's strongman Muammar al-Qaddafi. Perpetrators of terrorist attacks often take credit for their actions because one of their goals is maximum publicity for whatever political cause they claim to be advancing. The September 11 attacks followed that pattern, as Osama bin Laden and his al Qaeda organization lost little time in extolling the nineteen "martyrs" who hijacked the four airliners involved in the attacks. Some fringe groups in the United States and elsewhere have subsequently attributed the attacks to the CIA, Israel, or both working in collusion, but these theories have failed to gain much traction, even among publics that have been most critical of U.S. foreign policy.

There is ample evidence that following the September 11 attacks, the United States had considerable, though far from unanimous, international support for taking military action against the terrorists and their hosts. A Gallup International survey of thirty-seven countries undertaken shortly after the attacks asked respondents, "Do you agree or disagree that [your country] should take part in military actions against terrorists with the United States?" Among the fourteen Western European countries, only in Greece and three traditionally neutral countries—Austria, Finland, and Switzerland—did majorities oppose joining in military action. In France, which later came to disagree publicly with American policy in Iraq, 73 percent agreed, topped only by publics in Luxem-

---

2. A veritable flood of books based on documents and interviews has been published recently, including Michael R. Gordon and Bernard E. Trainor, *Cobra II: The Inside Story of the Invasion and Occupation of Iraq* (New York: Pantheon/Random House, 2005); George Packer, *The Assassins' Gate: America in Iraq* (New York: Farrar, Straus, and Giroux, 2005); Larry Diamond, *Squandered Victory* (New York: Times Books, 2005); Thomas E. Ricks, *Fiasco* (New York: Penguin Press, 2006); and Bob Woodward, *State of Denial* (New York: Simon and Schuster 2006).

bourg (74 percent) and Denmark (80 percent). Evidence presented in chapter 2 (table 2.13) also indicated that in 2004 the invasion of Afghanistan maintained strong support from publics in NATO allies, including by margins of 20 percent or more in France and Germany. Only in Poland and Turkey did publics express dissenting views on that issue.

Elsewhere the picture was mixed, with dramatically different responses from two South Asian neighbors. A full 86 percent of Indians supported military action, whereas in Pakistan, which had given ample support to the Taliban regime in Afghanistan and was also strongly suspected of housing training camps for terrorists, the verdict was quite different: by a margin of 62 percent to 32 percent Pakistani respondents opposed joining the United States in military action against terrorists or their host countries.[3]

International reactions to the terrorist attacks were not limited to expressions of sympathy for the United States and outrage at al Qaeda. Many countries offered assistance ranging from intelligence sharing to military support. The most important expression of solidarity came from the North Atlantic Treaty Organization, whose members, for the first time since the organization was founded in 1949, invoked Article 5 of the NATO Charter, which stipulates:

> The Parties agree that an armed attack against one or more of them in Europe or North America shall be considered an attack against them all and consequently they agree that, if such an attack occurs, each of them, in exercise of the right of individual or collective self-defense recognized by Article 51 of the Charter of the United Nations, will assist the Party or Parties so attacked by taking forthwith, individually and in concert with the other Parties, such action as it deems necessary, including the use of armed force, to restore and maintain the security of the North Atlantic area.

At the insistence of the United States, NATO members had agreed in 1999 to add "Article 24 of the Strategic Concept" to broaden the commitment undertaken in Article 5: "Alliance security must also take into account the global context. Alliance interests can be affected by other risks of a wider nature, including acts of terrorism, sabotage, and organized crime, and by the disruption of the flow of vital resources."[4] Thus, when NATO ministers met in Belgium on September 12, the stage seemed to be set for joint military action. Eighteen of the nineteen NATO members were prepared to act; only the United States op-

---

3. Gallup International Association, "Gallup International Poll on Terrorism in the U.S.," 2001.
4. Quoted in Rebecca Johnson and Micah Zenko, "All Dressed Up and No Place to Go: Why NATO Should Be on the Front Lines in the War on Terror," *Parameters* 32, no. 4 (winter 2002–3): 50.

posed taking advantage of the historic offer to invoke Article 5. According to one senior U.S. administration official, "The allies were desperately trying to give us political cover and the Pentagon was resisting it. It was insane." The United States made it clear that it wanted to conduct the campaign unilaterally in order not to have to seek allied permission on the choice of target, as had happened in Kosovo two years earlier. "Coalition is a bad word, because it makes people think of alliances," according to Robert Oakley, former head of the State Department's counterterrorism office and former ambassador to Pakistan. Or, as another senior official asserted, "The fewer people you have to rely on, the fewer permissions you have to get."[5] At a press conference in Brussels on September 26, Deputy Defense Secretary Paul Wolfowitz made public Washington's preference for going into Afghanistan alone: "If we need collective action, we will ask for it; we don't anticipate that at the moment." Defense Secretary Rumsfeld made essential the same point when he asserted, "The mission determines the coalition. The coalition doesn't determine the mission."[6]

Aside from the military shortsightedness of the decision to stiff-arm NATO allies, it had a potential future diplomatic cost. According to one analyst, "the situation irritated European leaders who, having given their strong political support, felt embarrassed about invoking Article 5 and then being left on the sidelines."[7] Leaders who had spent some of their political capital by offering Washington their military assistance in Afghanistan, only to be rebuffed, would be unlikely to forget the slight, and their enthusiasm for other American efforts to deal with terrorism might well have been diminished.

Shortly after the terrorist attacks, President Bush delivered a five-point ultimatum to the Taliban regime in Kabul in his September 20 address to Congress. In addition to delivery of al Qaeda leaders to the United States, the demands included closing terrorist training camps in Afghanistan, handing over all terrorists and their support structures, and giving the United States full access to the training camps to verify their closure.[8] The Taliban authorities allegedly made a disingenuous counteroffer concerning Osama bin Laden to American embassy officials in Pakistan but otherwise failed to satisfy the U.S. ultimatum. By then the United States was well on its way to planning for an invasion—"Operation Enduring Freedom"—with the dual purpose of overthrowing the Taliban

---

5. Elaine Sciolino and Steven Lee Myers, "A Nation Challenged: Coalition; Bush Says 'Time is Running Out': U.S. Plans to Act Largely Alone," *New York Times,* October 7, 2001.

6. Quoted in Johnson and Zenko, "All Dressed Up and No Place to Go," 51–52.

7. Stanley R. Sloan, "Crisis Response." *NATO Review* (spring 2002): 26–28.

8. George W. Bush, "Address to Joint Session of Congress and the American People," Washington, DC, September 20, 2002.

regime in Kabul and capturing the al Qaeda leadership. At that point there were compelling reasons for the United States to accept offers of military forces from NATO members. The superiority of American military technology ensured that the capture of Kabul and ouster of the Taliban regime could be achieved in short order. Indeed, if that were the criterion of victory, then the U.S. invasion was a spectacular success.

However, there remained the much more difficult immediate task of capturing or killing the top Taliban and al Qaeda leadership, and the even more daunting long-run goal of bringing stability and security to a country that had known little but conflict since the Soviet invasion of 1979. Given the size and mountainous terrain of Afghanistan, offers of more troops on the ground should have been welcomed. Moreover, the disastrous Soviet experience in trying to pacify the country after its invasion with one hundred thousand troops should have been a clear warning sign that capturing Kabul and other major cities would only be the first step in what promised to be a difficult and long-term undertaking.

Aside from a preference for unilateral action unconstrained by allies, the decision not to accept NATO assistance in conducting military operations in Afghanistan was also grounded, in part, on the hopes that the campaign would provide evidence about the deficiencies of the so-called Powell Doctrine that any military intervention should be undertaken with massive forces and a clear exit strategy. Defense Secretary Rumsfeld's preferred military plans called for remaking the American military to emphasize the superiority of smaller, highly mobile units armed with the most sophisticated military technology, thereby driving a stake through the "doctrine" of his bitter rival, Secretary of State Colin Powell.

Ultimately most members of NATO—including Canada, Great Britain, France, Germany, Italy, the Netherlands, Denmark, Norway, the Czech Republic, Portugal, and Poland—provided some forms of military assistance for the American undertaking in Afghanistan, including deployment of ground troops in some cases. Even Turkey, where the population is 99 percent Muslim, played an important role. Unlike officials in many Muslim countries, including Morocco and Indonesia, leaders in Ankara avoided framing the military undertaking in Afghanistan in "clash of civilization" terms.

That said, the decision to place unconstrained unilateralism ahead of taking full advantage of NATO's unprecedented offer of military assistance during the run-up to the invasion seems to have been a textbook case of shortsighted folly. It was obvious from the start that even the most successful military operations in Afghanistan, including the capture of all al Qaeda operatives there, would not put an end to the threat of international terrorism; therefore, the United States would continue to need all the help that it could get in its efforts to cope with that problem. By 2007 President Bush was pleading with allies to augment their forces in Afghanistan. Officials in Washington might have done well to pay heed to the advice of a retired leader who, in a speech shortly after the September 11 attacks, stated: "Just as Pearl Harbor awakened this country from the notion that we could avoid the call to duty and defend freedom in Europe and Asia in World War II so, too, should this most recent surprise attack erase the concept in some quarters that America can somehow go it alone in this fight against terrorism or in anything else for that matter."[9] The author of those words was former president George H. W. Bush.

It would be hard to make the case that the administration's somewhat clumsy dealing with NATO allies on the Afghanistan issue significantly affected how publics in those countries viewed the United States. The details of intra-alliance negotiations on burden sharing and other issues are likely to be of interest to a relatively small part of the general public. Moreover, the data presented in table 2.1 do not suggest any significant decline in support in NATO countries, other than Turkey, for the United States between the 1999–2000 State Department surveys and those undertaken by Pew in mid-2002. If there was any negative impact, it was most likely to have been confined to policy officials and perhaps some opinion leaders. Whatever the case, President Bush missed an important opportunity for fence-mending in his 2002 State of the Union address. At no cost, he might have taken a few minutes to thank by name the countries that helped the military campaign in Afghanistan and, perhaps, even to call for an ovation for the ambassadors of those countries. He cited only Afghanistan and Pakistan and Presidents Hamid Karzai and Pervez Musharraf.

Although the American military undertaking in Afghanistan had a limited impact on how publics in NATO countries viewed the United States, the same could not be said about Muslim countries. After an initial gaffe—using the word *crusade* to describe post–September 11 policies to deal with terrorism—President Bush made repeated and commendable efforts to assure Muslims in the United States and abroad of his sincere respect for their religion and his belief that terrorists were perverting rather than following the core tenets of Islam. Unfortunately not all members of the administration showed the same restraint. Lt. General Jerry Boykin, deputy undersecretary of defense for intel-

---

9. Quoted in *The New York Times*, September 19, 2001.

ligence, has repeatedly cast the conflict with terrorists in religious terms, between the true God and the false one. "I knew my God was bigger than his. I
knew that my God was a real God and his was an idol." Bin Laden and Saddam Hussein "will only be defeated if we come against them in the name of
Jesus." President Bush, who Boykin asserted "was appointed by God," has said
he disagrees but he did not publicly reprimanded Boykin for his controversial
statements.[10]

Those efforts proved to be less than persuasive, even in countries that have
usually maintained at least moderately good relations with the United States.
Indonesia is a good case in point. As a footnote to personal expressions of sympathy and support following the September 11 attacks, President Megawati
Sukarnoputri and several other Indonesian leaders warned that an attack on
Afghanistan would be unwarranted. The Gallup survey at the end of 2001 revealed that actions deemed in Washington and most NATO countries as
justified responses to the September 11 attacks were perceived very differently in
many Muslim countries, where they were often seen as evidence of an attack on
Islam. Three-fourths of Indonesians expressed favorable views of the United
States in the State Department polls at the turn of the century, but only 21 percent did so in the 2001 Gallup survey (table 2.1).

THE IRAQ WAR

Whereas it appears that the invasion of Afghanistan had rather limited impact
on public views of the United States other than in Muslim countries, there is little question about the widespread negative impact of the Iraq war.

A brief recapitulation of the survey evidence presented in chapter 2 points
clearly toward the conclusion that the Iraq issue, including prewar policy-making, the brief and successful drive into Baghdad, and the subsequent occupation of Iraq, are at the root of the "collapse" of support for the United States and
its foreign policies. Overall judgments of the United States declined sharply between 2002 and 2003 (tables 2.1 and 2.2). After a brief comeback following the
successful overthrow of the Saddam Hussein regime in April 2003, the decline
has continued in many countries. A late 2003 survey found very limited agreement for the proposition that American international influence is positive
(table 2.3), and support for a strong U.S. leadership role fell sharply between

---

10. Sidney Blumenthal, "The Religious Warrior of Abu Ghraib," *Guardian/UK*, May 20, 2004. The Rev. Franklin
Graham was equally outspoken in his depiction of Islam as an evil religion.

2002 and 2003 (table 2.4). During the same period the view that the United States takes into account the vital interests of other countries declined everywhere except among South Koreans, whose skepticism on that point remained steady (table 2.8). Although publics in most NATO allies agreed that military action is the "most appropriate way to fight terrorism" (table 2.10), when they were asked about the American antiterrorism effort, support declined steadily through 2006 (table 2.11), fueled by growing concerns that the Iraq undertaking was hurting rather than helping in coping with the problems of terrorism (table 2.20). By 2004, fewer than one-fifth of respondents in twelve NATO countries judged that the Iraq war was "worth it" (table 2.17). Nor did the American occupation effort gain many kudos for taking into account the interests and needs of the Iraqi people (table 2.18).

While this is not the place to undertake a full-scale analysis of American decision making on the Iraq issue and other recent foreign policy undertakings, it may be useful to explore briefly how policy-making in Washington, both with respect to Iraq and other issues, during the past few years has exacerbated the problem of gaining, nurturing, and sustaining support among leaders and publics abroad.

There is a legitimate place for both "worst-case" and "best-case" scenarios in the formulation and execution of policy, but they should always be used with caution and in conjunction with other diagnoses and prescriptions. The Bush administration policies with respect to Iraq illustrate the pitfalls of becoming unalterably wedded to either of these modes of analysis. During the run-up to the invasion of Iraq in March 2003, there were certainly some reasons to fear that the Saddam Hussein regime was making efforts to obtain weapons of mass destruction and that he would not hesitate to use them. Before the 1991 Gulf War, the Reagan and first Bush administrations had provided him with materials for chemical weapons that he had used not only against Iran but also against his own Kurdish citizens. Moreover, Iraq had expelled United Nations inspectors who were assigned to determine whether there had been any violations of the prohibition against weapons of mass destruction to which Baghdad had agreed in 1991 following its defeat in the Gulf War. Finally, the brutal Iraqi leader's record of mendacity provided grounds for doubting his denials of having breached the agreement on WMDs. Thus, advocates of a worst-case scenario were not lacking in ammunition.

Nevertheless, expert U.S. and UN inspectors were readmitted to Iraq in 2002 and permitted to resume their searches for any signs of WMDs. After several months, they had uncovered no evidence of such weapons. That might have given rise to some doubts about the worst-case scenario and, at minimum, to delaying any invasion in order to provide the inspectors with additional time to complete their work. Doing so would have satisfied the objections of allies and others who felt that there was no need to rush to war in the absence of clear evidence that Iraq had in fact violated the prohibition against WMDs. Without such evidence, even allies that had supported the invasion of Afghanistan—as well as the Gulf War to expel Iraqi forces from Kuwait—deemed an attack on Iraq as lacking legitimacy. Although there was no reason to believe that Iraq could use the time to upgrade its mediocre military forces and even worse leadership, the worst-case scenario prevailed, and an invasion was launched. Subsequent events demonstrated that there were no WMDs in Iraq.

Bush administration leaders—notably the president, vice president, and Defense Department leaders Donald Rumsfeld and Paul Wolfowitz—were simultaneously engaged in a best-case analysis of the challenges and opportunities presented by the predictable defeat of Iraq and overthrow of the Saddam Hussein regime. In brief, they believed that American forces would be welcomed as liberators, not conquerors, and that Iraq's oil exports would be sufficient to pay for the costs of postwar reconstruction. Repeated warnings from *within* the administration, including from Army Chief of Staff Eric Shinseki and a major five-thousand-page State Department study about the prospects for post-Saddam chaos and violence between the Sunni, Shiite, and Kurdish factions, were dismissed, as were some of those who had the temerity to express doubts about the administration's firmly held convictions about the best-case scenario for postwar Iraq. As was true of the worst-case analysis of WMDs in Iraq, events since the capture of Baghdad in April 2003 amply vindicated critics who cast doubts on the best-case scenario that depicted a stable and prosperous Iraq.

AMERICAN RHETORIC

In response to the question, "What is the role of the United States in the world?" in one of the 2000 presidential campaign debates, George W. Bush replied: "I'm not sure that the role of the United States is to go around the world and say this is the way it's got to be. . . . I just don't think it's the role of the United States to walk into a country and say, we do it this way, so should you. . . . I think the United States must be humble and must be proud and confident in our values, but humble in how we treat nations that are figuring out how to chart their own course." In response to another question, he returned to the same theme: "We're a freedom-loving nation. If we're an arrogant nation, they'll view us that way, but if we are a humble nation, they'll respect us."[11]

Candidate Bush's thoughtful advice has on more than one occasion fallen by the wayside during the post–September 11 era. In this generally well-received speech to Congress nine days after the terrorist attacks he asserted, "Either you are with us, or you are with the terrorist." That assertion, which has appeared in other presidential pronouncements, is hardly a sound basis for gaining support abroad. The moralistic tone of pronouncements to that effect is sure to offend many, and it needlessly classifies as enemies those countries that may have genuine reasons for not taking sides on an issue. Those reasons may often include domestic political realities that make it difficult for leaders, especially in democratic regimes in which leaders usually cannot be wholly indifferent to the preferences of important groups at home, to line up solidly behind Washington in a given situation. If it is necessary to divide the world into two camps, far better to adopt the formula that "if you are not against us, you are with us," as President John F. Kennedy did in connection with countries in the "Nonaligned Movement" that preferred not to become engaged in the Cold War conflict, or even those that found it profitable to play off Moscow versus Washington.

Unfortunately a number of other rhetorical gaffes marred the administration's diplomacy while it was trying to garner support for its campaign against Iraq. Some of the most derogatory barbs and taunts were aimed at NATO allies. After German Chancellor Gerhard Schroeder announced during his 2002 re-election campaign that he would not deploy German troops in an invasion of Iraq, relations between Washington and Bonn cooled considerably, in part owing to repeated verbal jabs from Washington aimed at recalcitrant NATO allies. At a press conference at the Foreign Press Center, Secretary of Defense Rumsfeld made a distinction between "Old Europe"—specifically Germany and France, who opposed invading Iraq—and the new East European members of the alliance. "But you look at vast numbers of other countries in Europe, they're not with France and Germany. . . . [T]hey're with the U.S. You're thinking of Europe as Germany and France. I don't. I think that's Old Europe."[12] Rumsfeld repeated his "Old Europe" jibe five months later at a ceremony marking the tenth anniversary of the George C. Marshall Center in Germany—with the German

11. Presidential debate at Wake Forest University, October 11, 2000.
12. "News Transcript: Secretary Rumsfeld Briefs at the Foreign Press Center," Defense Link: U.S. Department of Defense, January 22, 2003.

foreign minister in attendance. He asserted that "old" refers not to age, size, or geography, but to "behavior and vision."[13]

Lest anyone dismiss Rumsfeld's observations as a careless slip of the tongue, several weeks after the initial "Old Europe" comment, he identified the three countries "least likely to help" the United States in the war against terrorism as Cuba, Libya, and Germany, although, in fact, German combat forces were then engaged in supporting the U.S. military campaign in Afghanistan.[14] Given the odious tyrants ruling in Havana and Tripoli, Germans could scarcely miss the intent behind Rumsfeld's words. Two days later, State Department spokesman Richard Boucher contributed his mature words of wisdom. He described a forthcoming meeting among four NATO members—Germany, France, Belgium, and Luxembourg—as "a little bitty summit," and sneeringly referred to them collectively as "the chocolate makers."[15] During the same period the cafeteria in the House of Representatives renamed its French fries "freedom fries," and there was a suggestion, not acted upon, that Washington should pay to have the bodies of U.S. servicemen in French cemeteries disinterred and returned for burial in this country. French wines were removed from restaurant menus even in some cosmopolitan American cities. The frequency with which Rumsfeld and his colleagues hurled such barbs seems to rule out the hypothesis of inadvertent verbal carelessness.

Such observations almost surely contributed to the sharply declining assessments of the United States among many NATO countries, as revealed in table 2.1 and elsewhere, but their impact probably took a back seat to the much more serious diplomatic blunder committed by Deputy Defense Secretary Paul Wolfowitz in the wake of the March 2003 parliamentary vote to bar deployment of the U.S. Fourth Infantry Division from using Turkey as a launching pad in an attack against Iraq. His expression of regret that the military did not overrule the Ankara government would appear to have been an unprecedented suggestion that a military coup against an allied, democratically elected government would better have served American interests.

SENSITIVITY TO DOMESTIC INTERESTS

All democratic governments must pay heed to the interests and preferences of core domestic constituents at least some of the time. This sensitivity may, on

13. "Rumsfeld Repeats 'Old Europe' Comment," http://www.dw-world.de/dw/article/0,,890806,00.html.
14. "Rumsfeld: Time to Act against Iraq Almost Here," Fox News Channel, February 7, 2003.
15. "U.S. Sneers at 'Chocolate Makers,'" http://News24.com, February 9, 2003.

occasion, force governments to choose between placating domestic constituents and satisfying the preferences of even close allies abroad; in those instances, domestic concerns are likely to prevail. Some recent foreign policy decisions provide several relevant examples.

Because of opposition from the National Rifle Association and the attorney general the administration pulled out of the Small Arms Control Pact that is intended to slow the flow of small arms and assault weapons. Most of those arms ended up in Third World countries where weapons are annually responsible for about one half million deaths, mostly of women and children. The pact would not in any manner have infringed upon the Second Amendment right of Americans to purchase and own arms, but the NRA was adamant in its opposition, and it was not reticent in reminding the administration that its members had played a critical role in the very close 2000 election that brought George W. Bush to the White House.

To placate the fundamentalist religious right, in 2002 the administration eliminated the minuscule U.S. contribution of $34 million to the United Nations Population Fund. The given reason was the 1985 Kemp-Kasten amendment to the Foreign Operations Appropriation Act: "None of the funds made available by this act . . . may be made available to any organization or program, which, as determined by the President of the United States, supports or participates in the management of a program of coercive abortion or involuntary sterilization." The obvious target was China, which has a one-child-per-family policy, but a State Department investigation in 2002 found "no evidence" that the UNPF knowingly took part in managing programs of coercive abortion or sterilization. Investigations by the United Nations, the British Parliament, and a group of religious leaders came to the same conclusion. The United States has nevertheless continued to block UNPF contributions.[16]

The temptation to issue a congressional proclamation on the massacre of Armenians by Turkey during World War I may cause serious damage to relations with a crucial ally. Armenian-Americans are almost certainly correct in asserting that, contrary to vehement Turkish denials, the killings in fact took place. It is, however, far from clear that American interests are well served by a "feel good" gesture that may give Turkey, already on the verge of a rebuff from the European Union, still another reason to look eastward—perhaps toward Iran—rather than toward the west. It is as if in a fit of meddlesome mischief the

---

16. Paul Richter, "Citing Chinese Abortions, U.S. Refuses to Fund Program," *Los Angeles Times*, July 17, 2004; and Christopher Marquis, "U.S. Cuts Off Financing of U.N. Unit for 3rd Year," *New York Times*, July 17, 2004.

Turkish Grand National Assembly demanded an American acknowledgment and apology for its treatment of Native Americans. It seems certain that the reaction in Washington and among most Americans would range between a bemused "so why is that *your* concern?" and outrage.

The previously cited American tariffs on softwood lumber imports from Canada provide still another example of domestic interests trumping amicable relations with even close allies. In that case, although Canadian appeals brought forth several favorable rulings based on both the North American Free Trade Agreement and the World Trade Organization rules, in the face of American insistence that the issue should be negotiated, Canada ended up having to accept a partial settlement. Similarly, the United States responded to demands for protection from the steel industry by imposing heavy tariffs on imports. The tariffs were declared illegal by the WTO but were only rescinded on December 4, 2003, when Japan and the European Union threatened to retaliate with tariffs on goods from key electoral states such as Florida, Wisconsin, and Michigan.

A final example in which the perceived need to placate domestic interest groups trumped international interests emerges from trade policy. Shortly after the September 11 terrorist attacks, most of the world's major trading countries met in Doha, Qatar, where they agreed to undertake a series of measures intended to expand international trade. The beneficiaries were to include less-developed countries by opening markets to their products, especially agricultural goods. After several international meetings, the so-called Doha Round of trade negotiations collapsed in 2006 in a flurry of finger-pointing. There was plenty of blame to go around. European Union countries, especially France, were determined to maintain tariffs on agricultural goods in order to protect their farmers. Governments in Brazil, India, and other emerging economies were unenthusiastic about opening their markets to manufactured goods.

The United States could easily have emerged as the champions of freer trade and of efforts to level the international playing field for poorer countries, especially in Africa, that have been left far behind economically. As the most important international economic player and a prime beneficiary of expanding trade, the United States has long been committed to the principle of a more liberal trading regime; many conservative supporters of the Bush administration were ideologically attracted to reducing rather than expanding federal programs; and, following the tax cuts of the previous year, the federal budget deficit was inching toward unprecedented levels. Even in the face of such strong reasons for scaling back farm subsidies, in 2002 the president signed a $180 billion program to expand them. This represented a $70 billion increase and a reversal of a 1996 Clinton administration decision to begin phasing out such payments. The conservative Heritage Foundation estimated the actual cost to taxpayers of the 2002 farm subsidy program as $462 billion over its ten-year life.

The result is that American farmers, who already enjoy vast advantages in mechanization of farming, are encouraged to overproduce and then flood international markets with soybeans, cotton, and other commodities at prices that those in developing countries cannot match. Although farmers now constitute only about 2 percent of the world's largest economy, and huge industrial conglomerates have largely replaced the revered "small family farm" of American lore, agricultural interests remain a powerful force in Washington, at least in part because rural states enjoy a disproportionate representation in Congress. The farm bill also includes a provision stating that data about recipients of the subsidies is "proprietary information" and is thus not available to journalists or others.[17] The dearth of polling data from African countries makes it very difficult to assess the impact of the 2002 farm bill on assessments of the United States and its policies.

In the light of European Union intransigence on the issue and farm group pressures at home, could Washington have prevailed had it made good on its pledge at the 2001 Doha meeting? Perhaps not. But by reducing or eliminating rather than increasing farm subsidies, it would at least have driven home the important point that the United States is prepared to stand behind its longstanding thesis that "trade, not aid" is the best path for economic development, while at the same time highlighting quite clearly that France and some others in the EU were less than sterling international citizens in this instance.

Although the Bush administration has been sensitive to the policy preferences of its core domestic interest groups, it has often been somewhat less patient and forgiving with allies who fail to toe Washington's line. On occasion it has acknowledged and graciously accepted decisions by foreign leaders to give their domestic political considerations priority over Washington's policy preferences. When newly elected Ukrainian president Viktor Yushchenko, who had received strong U.S. backing in his electoral campaign against an old-line communist, withdrew his country's small military contingent from Iraq, at least publicly President Bush accepted that decision as the redemption of a campaign pledge by a strongly pro-Western leader. And, as noted in chapter 4, Washington wisely chose to overlook Morocco's decision not to join the "coali-

---

17. Andrew Cassel, "Why U.S. Farm Subsidies Are Bad for the World," *Philadelphia Inquirer,* May 6, 2002; and Alan Beattie, "US Farm Subsidies Weigh Down Efforts to Defrost Doha Talks," *Financial Times,* January 31, 2007.

tion of the willing" in Iraq. But such tolerance has not always prevailed. Mexico and Turkey had powerful domestic reasons, including overwhelming evidence from public opinion surveys, not to defer to American demands on the issue of Iraq during the weeks prior to the invasion of that country. However, rather than accepting the decisions of the Turkish parliament to bar deployment of the U.S. Fourth Infantry Division and of the Mexican government not to support Security Council Resolution 1442, Washington reacted with scarcely concealed anger. In the case of Mexico, that included the rather petty cancellation of the traditional American reception to celebrate the Cinco de Mayo, a major Mexican holiday.

After the capture of Baghdad, when the United States was trying to gain international financial and other support for the occupation and reconstruction of Iraq, it simultaneously declared that only firms from countries that joined the "coalition of the willing" in the Iraq invasion would be permitted to bid on reconstruction contracts.[18] Possibly this was an instance of bureaucratic bungling in which two parts of the government were unaware of each other's missions, but statements from the Defense Department suggested otherwise— that it was indeed a carefully planned policy to reward friends and punish those who chose to pursue national interests as they, not Washington, defined them.

Along the same lines, the administration has seemed quite tone deaf about assisting leaders abroad who may need to show their domestic constituents that following Washington's lead in foreign affairs will at least on occasion yield tangible rewards. This is especially true if joining the United States is highly unpopular at home. The example of British prime minister Tony Blair is instructive in this respect. Blair was the ultraloyal ally who joined the "coalition of the willing," sending British forces into Iraq in 2003 despite public opposition to the war. As a result of doing so, he paid a very high political price at home. Although Blair's Labor Party was returned to power in the May 5, 2005, election, it suffered a net loss of ninety-five seats from its previous majority. Yet when Blair asked the United States to join in his plan for doubling the level of foreign aid to Africa, he met a rebuff from President Bush, who stated that such an increase in aid "does not fit our budget schedule."[19] Although Blair has strongly supported international action to deal with global warming, he has received no

---

18. Erin E. Arvedlund and Clifford Krauss, "A Region Inflamed: Reconstruction; Allies Angered at Exclusion from Bidding," New York Times, December 11, 2003.

19. Elizabeth Becker and David E. Sanger, "Bush Maintains Opposition to Doubling Aid to Africa," New York Times, June 2, 2005. The administration later increased aid to Africa, but as a percent of GDP, U.S. aid still lags far behind that from other developed countries, Sonni Efron, "Catastrophe in Southern Asia: U.S. Aid Generous and Stingy," Los Angeles Times, December 31, 2004.

support from Washington on the issue. President Bush has been adamantly opposed to any substantial action to deal with the issue. He has not only opposed the Kyoto Protocol but he has also refused to enter into negotiations to deal with some major objections to that agreement—for example, that it unfairly exempts India, China, and other developing countries from its target goals on reduction of emissions. Blair's historic string of three consecutive electoral victories should have been enough to ensure widespread affection and support, most of all from his Labor Party colleagues, but because of the growing unpopularity of British participation in Iraq, he suffered the humiliation of being publicly pushed by members of his own party in Parliament to hasten the date of his retirement. It is little wonder that David Cameron, the new Conservative Party leader, has assured the British public that he will pursue a more independent course in foreign policy.[20] Nor should Blair's decision in February 2007 to bring home more British troops from Iraq be a great surprise. The thesis that it was a testament to Britain's ability to have secured the Basra region was not wholly convincing, even to British observers.[21]

Tony Blair was not alone in learning that Washington has been much quicker to take note of deviations from its policy preferences than to express gratitude for support from abroad. As noted earlier, France, Germany, Mexico, Canada, Turkey, and other countries that chose not to follow the United States into Iraq have learned that defiance is not cost-free. An effective alliance leader, especially a rich and powerful one, can make good use of "side payments" to reward and sustain cooperation from its allies. The United States regularly did so during the Cold War, and when disagreements arose within NATO, it made efforts to contain them to ensure that they did not spill over into other issue areas. In Cold War alliances led by the USSR, on the other hand, deviations could bring forth invasions—for example of Hungary in 1956 and Czechoslovakia in 1968—or at least public denunciations of ideological heterodoxy, most notably in the case of China.[22]

DEEP PARTISAN CLEAVAGES

Repairing America's sinking reputation abroad will also require confronting the effects of deep partisan cleavages on the home front. "Politics stops at the

---

20. Speech of September 11, 2006.
21. Stephen Fidler and Steve Negus, "Stability and Rule of Law Remain a Distant Vision," *Financial Times*, February 22, 2007; and "Iraq Is No Success for UK as Pull-Out Starts," *Financial Times*, February 22, 2007.
22. Ole R. Holsti, P. Terrence Hopmann, and John D. Sullivan, *Unity and Disintegration of International Alliances* (New York: Wiley, 1973), esp. chaps. 1 and 6.

water's edge," a favorite slogan of countless presidents and other leaders eager to cut off debate on their policies, has rarely been an accurate description of American foreign policy-making, but even by the standards of previous contentious periods, current divisions stand out as exceptionally deep.

Aside from its domestic importance in formulating and executing foreign policies, bipartisanship is also significant internationally. All other things being equal, American policies that gain the support of both major political parties are likely to be perceived by others as more legitimate. Moreover, actions that are sustained by bipartisan support can reassure leaders and publics abroad of continuity in Washington's policies. Why make a commitment to join the United States in a major international undertaking if the next American election is likely to bring a policy reversal? An important consequence of Dwight Eisenhower's narrow victory over isolationist Senator Robert Taft for the 1952 Republican presidential nomination and his subsequent landslide win in the general election was that these outcomes ensured continuity on major elements of the internationalist policies of Democratic presidents Roosevelt and Truman. Although Eisenhower criticized implementation of these policies by Truman, he did not propose withdrawing from the UN and NATO or reversing the principles of containment and deterrence that lay at the core of what has sometimes been called "the revolution in American foreign policy."[23]

Bipartisanship is not an important virtue in its own right, nor does agreement across party lines guarantee high-quality foreign policy decisions. In an impressive display of bipartisan consensus, the Senate passed the "Gulf of Tonkin Resolution" in August 1964 with little debate and only two dissenting votes, and the House of Representatives quickly followed suit by a vote of 416-0. Presidents Lyndon Johnson and Richard Nixon subsequently cited these congressional actions to justify rapid escalation of American forces in Vietnam, which, in turn, led to what was arguably the most disastrous undertaking in the history of American foreign affairs.

That said, just as support from the UN Security Council in 1990 for military action against Iraq to expel its invading forces from Kuwait made it easier for other countries to join the coalition against Iraq, a degree of bipartisan agreement can provide an important element of "policy legitimacy" in the domestic political arena. During much of the Cold War, top leaders in both parties were in broad agreement on many core elements of American policy, even though they might engage in vigorous debates, especially during presidential cam-

---

23. William G. Carleton, *The Revolution in American Foreign Policy* (New York: Random House, 1963).

paigns, about the most desirable and feasible strategies and tactics for implementing them.

Policies for dealing with terrorist threats have and will continue to involve serious questions about priorities, costs, acceptable infringements on individual freedoms, and the like. If discussions of such important issues become little more than perceived opportunities for scoring partisan debating points, the quality and legitimacy of the outcomes will surely suffer. For example, an outburst by Karl Rove in which he accused liberals of merely wanting to "prepare indictments and offer therapy and understanding for our [September 11] attackers"—in short, to coddle terrorists—brings to mind Senator Joseph McCarthy's charges during the early 1950s that communists in the State Department had "lost" China.[24]

In part owing to the acrimonious debates among leaders in Washington and elsewhere, survey data reveal that a partisan divide—perhaps partisan chasm would be a more accurate description—of almost unprecedented dimensions may also be found among the general public, especially on the Iraq war. For example, a January 2006 Gallup survey revealed that when the public was asked if the United States "made a mistake in sending troops to Iraq, or not," the overall response was fairly evenly divided—51 percent stated that it was a "mistake," but that masked deep partisan divisions among Republicans (14 percent "mistake"), Democrats (76 percent), and independents (63 percent). Sharp divisions emerge even when surveys shift from normative questions to more factual ones. An October 2006 Gallup poll asked, "Who do you think is currently winning the war in Iraq—the United States and it allies, the insurgents in Iraq, or neither side?" Fifty-one percent of Republicans responded that the United States and its allies are winning, whereas only 3 percent of Democrats and 13 percent of independents expressed that view.[25] Surveys by other polling organizations yield equally wide partisan chasms on a wide range of foreign policy issues.

Bipartisanship is not the natural state of affairs on foreign policy, as George Washington, James Madison, Woodrow Wilson, and many otherwise able leaders have learned. Cooperation across party lines requires skilled and thoughtful presidential leadership.

Appointments to key positions are among the tools available to presidents who seek to mitigate the impact of partisanship. In selecting the American del-

---

24. Speech to New York Conservative Party, June 22, 2005.
25. Gallup poll, January 20–22, 2006; and Gallup poll, October 20–22, 2006.

egation to the Versailles Conference following World War I, Woodrow Wilson could have included any of several distinguished Republicans who were on record as favoring the creation of an international organization as part of the peace settlement. Even if deep personal animosities had ruled out including Senator Henry Cabot Lodge, former president William Howard Taft might have been appointed. Or, with an eye toward the treaty ratification process, Wilson might have selected a leading Republican senator other than Lodge. By failing to include a leading Republican on the American delegation, Wilson went a long way toward framing the question of American membership in the League of Nations as a partisan issue, thereby materially reducing the chances that the Versailles Treaty would gain approval of the Republican-dominated Senate.

Some of Wilson's successors have demonstrated greater political acumen. After the collapse of the French army in 1940, anticipating that the United States would be drawn into World War II, Franklin D. Roosevelt fired his isolationist secretaries of navy and war—both Democrats—and replaced them with Frank Knox (Republican vice presidential candidate in 1936) and Henry L. Stimson (among the most distinguished Republican foreign policy officials of the twentieth century, who had served as secretary of war and state in the cabinets of Presidents William Howard Taft and Herbert Hoover). When faced with negotiating a peace treaty with all the countries that had been at war with Japan and then guiding it through the U.S. Senate, Harry Truman turned to Republican stalwart John Foster Dulles, who would soon thereafter serve as President Eisenhower's secretary of state. And, after winning a close election in 1960, John F. Kennedy appointed Republicans Douglas Dillon and Robert McNamara to head the treasury and defense departments. These appointments certainly did not ensure Republican support for all administration foreign policies, but they represented significant steps in eliciting bipartisan cooperation on some important issues during World War II and the ensuing Cold War.

Whether the partisan divide on Iraq and other issues can be bridged probably depends at least in part on how events play out on the ground in Iraq, and also on whether the Bush administration makes even token efforts to reach out to Democrats in order to establish some semblance of bipartisan foundations for American foreign policy. Early signs on the latter point are not especially auspicious as the official who might have worked most effectively with the opposition party, Secretary of State Colin Powell, was abruptly fired within days of the president's reelection. In general, members of the president's team who have questioned any aspects of his policies, including Army Chief of Staff Eric

Shinseki (who presciently warned that several hundred thousand U.S. troops would be required to maintain order in postwar Iraq), Chair of the Foreign Intelligence Advisory Board Brent Scowcroft (who publicly opposed the invasion of Iraq), Treasury Secretary Paul O'Neill (who was not sufficiently enthusiastic about impending tax cuts because they would result in huge budget deficits), and Director of the National Economic Council Lawrence Lindsey (who had the temerity to state that the impending war against Iraq would cost $100–200 billion rather than the administration's figure of $50–60 billion), were quickly shown the door. O'Neill and Lindsey fared better than Shinseki, who was subject to repeated and humiliating public rebukes, as both received at least "lukewarm thanks" for their services.[26] Thus, it would take a major change of mind set for the president to reach out to those who may not always have been vocal cheerleaders. However, the president made it clear in a long interview that his victory in the 2004 election essentially settled all issues relating to the Iraq war, including accountability for any mistakes and misjudgments.[27]

Openings at the World Bank and in the American delegation to the United Nations provided President Bush with an opportunity for minor gestures toward bipartisanship, especially as neither the World Bank nor the UN plays a central role in the administration's foreign policy calculations. Instead of grasping this chance, the president appointed two of the most partisan and ideological officials of his first administration—Paul Wolfowitz and John R. Bolton—to serve as president of the World Bank and U.S. ambassador to the United Nations. When Wolfowitz was forced to resign in 2007 following revelations of unduly favorable arrangements for his girlfriend, also a World Bank official, yet another opportunity for a gesture toward bipartisanship arose. Instead, President Bush selected Robert Zoellick, an able lawyer who has served in three Republican administrations and who was an early advocate of military action against Iraq.

CONCLUSION

These examples have illustrated but certainly not proved beyond reasonable doubt that American policies and policy-making have been one of the main

---

26. Edmund L. Andrews, "Upheaval in the Treasury: Treasury Secretary; Bush, in Shakeup of Cabinet, Ousts Treasury Leader," *New York Times,* December 7, 2002; and Elizabeth Bumiller, "Threats and Response: The Costs; While White House Cuts Estimates of Costs of War with Iraq," *New York Times,* December 31, 2001.
27. Jim VandeHei and Michael Fletcher, "Bush Says Election Ratified Iraq Policy," *Washington Post,* January 15, 2005. The full transcript of the interview appears in the same issue of that newspaper.

driving forces behind the increasingly critical views of publics abroad. This is not to say that changing policies will always change minds because humans and governmental organizations have a remarkable ability to interpret information in ways that sustain their preconceptions, even if that information might seem to call them into question. For example, "inherent good faith" and "inherent bad faith" models of other countries can skew interpretations of information, with significant policy consequences. Throughout early 1941 British intelligence warned Joseph Stalin that Hitler's armies were massing on the USSR's western frontier in preparation for an invasion of the Soviet Union. Stalin dismissed the information as a British trick intended to incite a war between the two partners in the Nazi-Soviet Pact, and he continued to ship vital raw materials to Germany right up to the day of the invasion. Unable to believe that Hitler was capable of such treachery, even hours after the German attack, Stalin refused to order the Soviet air force into action against the invaders.

A less dramatic example emerges from the Cold War. Following Stalin's death in 1953, Soviet leaders undertook a number of steps that seemed to be consistent with U.S. goals in Europe. These included an agreement on a peace treaty and neutralization of Austria, withdrawal from the Porkkala naval base in Finland, and some reductions in the size of the Soviet army. When asked whether these steps signaled a fundamental change in Moscow's foreign policy, Secretary of State Dulles vehemently denied that they did. With respect to the troop reductions, he asserted that it was better for Soviet soldiers to be doing guard duty than building nuclear weapons. More generally, he argued that such moves were motivated by Soviet weakness rather than any genuine change of policy. Dulles's statements were intended to prevent publics at home and abroad from relaxing out of an unwarranted belief that the Soviet leadership had given up its long-term goal of world domination. They also reflected an unswerving belief that not even a post-Stalin Soviet regime could act out of other-than-malicious goals. In fairness, by its brutal invasion of Hungary in 1956, Moscow reinforced Dulles's pessimistic theory about the sources of Soviet conduct.

There can be little doubt that some of America's most vocal critics adhere to an "inherent bad faith" model of the United States in which, for example, Washington's actions in the Third World on some issue are evidence of expansionist imperial ambitions, whereas inaction on the same question proves its indifference to the plight of the poor. Nevertheless, it would be a grievous error to accept the thesis that those who are critical of the United States invariably hate us because of who we are rather than what we do. This is the ultimate counsel of despair. It is in effect asserting that the world's only superpower does not have the ability to devise and execute foreign policies that are capable of generating good will or "winning the hearts and minds" of most leaders and publics abroad while also pursuing vital national interests. The United States has repeatedly demonstrated an ability to do precisely that. From leadership in establishment of the United Nations and other major international organizations after World War II, the establishment of the Marshall Plan and Point Four, the Berlin airlift to break the Soviet blockade of that beleaguered city, an important role in creation of the North Atlantic Treaty Organization, resistance to the invasion of South Korea, and other actions during the early post–World War II years, to such later actions as creation of the Peace Corps, expulsion of Saddam Hussein's forces from Kuwait in the first Gulf War, and the major relief efforts in the wake of such natural disasters as the tsunami of 2004, the United States has shown that it can act in ways that gain the approval of most publics abroad. To believe otherwise and to act as if others will oppose us irrespective of our policies is to fall prey to a dangerous self-fulfilling prophecy.

There will, of course, always be naysayers who will attribute nefarious motives to whatever Washington does—or fails to do—because they do in fact hate America for what it is, but that should not act as a deterrent against policies that promote vital national interests by means that will gain international support, especially from liberal democracies, rather than alienate substantial numbers of leaders and publics abroad. If undertaken in the spirit of humility rather than arrogance, as suggested by candidate George W. Bush in one of the 2000 presidential debates, such policies will in the long run be more cost-effective. Rather than reliance solely on carrots (inducements) and sticks (threats), Washington can count on the cooperation that arises from "soft power."

But at this point it is appropriate to ask, "So what?" While it is always nice to be liked by everyone, given America's unquestioned status as the world's only superpower, does it really matter very much if publics and governments in long-time allies France, Canada, Turkey, South Korea, and elsewhere harbor growing doubts about the United States and are unwilling to toe Washington's line on all of its policies? In any case, don't the benefits of acting swiftly without the need to consult, cooperate, and compromise with other countries or within international institutions outweigh whatever contributions allies and others might make to major American international undertakings?[28]

---

28. According to a PIPA survey, 87 percent of Americans believe that it is very (40 percent) or somewhat (47 percent) important "for people in other countries to feel good will toward the United States." PIPA, "What Kind of Foreign Policy Does the American Public Want?" October 20, 2006, 6.

The argument here is that it does indeed matter and it will become increasingly important. During the coming decades the United States will confront a complex agenda of international issues, ranging from immigration, trade imbalances, energy dependence, international pandemics, and environmental degradation to proliferation of weapons of mass destruction and genocidal wars within and between "failing states." It requires no great leap of imagination to include international terrorism among the top threats to American security. Although the "war on terrorism" resembles "the war on cancer" in that it will never be possible to declare an outright victory, progress in coping with the threat during the years since the September 11 attacks has been rather spotty.

An effective American policy for dealing with global issues—and most assuredly with the terrorist threat—will be materially enhanced if the United States is able to mobilize strong international support through NATO, the United Nations, and other multinational venues. Few contemporary international problems lend themselves to unilateral solutions, even if undertaken with all the material resources of the world's only superpower.

At minimum, any progress on terrorism will depend on gaining widespread sharing of intelligence. To be sure, the United States has not experienced another terrorist attack since 9/11, but bombings in Bali, Madrid, London, Egypt, and elsewhere indicate clearly that the threat has not disappeared. Moreover, recent events in Afghanistan provide scant reason for complacency. Although the Taliban was driven from power in 2001 and a number of important al Qaeda and other terrorist leaders have been killed or driven into hiding, the effective reach of the elected Karzai government is largely confined to Kabul and its environs, while the Taliban and drug traffickers have been making a comeback. A late 2006 report from the CIA highlights the urgency of the deteriorating situation in Afghanistan. It concludes that the elected Karzai government is increasingly perceived by Afghans as corrupt and unable to deliver reconstruction or protect the country from the surge of Taliban attacks.[29] The relatively small American military contingent is clearly insufficient to help the Kabul government gain control of the country, and the increasingly bloody insurgency in Iraq has made it difficult, if not impossible, for the United States to augment its force in Afghanistan in a very substantial way. A classified report from the Pentagon to Congress acknowledged that commitments to

29. David Rohde and James Risen, "CIA Review Highlights Afghan Leader's Woes," *New York Times*, November 5, 2006.

Afghanistan and Iraq have strained Pentagon resources.[30] In the face of a manifest danger that Afghanistan will again experience a civil war, as happened after the loss of American interest in the country in the wake of the Soviet withdrawal in February 1989, a number of NATO and other countries have increased their military forces there. It remains to be seen whether the Afghanistan undertaking will be successful in establishing a stable, effective government while also providing security for the long-suffering population, but in the absence of significant military assistance from other countries, the Afghanistan undertaking will almost surely fail.

In short, the United States will face great difficulties in dealing effectively with a challenging foreign policy agenda unless it is able to persuade other countries that *their* vital interests are best served by cooperation *with* rather than balancing *against* the United States; that is, soft power will be needed to supplement its immense hard power resources and to mitigate fears that American material resources represent a threat to the interests of others. Even Robert Kagan, a staunch supporter of a muscular American foreign policy and vocal critic of European approaches to foreign affairs, has admitted that "America for the first time since World War II, is suffering a crisis of international legitimacy."[31] Another conservative Republican observer, Brent Scowcroft, national security adviser to the first President Bush, is even more pointed: "Historically, the world has always given us the benefit of the doubt because it believed that we meant well. It no longer does. It is easy to lose trust, but it takes a lot of work to gain it. Can the sense of confidence in us be restored? Sure. But not easily."[32] As if to underscore the magnitude of the task, a June 2007 Harris survey for the *Financial Times* found that in five European countries—all NATO allies—32 of the respondents rated the United States as the "greatest threat to global security," a far higher danger than China (19 percent), Iran (17 percent), Iraq (11 percent), North Korea (9 percent), or Russia (5 percent).[33] To date there are few indications of balancing against the United States, at least in part because of America's past reputation for using its power in relatively benign ways; for example, heretofore it has rarely initiated aggressive wars outside the Western hemisphere. The invasion of Iraq in 2003 could change that because it is widely

---

30. Thom Shanker, "Pentagon Says Iraq Effort Limits Ability to Fight Other Conflicts: Chairman of Joint Chiefs Tells Congress of Risks," *New York Times*, May 3, 2005.

31. Robert Kagan, "America's Crisis of Legitimacy," *Foreign Affairs* 83, no. 2 (March/April 2004): 65–87.

32. Quoted in Roger Cohen, "The Breaking Point," *New York Times*, September 18, 2007.

33. Daniel Dombey and Stanley Pignal, "Europeans See US as Biggest Threat to World Peace," *Financial Times*, July 2, 2007.

seen abroad as, at best, a misguided diversion from the central task of confronting terrorist organizations or as, at worst, a twenty-first-century example of traditional imperialism.

Echoing a theme made famous by Walt Kelly's cartoon character Pogo—"We have met the enemy and he is us"—a thoughtful observer of American foreign policy has warned, "With such [military] power undergirded by a belief in America's moral exceptionalism, the most dangerous threat to American omnipotence may very well come about as a result of the alienation of Europe and Japan, and the wariness of China and Russia. . . . In this respect, we have more to fear from our own mistakes than from those enemies who are now determined to bring us down."[34]

---

34. James Chase, "Imperial America and the Common Interest," *World Policy Journal* 19 (spring 2002): 8.

Bibliography

Note: Newspaper and Internet articles used in this book are listed in the footnotes.

Ackerman, Spencer, and Franklin Foer. "The Radical." *New Republic* 229 (December 1 and 8, 2003): 17–23.

Ahearn, Raymond J. "Morocco-U.S. Free Trade Agreement." Congressional Research Service, May 26, 2005.

Ajami, Fouad. "The Falseness of Anti-Americanism." *Foreign Policy* (September/October 2003): 52–61.

Albinski, Henry. "Australia's American Alliance in the Aftermath of September 11th. *Australian Review of Public Affairs,* October 11, 2001.

Berman, Russell A., and Arno Tausch. "Yet Another Reason They Dislike Us: Europe Is Rich, but the United States Is Richer." *Hoover Digest* (winter 2005).

Brooks, Stephen. *As Others See Us: The Causes and Consequences of Foreign Perceptions of America.* Peterborough, Ontario: Broadview Press, 2006.

Buchanan, Patrick. *State of Emergency: The Third World Invasion and Conquest of America.* New York: St. Martin's Press, 2006.

Bush, George W. "Address to a Joint Session of Congress and the American People." Washington, DC, September 20, 2001.

Byers, Michael. "Preemptive Self-Defense: Hegemony, Equality, and Strategies of Legal Change." *Journal of Political Philosophy* 11 (June 2003): 171–90.

The Cabinet Diaries of Josephus Daniels. Edited by E. David Cronon. Lincoln: University of Nebraska Press, 1965.

Cameron, David. Speech on British foreign policy, September 11, 2003.

Carleton, William G. *The Revolution in American Foreign Policy.* New York: Random House, 1963.

Cellucci, Paul. *Unquiet Diplomacy.* Toronto: Key Porter Books, 2005.

Changing Minds, Winning Peace. A report submitted to the Committee on Appropriations, House of Representatives, October 1, 2003.

Chicago Council on Foreign Relations and German Marshall Fund. *Global Views 2004.* Chicago, 2004.

Chicago Council on Foreign Relations and German Marshall Fund. *Worldviews 2002: American and European Public Opinion and Foreign Policy.* Chicago, 2002.

Centro de Investigación y Docencia Económicas (CIDE) and Consejo Mexicano de Asuntos Internacionales (COMEX). *Mexico y El Mundo: Global Views 2004; Mexican Public Opinion and Foreign Policy.* September 2004.

Clarke, Harold D., Allan Kornberg, Thomas Scotto, and Joe Twyman. "Flawless Campaign, Fragile Victory: Voting in Canada's 2006 Federal Election." *PS: Political Science and Politics* 39 (October 2006): 815–19.

Conetta, Carl. "The Wages of War: Iraqi Combatant and Noncombatant Fatalities in the 2003 Conflict." Commonwealth Institute, Project on Defense Alternatives, Research Monograph 8, Cambridge, MA, October 20, 2003.

Cook, Ivan. *Australians Speak 2005: Public Opinion and Foreign Policy.* Sydney: Lowy Institute for International Policy, 2005.

Department of Foreign Affairs for the Republic of Indonesia. "Joint Statement between the United States of America and the Republic of Indonesia." September 19, 2001.

Department of Foreign Affairs for the Republic of Indonesia. "Indonesia Welcomes Iraq's Decision with Regard to the UN Inspection Team." September 18, 2002.

Department of Foreign Affairs for the Republic of Indonesia. "Indonesia Strongly Deplores Unilateral Action against Iraq." March 20, 2003.

Department of Foreign Affairs for the Republic of Indonesia. "Press Release: Indonesia Opposes Military Action towards Iraq." March 18, 2003.

Department of Foreign Affairs for the Republic of Indonesia. "Statement on the New Initiative for the Question of Iraq." February 14, 2003.

Diamond, Larry. *Squandered Victory.* New York: Times Books, 2005.

Dimock, Michael A., and Samuel L. Popkin. "Political Knowledge in Comparative Perspective." In *Do the Media Govern?* edited by Shanto Iyengar and Richard Reeves. Thousand Oaks, CA: Sage, 1997.

Dominguez, Jorge I. "Mexico," *Encyclopedia of U.S. Foreign Relations,* edited by Bruce W. Jentleson, Thomas G. Paterson, Nicholas X. Rizopoulos, Gaddis Smith, Caroline A. Hartzell, Ole R. Holsti, Howard Jones, and Henry R. Nau, vol. 3. New York: Oxford University Press, 1997.

D'Souza, Dinesh. *The Enemy at Home: The Cultural Left and Its Responsibility for 9/11.* New York: Doubleday, 2007.

Economist, *Pocket World in Figures.* London: Profile Books, 2007.

Energy Information Administration. *Annual Energy Outlook, 2004.* Washington, DC, 2004.

European Commission. *Eurobarometer.* Annual Public Opinion Surveys since 1974.

Fabbrini, Sergio. "The Domestic Sources of European Anti-Americanism." *Government and Opposition* 37, no. 1 (January 2002): 3–14.

Furia, Peter A., and Russell E. Lucas. "Determinants of Arab Public Opinion on Foreign Relations." *International Studies Quarterly* 50 (September 2006): 585–605.

Gallup Organization. *Gallup International End of Year Terrorism Poll 2001.*

German Marshall Fund. *Transatlantic Trends, 2003.*

German Marshall Fund. *Transatlantic Trends, 2004.*

German Marshall Fund. *Transatlantic Trends, 2006.*

Gingrich, Newt. "Rogue State Department." *Foreign Policy* (July/August 2003): 42–48.

"Globalization Index." *Foreign Policy* (November/December 2006): 74–81.

Global Market Insite (GMI). *World Poll Survey.* June 2004.

Gordon, Michael R., and Bernard E. Trainor. *Cobra II: The Inside Story of the Invasion and Occupation of Iraq.* New York: Pantheon/Random House, 2006.

Granatstein, J. L. *A Friendly Agreement in Advance: Canada-US Defence Relations Past, Present, and Future.* Ottawa: C. D. Howe Institute, 2002.

Harris Interactive. *What Do Europeans Like and Dislike about the United States?* March 2004.

Hollander, Paul. *Anti-Americanism: Rational and Irrational.* Revised edition. New Brunswick, NJ: Transaction Books, 1995.

Hollander, Paul, ed. *Understanding Anti-Americanism: Its Origins and Impact at Home and Abroad.* Chicago: Ivan R. Dee, 2004.

Holsti, Ole R. *Public Opinion and American Foreign Policy.* 2nd edition. Ann Arbor: University of Michigan Press, 2004.

Holsti, Ole R., P. Terrence Hopmann, and John D. Sullivan. *Unity and Disintegration of International Alliances.* New York: Wiley, 1973.

Hong, Kyudok. "The Impact of NGOs on South Korea's Decision to Dispatch Troops to Iraq." *Journal of International and Area Studies* 12, no. 2 (2005): 31–46.

Huntington, Samuel P. *The Clash of Civilizations and the Remaking of World Order.* New York: Simon and Schuster, 1996.

Huntington, Samuel P. *Who We Are: The Challenge to America's National Identity.* New York: Simon and Schuster, 2004.

ICM Research. *Survey for the British Broadcasting Corporation.* May–June 2003.

Ignatieff, Michael. "Canada in the Age of Terror—Multilateralism Meets a Moment of Truth." *Policy Options* 24 (February 2003): 14–18.

Inglehart, Ronald, and Pippa Norris. "The True Clash of Civilizations." *Foreign Policy* (March/April 2003): 62–70.

International Institute of Strategic Studies. *The Military Balance.* London: Routledge.

International Strategic Research Organization (ISRO). "Turkey-USA Relations Survey Results." Ankara, March 12, 2005.

International Strategic Research Organization (ISRO). "ISRO Turkey Terrorism Perception Survey." Ankara, August 3, 2005.

Isaacs, Maxine. "Two Different Words: The Relationship between Elite and Mass Opinions on American Foreign Policy." *Political Communication* 15 (June 1998): 323–45.

Johnson, Rebecca, and Micah Zenko. "All Dressed Up and No Place to Go: Why NATO Should Be on the Front Lines in the War on Terror." *Parameters* 32, no. 4 (winter 2002–3): 48–63.

Jones, Sidney. "Indonesia's Reaction to the War on Terrorism." United States–Indonesian Society, October 28, 2003.

Jong-yon, Hwang. "Rethinking Korean Views on America: Beyond the Dichotomy of Pro- and Anti-Americanism." *Korea Journal* (spring 2004): 103–8.

Juarez G., Leticia. "Mexico, the United States, and the War in Iraq." *International Journal of Public Opinion Research* 16, no. 2 (2004): 331–43 .

Kagan, Robert. "America's Crisis of Legitimacy." *Foreign Affairs* 83 (March/April 2004): 65–87.

Katzenstein, Peter, and Robert O. Keohane, eds. *Anti-Americanisms in World Politics.* Ithaca: Cornell University Press, 2006.

Kennedy, Paul. *The Rise and Fall of the Great Powers: Economic Change and Military Conflict from 1500 to 2000*. New York: Random House, 1987.

Kern, Thomas. "Anti-Americanism in South Korea: From Structural Cleavages to Protest." *Korea Journal* (spring 2005): 237–88.

Kim, Seung Hwan. "Anti-Americanism in Korea." *Washington Quarterly* 26 (winter 2002/2003): 109–22.

Kim, Woosang, and Tae-Hyo Kim. "A Candle in the Wind: Korean Perceptions of ROK-U.S. Security Relations." *Korean Journal of Defense Analysis* 16 (spring 2004): 99–118.

Kinzer, Stephen. *Crescent and Star: Turkey between Two Worlds*. New York: Farrar, Straus, and Giroux, 2001.

Kohut, Andrew. Testimony to the U.S. House International Relations Committee, Subcommittee on Oversight and Investigations, November 10, 2005.

Kohut, Andrew, and Bruce Stokes. *America against the World: How We Are Different and Why We Are Disliked*. New York: Time Books, 2006.

Kuniholm, Bruce. "Turkey." In *Encyclopedia of U.S. Foreign Relations*, edited by Bruce W. Jentleson, Thomas G. Paterson, Nicholas X. Rizopoulos, Gaddis Smith, Caroline A. Hartzell, Ole R. Holsti, Howard Jones, and Henry R. Nau, vol. 3. New York: Oxford University Press, 1997.

Kurlantzick, Joshua. "Terrorist Suspect." *New Republic Online*, June 7, 2006.

Lagos, Marta. "World Opinion: Terrorism and the Image of the United States in Latin America." *International Journal of Public Opinion Research* 15, no. 1 (2003): 95–101.

Larson, Eric V., Norman D. Levin, Seonhae Baik, and Bogdan Savych. *Ambivalent Allies: A Study of South Korean Attitudes toward the U.S.* Santa Monica, CA: RAND Corporation, 2004.

Lee, Sung-Yoon. "Korea-US: Swan Song for Alliance." *Asia Times*, September 16, 2006.

Levy, Jack S. "The Diversionary Theory of War: A Critique." In *Handbook of War Studies*, edited by Manus Midlarsky. London: Allen and Unwin, 1989.

Library of Congress, Federal Research Division. "Country Profile: Morocco," May 2006. lcweb2.loc.gov/frd/cs/profiles/Morocco.pdf.

Lynch, Marc. "Beyond the Arab Street: Iraq and the Arab Public Sphere." *Politics and Society* 31 (March 2003): 55–91.

Lynch, Marc. "Taking Arabs Seriously." *Foreign Affairs* 82 (September/October 2003): 81–94.

Massie, Alex. "Dog Days: Breaking the Special Relationship," *New Republic* (April 3, 2006): 18–19.

Maureen and Mike Mansfield Foundation. *Dong-A Ilbo Korean Attitudes toward Japan and Other Nations*. Asian Opinion Poll Data, March 2005.

Meunier, Sophie. "The French Exception." *Foreign Affairs* 79 (2000): 104–16.

Meunier, Sophie. "The Distinctiveness of French Anti-Americanism." In *Anti-Americanisms in World Politics*, edited by Peter J. Katzenstein and Robert O. Keohane. Ithaca: Cornell University Press, 2006.

Migdalovitz, Carol. "Morocco: Current Issues." Congressional Research Service, May 4, 2006.

Mitchell, Derek J., ed. *Strategy and Sentiment: South Korean Views of the United States and the U.S.-ROK Alliance.* Washington, DC: Center for Strategic and International Studies, 2004.

Morgenthau, Hans J. *Politics among Nations.* 4th edition. New York: Knopf, 1967.

Mueller, John. *Policy and Opinion in the Gulf War.* Chicago: University of Chicago Press, 1994.

Muftuler-Bac, Meltem. "Turkey and the USA at Cross Roads: The Impact of the War in Iraq." *International Journal* 61 (winter 2006): 61–82.

National Archives and Records Administration. Zimmermann Telegram, Record Group 59, General Records of the Department of State, 1756–1979.

Neustadt, Richard. *Alliance Politics.* New York: Columbia University Press, 1970.

Nye, Joseph. "Understanding U.S. Strength." *Foreign Policy* 72 (fall 1988): 105–29.

Nye, Joseph. *Bound to Lead: The Changing Nature of American Power.* New York: Basic Books, 1991.

Nye, Joseph. *The Paradox of American Power: Why the World's Only Superpower Can't Go It Alone.* New York: Oxford University Press, 2002.

Nye, Joseph. *Soft Power: The Means to Success in World Politics.* New York: Public Affairs, 2005.

Olson, Edward A. "Korea." In *Encyclopedia of U.S. Foreign Relations,* edited by Bruce W. Jentleson, Thomas G. Paterson, Nicholas X. Rizopoulos, Gaddis Smith, Caroline A. Hartzell, Ole R. Holsti, Howard Jones, and Henry R. Nau, vol. 3. New York: Oxford University Press, 1997.

Olson, Robert. "Views from Turkey: Reasons for the United States War against Iraq." *Journal of Third World Studies* (fall 2005): 141–60.

Ozernoy, Ilana. "Ears Wide Shut." *Atlantic Monthly* (November 2006): 30–33.

Packer, George. *The Assassins' Gate: America in Iraq.* New York: Farrar, Straus, and Giroux, 2005.

Paul, T. V. "Soft Balancing in the Age of U.S. Primacy." *International Security* 30 (summer 2005): 46–71.

Pennel, C. R. *Morocco: From Empire to Independence.* Oxford: One World Press, 2003.

Pew Research Center. *What the World Thinks in 2002.* Washington, DC: Global Attitudes Project, 2002.

Pew Research Center. *America's Image Further Erodes, Europeans Want Weaker Ties.* April–May 2003.

Pew Research Center. *Views of a Changing World.* June 2003.

Pew Research Center. *A Year after Iraq War: Mistrust of America in Europe Ever Higher, Muslim Anger Persists.* 2004.

Pew Research Center. Pew Global Attitudes Survey, *U.S. Image Up Slightly, but Still Negative,* 2005.

Pew Research Center. *Conflicting Views in a Divided World 2006.* Washington, D.C.: Pew Research Center, 2006.

Pew Research Center. *Global Unease with Major World Powers.* 2007.

Prestowitz, Clyde. *Rogue Nation: American Unilateralism and the Failure of Good Intentions.* New York: Basic Books, 2003.

Program on International Policy Attitudes (PIPA)/Globescan. *19 Nation Poll on Global Issues.* 2003–4.

Program on International Policy Attitudes (PIPA)/Globescan. *World Public Opinion Says World Not Going in Right Direction.* 2004–5.

Program on International Policy Attitudes (PIPA)/Globescan. *In 20 of 23 Countries Polled Citizens Want Europe to Be More Influential Than U.S.* 2005–6.

Program on International Policy Attitudes (PIPA)/Globescan. *World View of U.S. Role Goes from Bad to Worse.* 2006–7.

Record, Jeffrey. "The Bush Doctrine and the War with Iraq." *Parameters: U.S. Army War College Quarterly* (spring 2003): 4–21.

Ricks, Thomas E. *Fiasco.* New York: Penguin Press, 2006.

Roy Morgan Research. *Majority of Australians Approve Sending Troops to Gulf If America Launches Military Action against Iraq.* Finding no.3057, February 24, 1998.

Roy Morgan Research. *Australians Approve Action against Iraq; Believe UN Should Have Supported Military Action.* Finding no. 3616, March 27, 2003.

Roy Morgan Research. *Our Troops Should Stay in Iraq until Job Done but Not at USA Request.* Finding no. 3726, April 2, 2004.

Roy Morgan Research. *Health and Education Still Top Issues.* April 14, 2004.

Roy Morgan Research. *What Australia Thinks of America.* Finding no. 3641, June 19, 2003.

Rubin, Barry. "The Real Roots of Anti-Americanism." *Foreign Affairs* 81 (November/December 2002): 73–85.

Scheuer, Michael. *Imperial Hubris: Why the West Is Losing War on Terror.* London: Brassey's, 2004.

Shapiro, Ilya. "Why Do They Hate Us?" March 23, 2004. Web site of the Institute of Communication Studies, University of Leeds, UK. http://ics.leeds.ac.uk/papers/vp01.cfm?outfit=pmt&requesttimeout=500&folder=1259&paper=1456.

Sloan, Stanley R. "Crisis Response." *NATO Review* (spring 2002): 26–28.

Smith, Anthony L. "Reluctant Partner: Indonesia's Response to U.S. Security Policies." Asia-Pacific Center for Security Studies, March 2003.

Sook-jung, Lee. "Anti-Americanism in Korean Society: A Survey Based Analysis." In *The United States and South Korea: Reinvigorating the Partnership,* U.S.-Korea Academic Symposium, 2003, edited by Peter H. Beck and Florence Lowe-Lee, 183–203. Korean Economic Institute, 2004.

Stockholm International Peace Research Institute. *Military Expenditure Database.* http://www.sipri.org/GlobalSecurity.org.

Sutter, Robert G. "Australia." In *Encyclopedia of U.S. Foreign Relations,* edited by Bruce Jentleson, Thomas G. Paterson, Nicholas X. Rizopoulos, Gaddis Smith, Caroline A. Hartzell, Ole R. Holsti, Howard Jones, and Henry R. Nau, 1:116–118. New York: Oxford University Press, 1997.

Teitelbaum, Michael S., and Philip L. Martin. "Is Turkey Ready for Europe?" *Foreign Affairs* (May/June 2003): 97–111.

Telhami, Shibley. "Arab Public Opinion on the United States and Iraq." *Brookings Review* 21 (summer 2003): 24–27.

U.S. Department of Defense. *Operation Desert Fox.* 2001.

U.S. Department of State, Office of Research. *The U.S. Image 2000: Global Attitudes toward the U.S. in the New Millennium.* November 2000.

U.S. Department of State, Office of Research. *West European Views of U.S.: A Pre-9/11 Baseline.* September 20, 2001.

U.S. Department of State, Office of Research. *Europeans and Anti-Americanism: Fact vs. Fiction; A Study of Public Attitudes toward the U.S.* September 2002.

United States Information Agency Surveys, 1953–99.

Uslu, Nasuh, Metin Toprak, Ibrahim Dalmis, and Ertan Aydin. "Turkish Public Opinion Toward the United States in the Context of the Iraq Question." *Review of International Affairs* 9, no. 3 (September 2005): 75–107.

Vandenberg, Arthur H., Jr., ed. *The Public Papers of Senator Vandenberg.* Boston: Houghton-Mifflin, 1952.

Waltz, Kenneth. "The Emerging Structure of International Politics." *International Security* 18 (fall 1993): 44–79.

White House. *The National Security Strategy of the United States of America.* http://www.whitehouse.gov/nsc/nss.pdf.

Wirajuda, N. Hassan. "Statement by H.E. Dr. N. Hassan Wirajuda, Minister for Foreign Affairs, Republic of Indonesia, at the 57th Session of the UN General Assembly." Department of Foreign Affairs for the Republic of Indonesia, September 18, 2002.

Woodward, Robert. *State of Denial.* New York: Simon and Schuster, 2006.

Yong-lib, Gweon. "The Changing Perception of America in South Korea: Transition or Transformation?" *Korea Journal* (spring 2004): 152–77.

Young, Thomas-Durell. "The Australian-United States Security Alliance." In *Australia's Security in the 21st Century,* edited by J. Mohan Malik. St. Leonards: Allen and Unwin, 1999.

Yudhoyono, Susilo Bambang. "Address by H.E. Dr. Susilo Bambang Yudhoyono, President of the Republic of Indonesia, at a Dinner Tendered by USINDO." Washington, DC, May 25, 2005.

Yudhoyono, Susilo Bambang. "Statement by H.E. Dr. N. Hassan Wirajuda, Minister for Foreign Affairs, Republic of Indonesia, at the 61st Session of the UN Commission on Human Rights," March 15, 2005.

Zogby International. *Impressions of America, 2002.*

Zogby International. *Impressions of America, 2004.*

Index